50 Spiritual Classics

First published by
Nicholas Brealey Publishing in 2005

3–5 Spafield Street
Clerkenwell, London
EC1R 4QB, UK
Tel: +44 (0)20 7239 0360
Fax: +44 (0)20 7239 0370

100 City Hall Plaza, Suite 501
Boston
MA 02108, USA
Tel: (888) BREALEY
Fax: (617) 523 3708

http://www.nbrealey-books.com
http://www.butler-bowdon.com

ISBN 1-85788-349-7

British Library Cataloguing in Publication Data
A catalogue record for this book is available from the British Library.

Printed in Finland by WS Bookwell.

50 Spiritual Classics

Timeless wisdom from

50 great books of

inner discovery, enlightenment, and purpose

Tom Butler-Bowdon

NICHOLAS BREALEY
PUBLISHING

LONDON   BOSTON

Muhammad Asad

Chuang Tzu

Hermann Hesse

Chögyam Trungpa

ST. AUGUSTINE

Ram Dass

Aldous Huxley

W. Somerset Maugham

Neale Donald Walsch

Richard Bach

Epictetus

William James

Dan Millman

RICK WARREN

Black Elk

Mohandas Gandhi

CARL GUSTAV JUNG

Michael Newton

Simone Weil

Richard Maurice Bucke

Ghazzali

Margery Kempe

Thich Nhat Hanh

Ken Wilber

FRITJOF CAPRA

Kahlil Gibran

J. Krishnamurti

John O'Donohue

Paramahansa Yogananda

Carlos Castaneda

G. I. Gurdjieff

C. S. Lewis

Robert M. Pirsig

Gary Zukav

G. K. Chesterton

Dag Hammarskjöld

Malcolm X

James Redfield

Pema Chödrön

Abraham Joshua Heschel

Daniel C. Matt

Miguel Ruiz

Idries Shah

Starhawk

Shunryu Suzuki

Emanuel Swedenborg

Teresa of Avila

Mother Teresa

Eckhart Tolle

Contents

Introduction   1

1   **Muhammad Asad**   *The Road to Mecca* (1954)   14
2   **St. Augustine**   *Confessions* (400)   20
3   **Richard Bach**   *Jonathan Livingston Seagull* (1970)   26
4   **Black Elk**   *Black Elk Speaks* (1932)   30
5   **Richard Maurice Bucke**   *Cosmic Consciousness* (1901)   36
6   **Fritjof Capra**   *The Tao of Physics: An Exploration of the Parallels between Modern Physics and Eastern Mysticism* (1976)   42
7   **Carlos Castaneda** *Journey to Ixtlan* (1972)   48
8   **G. K. Chesterton**   *St Francis of Assisi* (1922)   54
9   **Pema Chödrön**   *The Places That Scare You: A Guide to Fearlessness in Difficult Times* (2001)   60
10   **Chuang Tzu** *The Book of Chuang Tzu* (4th century)   66
11   **Ram Dass**   *Be Here Now* (1971)   72
12   **Epictetus**   *Enchiridion* (1st century)   78
13   **Mohandas Gandhi**   *An Autobiography: The Story of My Experiments with Truth* (1927)   84
14   **Ghazzali**   *The Alchemy of Happiness* (1097)   90
15   **Kahlil Gibran**   *The Prophet* (1923)   96
16   **G. I. Gurdjieff**   *Meetings with Remarkable Men* (1960)   102
17   **Dag Hammarskjöld**   *Markings* (1963)   108
18   **Abraham Joshua Heschel**   *The Sabbath: Its Meaning for Modern Man* (1951)   112
19   **Hermann Hesse**   *Siddartha* (1922)   118
20   **Aldous Huxley**   *The Doors of Perception* (1954)   124
21   **William James**   *The Varieties of Religious Experience* (1902)   130
22   **Carl Gustav Jung**   *Memories, Dreams, Reflections* (1955)   136
23   **Margery Kempe**   *The Book of Margery Kempe* (1436)   142
24   **J. Krishnamurti**   *Think on These Things* (1964)   148
25   **C. S. Lewis**   *The Screwtape Letters* (1942)   154
26   **Malcolm X**   *The Autobiography of Malcolm X* (1964)   160
27   **Daniel C. Matt**   *The Essential Kabbalah: The Heart of Jewish Mysticism* (1994)   168
28   **W. Somerset Maugham**   *The Razor's Edge* (1944)   174
29   **Dan Millman**   *The Way of the Peaceful Warrior: A Book that Changes Lives* (1989)   180
30   **Michael Newton**   *Journey of Souls: Case Studies of Life between Lives* (1994)   186

31 **Thich Nhat Hanh**   *The Miracle of Mindfulness: An Introduction to the Practice of Meditation* (1975)   192
32 **John O'Donohue** *Anam Cara: Spiritual Wisdom from the Celtic World* (1998)   198
33 **Robert M. Pirsig**   *Zen and the Art of Motorcycle Maintenance* (1974)   204
34 **James Redfield**   *The Celestine Prophecy: An Adventure* (1994)   210
35 **Miguel Ruiz**   *The Four Agreements: A Practical Guide to Personal Freedom* (1997)   216
36 **Helen Schucman & William Thetford**   *A Course in Miracles* (1976)   222
37 **Idries Shah**   *The Way of the Sufi* (1968)   228
38 **Starhawk**   *The Spiral Dance: A Rebirth of the Ancient Religion of the Great Goddess* (1979)   234
39 **Shunryu Suzuki**   *Zen Mind, Beginner's Mind: Informal Talks on Zen Meditation and Practice* (1970)   240
40 **Emanuel Swedenborg**   *Heaven and Hell* (1758)   246
41 **Teresa of Avila**   *Interior Castle* (1570)   252
42 **Mother Teresa**   *A Simple Path* (1994)   258
43 **Eckhart Tolle**   *The Power of Now: A Guide to Spiritual Enlightenment* (1998)   264
44 **Chögyam Trungpa**   *Cutting through Spiritual Materialism* (1973)   270
45 **Neale Donald Walsch**   *Conversations with God: An Uncommon Dialogue* (1998)   276
46 **Rick Warren**   *The Purpose-Driven Life* (2002)   282
47 **Simone Weil**   *Waiting for God* (1979)   288
48 **Ken Wilber**   *A Theory of Everything: An Integral Vision for Business, Politics, Science and Spirituality* (2000)   294
49 **Paramahansa Yogananda**   *Autobiography of a Yogi* (1946)   300
50 **Gary Zukav**   *The Seat of the Soul: An Inspiring Vision of Humanity's Spiritual Destiny* (1990)   306

50 More Spiritual Classics   312
Chronological list of titles
Credits
Acknowledgments

Introduction

5o *Spiritual Classics* is the third work in a personal development trilogy that began with *50 Self-Help Classics*. That first book explored many of the landmarks of the personal development literature, including the "original" self-help books such as the Bible, *Tao Te Ching*, the Dhammapada and the Bhagavad-Gita, plus the best of contemporary writings by, for instance, Deepak Chopra, Wayne Dyer, Susan Jeffers, Thomas Moore, and The Dalai Lama. This was followed by *50 Success Classics*, which highlighted key titles in the fields of leadership, motivation, and prosperity, and focused more on worldly success.

50 Spiritual Classics is based on the premise that the quest for material security alone does not ultimately satisfy, and that not even emotional security or great knowledge is enough to sustain us—we were built to seek answers to larger questions. The paradox of personal development is that, taken to its logical end, it takes us *beyond* the self. Meaning is found outside the perimeter of our small concerns.

The word "spiritual" comes from the Latin word for breathing—our most commonplace and natural function. If nothing else, this book aims to dispel the idea that there is anything outlandish about spiritual experience; on the contrary, it is what makes us human.

If you feel an absence of sacred worship or mystery in your life, some of the ideas presented here may provide a key to the greater richness you crave. If you have achieved a level of success but then found that it did not satisfy you, this book may get you thinking about whether or not you have some deeper purpose to fulfill.

50 Spiritual Classics is less about religion or theology than *personal* spiritual awakening and the expansion of awareness. Consequently, it focuses on the life stories of many well-known spiritual figures, including dramatic conversions or increases in faith, but also the slow discovery of purpose over a lifetime. By finding out what it was that transformed these people, we can begin to understand our own spiritual potential.

There are inevitably many great authors and books that by rights should be included in the list of spiritual classics. However, the list is not meant to be a survey of the world's religions, only to give an idea of the great variety of spiritual points of view spanning time and place. Some readers will be surprised by the juxtaposition of old or ancient writings next to bestsellers of modern times, but the book is less concerned with when a title was written than with the force of its ideas. The last 20 years have seen a renaissance in popular spiritual writing and the selection aims to give some idea of the prominent titles, even if the jury is still out on whether they will become firm classics, or even whether they are "good" writing.

At the beginning of each commentary is a mention of other books from the list of a similar nature or connected theme ("In a similar vein"). As there is some overlap with titles chosen for *50 Self-Help Classics* (50SHC), a few of those titles will also be suggested for further reading, as will some from *50 Success Classics* (50SC).

The spiritual literature is a treasury of collective wisdom, at least equal to the great libraries of science, philosophy, poetry, or fiction. The commentaries here are only a glimpse into that great heritage, but I hope they will increase your awareness of its breadth and depth.

Below I outline some themes in the literature, as a guide to the commentaries you may wish to read. This is followed by a brief exposition of some of the key spiritual realizations that these books can provoke.

Great spiritual lives

Muhammad Asad *The Road to Mecca* (1954)
St. Augustine *Confessions* (400)
G. K. Chesterton *St Francis of Assisi* (1922)
Ram Dass *Be Here Now* (1971)
Hermann Hesse *Siddartha* (1922)
Margery Kempe *The Book of Margery Kempe* (1436)
Malcolm X *The Autobiography of Malcolm X* (1964)
W. Somerset Maugham *The Razor's Edge* (1944)

What is the purpose of spirituality if not to transform our lives? Consider the following examples:

❖ Malcolm X was a petty criminal whose religious conversion turned him into a voice for black empowerment.

- ❖ Muhammad Asad grew up a Viennese Jew but left Europe behind to become a champion of Islam.
- ❖ St. Augustine lived for cheap entertainments and sex, but after great soul searching became a father of the Catholic church.
- ❖ Richard Alpert, professor of psychology, gave up his Harvard career to become Ram Dass, master meditator and guru.
- ❖ Francis of Assisi was the son of a well-off businessman who threw away his inheritance in order to restore ruined churches and commune with nature.
- ❖ Margery Kempe was a prideful harridan whose visions of Jesus made her into a woman of God.
- ❖ In Somerset Maugham's novel based on fact, Larry Darrell turns his back on material comforts in favor of a life-long spiritual search.

While most people are content to raise their standard of living and carry on a program of incremental self-improvement, none of these figures was content with the values that their original lives had given them. Each came to the realization that nothing less than a complete change of identity would suffice in order for them to shift from psychological fragmentation to spiritual wholeness. Their stories are inspirational because they demonstrate the possibility of utter transformation in the human character. While skeptics view a conversion experience as taking away the person they knew, for the convert just the opposite occurs—now existing for some higher purpose and not only themselves, their potential as a person is finally realized.

Practical spirituality

Pema Chödrön *The Places that Scare You* (2001)
Mohandas Gandhi *An Autobiography* (1927)
Kahlil Gibran *The Prophet* (1923)
Dan Millman *The Way of the Peaceful Warrior* (1989)
Thich Nhat Hanh *Miracle of Mindfulness* (1975)
Miguel Ruiz *The Four Agreements* (1997)
Shunryu Suzuki *Zen Mind, Beginner's Mind* (1970)
Eckhart Tolle *The Power of Now* (1998)
Chögyam Trungpa *Cutting through Spiritual Materialism* (1973)

The Buddhist nun Pema Chödrön tells of the time beat poet Jack Kerouac went into the mountains alone to meet face to face with God or Buddha (he wasn't sure which). All that happened was that he encountered his own naked self, unprotected for the first time by booze and drugs. We can have grand ideas for becoming "enlightened," but the more common reality of the spiritual life is daily effort to be compassionate and stay attuned to right principles. This was the approach taken by no less a figure than Gandhi, whose "experiments in truth" described in his autobiography included severe dietary restrictions, celibacy, and simple living, daily habits that over decades transformed him from a self-absorbed young man into a symbol of selflessness and human freedom. The "mindfulness" ideas of Vietnamese Buddhist master Thich Nhat Hanh are similar, in that they charge even the smallest acts in daily routine with significance; every moment is considered precious. Eckhart Tolle's surprise bestseller *The Power of Now* also reminds us of the peace and power that come from living in the moment. To retain a "beginner's mind" in everything we do keeps us mentally fresh and free from making wrong assumptions.

Discipline and mindfulness can reduce the ego's hold on our thoughts and actions, but most of us don't consider that earnest spiritual seeking can itself be a product of the ego. Chögyam Trungpa's idea of "spiritual materialism" is that striving to be a spiritually advanced person is really to make us feel good; the higher or true self is not interested, for instance, in quitting a job to live in a monastery or ashram. If we do become enlightened, it is by working through the issues and problems of our lives as they are. We will do anything to avoid the "places that scare us," to use Chödrön's phrase, but it is only in acknowledging our real thoughts and darker side that true spiritual healing can occur.

Miguel Ruiz's form of practical spirituality is based on the idea from Mexican Toltec tradition that everyone makes unconscious agreements with themselves and with society about the sort of person they are. By being more conscious about these agreements we can regain mastery over our lives. We can become what Dan Millman calls a "peaceful warrior," taking the sword to any aspect of ourselves that does not empower.

The great variety of experience
Black Elk *Black Elk Speaks* (1932)
Epictetus *Enchiridion* (1st century)
Abraham Joshua Heschel *The Sabbath* (1951)
William James *The Varieties of Religious Experience* (1902)
Carl Gustav Jung *Memories, Dreams, Reflections* (1955)
C. S. Lewis *The Screwtape Letters* (1942)
John O'Donohue *Anam Cara: A Book of Celtic Wisdom* (1998)
Helen Schucman & William Thetford *A Course in Miracles* (1976)
Idries Shah *The Way of the Sufi* (1968)
Starhawk *The Spiral Dance* (1979)
Paramahansa Yogananda *Autobiography of a Yogi* (1946)

In order to write his landmark study *The Varieties of Religious Experience*, William James read a large number of autobiographical accounts of spiritual awakening. Not being particularly religious himself, he was less concerned with the objective truth of what the subject may have felt or seen than the effect that it had on their lives. What mattered, he concluded, was not so much the content of a person's beliefs but whether or not they led to personal transformation of a positive kind.

A religion is not simply a collection of beliefs but a particular way of seeing the world, a way of knowing that satisfactorily explains the place of humans in the universe for the believer. This applies to the nature-based cosmology of Native Americans such as Black Elk, but equally to the Stoical understanding of the universe expressed in the philosophy of Epictetus. Just as the Sabbath is of central importance in the Jewish religion, so reincarnation is absolutely necessary to the Hindu way of seeing the world. And while Christians may view Goddess worship as the work of the devil, its adherents find in it a beautiful and complete expression of the sacred feminine power.

Carl Jung spent years looking into the mythological and religious beliefs that humankind had created to understand the world, yet he did not see such multiplicity as a threat to anyone's personal beliefs. Asked once whether he believed in God, he replied, "I don't believe—I know."

Opening the doors of perception

Richard Bach *Jonathan Livingston Seagull* (1970)
Fritjof Capra *The Tao of Physics* (1976)
Carlos Castaneda *Journey to Ixtlan* (1972)
Chuang Tzu *The Book of Chuang Tzu* (4th century)
G. I. Gurdjieff *Meetings with Remarkable Men* (1960)
Aldous Huxley *The Doors of Perception* (1954)
J. Krishnamurti *Think on These Things* (1964)
Robert M. Pirsig *Zen and the Art of Motorcycle Maintenance* (1974)

The common perception of the spiritual literature is that it is all about
God. In fact, the further one goes into it the more it seems to concern
the cleaning away of layers of misperception. The stories and anecdotes
in the ancient *Book of Chuang Tzu*, for instance, aim to awaken the
mind from its usual dullness to become aware of the Tao, or universal
force, that is behind all appearances. In more recent times, G. I.
Gurdjieff tried to wake up those who were sleepwalking through life
and see the deeper realities that made life worth living. Krishnamurti
devoted himself to the same end, making a distinction between the
mere "technicians," those who mechanically worked for the achievement of limited goals, and creators, who put things such as love and
truth at the center of their life and then worked outward.

In his landmark *Zen and the Art of Motorcycle Maintenance*,
Robert Pirsig wrote about a person whose quest for truth (or "quality") had actually driven him to the brink of madness, yet ultimately
his life was much richer for it. These sorts of quests can indeed be
frightening, and only a comparative minority are willing to push open
the "doors of perception" that Aldous Huxley and before him William
Blake discovered.

An author who has done perhaps more than any other to break
apart normal conceptual patterns is Carlos Castaneda. The don Juan
character in his writings teaches that a human being only really
becomes a full person when they stop being a mere reflection of their
culture and master their own mind. We are the products of conditioning so this is easier said than done, but the effort to become truly conscious is one of the more noble things we can do with our time, and the
books above require no particular belief in God to achieve this.

Divine relationship and life purpose

Ghazzali *The Alchemy of Happiness* (1097)
Dag Hammarskjöld *Markings* (1963)
Daniel C. Matt *The Essential Kabbalah* (1994)
Michael Newton *Journey of Souls* (1994)
Teresa of Avila *Interior Castle* (1570)
Mother Teresa *A Simple Path* (1994)
Neale Donald Walsch *Conversations with God* (1998)
Rick Warren *The Purpose-Driven Life* (2002)
Simone Weil *Waiting for God* (1979)
Emanuel Swedenborg *Heaven and Hell* (1758)

The question "Why are we here?" has inspired all great spiritual writing. Over 900 years ago, Ghazzali's *The Alchemy of Happiness* built a rationale for human existence that employed logic instead of blind faith. For Ghazzali, men and women were created in order to achieve greater knowledge of God, and our happiness depended on increasing this knowledge. The Jewish system of Kabbalah outlined in Matt's book was also developed to unravel the mystery, one of its central ideas being that God created humans in order to be made complete—the unfolding of the universe literally depended on the fulfillment of each person's unique potential. Among contemporary titles, Rick Warren's *The Purpose-Driven Life* is an excellent example of this view that we exist mainly for the purposes of glorifying God, and that we take human form so that the eternity of the soul can be fully appreciated.

The discovery of a life purpose is a defining event in anyone's existence. As related in *A Simple Path*, Mother Teresa's calling to help the poorest of the poor of Calcutta came comparatively late in her life, but the clarity of her mission saw her go from modest school principal to global spiritual entrepreneur within 15 years. Teresa was inspired by her earlier namesake, Teresa of Avila, who began her religious career as a giggling novice, but after a series of ecstatic visions of God was slowly transformed into a spiritual leader who founded a string of convents and monasteries. In modern times, UN Secretary-General Dag Hammarskjöld is a great example of how worldly power can be driven by spiritual conviction.

The question of what we are here for is sharpened by the knowledge of life's brevity. No spiritual library is therefore complete without a range of titles on the afterlife and the idea of eternity.

Swedenborg claimed that his *Heaven and Hell* was not fantasy but an accurate description of worlds he had journeyed to while in a higher state of consciousness. This book should be read alongside the contemporary *Journey of Souls* by Michael Newton, which lays out convincing suggestions of what happens to us after physical death through the eyes of hypnotized subjects.

Humanity's spiritual evolution

Richard Maurice Bucke *Cosmic Consciousness* (1901)
James Redfield *The Celestine Prophecy* (1994)
Ken Wilber *A Theory of Everything* (2000)
Gary Zukav *The Seat of the Soul* (1990)

The idea of an emerging human consciousness is a recurring theme in the spiritual literature. Bucke's *Cosmic Consciousness* was an early effort in this sub-genre, suggesting that the incidence of mystical experiences had steadily risen throughout history, and that this increase in direct divine revelation would eventually obviate the need for religion. In *The Seat of the Soul*, Gary Zukav made the case that humankind was evolving from a being with five senses to a "multisensory" one, able to be aware of many levels of spiritual reality and recognize that we are "spiritual beings having a human experience."

Another book from the 1990s, *The Celestine Prophecy*, asks readers to take a "big picture" view of history in which we can see the drive for material security being slowly replaced by the quest to find spiritual purpose. Ken Wilber is one of the great spiritual theorists of our time, and has called for a "theory of everything" that incorporates the development of consciousness into our understanding of evolution and physics. We do not simply live in a cosmos of space and matter, he says, but a "Kosmos" that includes the emotional, mental, and spiritual realms; the true evolution of the species will occur only when we give as much recognition to personal development as we have done to the manipulation of matter.

Landmarks on the spiritual path

Acknowledgment of an unseen order

"Were one to characterize the life of religion in the broadest and most general terms possible, one might say that it consists of the belief that there is an unseen order, and that our supreme good lies in harmoniously adjusting ourselves hereto."
William James

We tend to think of human achievement in terms of setting and accomplishing goals, shaping the world according to our aims and desires. It is a given that with enough effort and time, we can generally obtain what we want. Yet if we live long enough, inevitably we see the truth of the Old Testament proverb: "Many are the plans in a man's heart, but it is the Lord's purpose that prevails."

Not everyone believes in a particular God, but most of us do come to appreciate that there is some kind of intelligent force that moves the universe; perhaps, therefore, the first step on the spiritual way is an acknowledgment that life works better and has more meaning when we are in accord with this "unseen order." In his famous *Autobiography of a Yogi*, Paramhansa Yogananda remembered the words of one of his teachers, the "levitating saint" Bhaduri Mahasaya:

"The divine order arranges our future more wisely than any insurance company... The world is full of uneasy believers in an outward security. Their bitter thoughts are like scars on their foreheads. The One who gave us air and milk from our first breath knows how to provide day by day for His devotees."

In Taoism, this unseen order or force is known as the Tao. A person in attunement with it gets insights into the true nature of things, but to do so they must become humble, acknowledging that they are simply an element or expression of something much greater.

Divining a life purpose

The modern idea of personal development usually means improving ourselves in order to succeed in our career and relationships, but genuine transformation is much more likely to come through strong spiritual belief. People who undergo a conversion or epiphany are more likely to be extreme personalities to begin with, but the point is that their awakening redirects their energies in a way that makes the most of their higher traits, allowing for a more purposeful life.

Carl Jung suggested that when a person enters the world, they represent a question to which their life has to provide an answer. Most people never consider their lives in this way, but spiritual experience brings the realization that, because we are created beings, we must have been created for a reason. In *The Purpose-Driven Life*, Rick Warren likens a life to an invention that we only discover the purpose of when we are in contact with the inventor. Until this point, life has no meaning. We can try to find meaning in achieving goals based on our own ambitions, but our existence moves to another level when we discover a divinely given reason for being.

According to Kabbalah wisdom, the divine realm needs human action to make the world fulfill its potential. In return, it is up to us to ponder God's will and the mysteries of creation. This requires us to stop believing in ourselves and consider the vastness of God, and in doing so we are more likely to become a vehicle for divine expression. Most people believe that becoming a "vehicle" means that we lose control of our life, but the point made by all mystics is that in fact this brings out all our dormant potentialities. Self-knowledge is the discovery of who God intended us to be, but it is up to us whether we will express that idea or promise in our actions in the real world.

Loss of the little self

Twelfth-century Islamic theologian Ghazzali noted that human beings delight in the faculties they have been given, for instance anger delights in taking vengeance, the eye in seeing beauty, and the ear in hearing music. If, therefore, the highest faculty of human beings is the location of truth, then our greatest delight must lie in finding it.

We may think we are getting the most enjoyment out of life by satisfying our appetites, but we cannot know the much higher pleasure to be had from letting these worldly wants drop away. The pleasures of the world are good, but the delight in knowledge of God cannot be described. It is loss of the normal sense of self that provides human beings with their greatest satisfaction.

A Course in Miracles says: "Your mission is very simple. You are asked to live so as to demonstrate that you are not an ego." It is possible to become something other than a ball of small desires. Dov Baer, an eighteenth-century Hasidic master, said: "If you think of yourself as something, then God cannot clothe himself in you, for God is infinite." Paradoxically, it is through losing the small self or the ego that the greatest personal power is gained.

Living in the present

The grasping person lives for some abstract future; the spiritually successful person is aware of the treasure in the moment.

In *The Miracle of Mindfulness*, Thich Nhat Hanh recounts the story of a king who always wanted to make the right decisions and looked far and wide to the answers to three questions: "What is the best time to do each thing? Who are the most important people to work with? What is the most important thing to do at all times?"

His answers came, but they were not what he expected: the most important time is now; the most important person is the one you are with; the most important act is making the person next to you happy. In *Markings*, UN leader Dag Hammarskjöld noted that it was easier to voice commitment to great causes than it was actually to make a difference to an individual human being. Chuang Tzu told the story of the man who refused the offer to become a king because he was more interested in growing vegetables. This choice to give up our grand schemes and instead focus on the present moment may seem naïve, but many spiritual writers, including Eckhart Tolle and Shunryu Suzuki, point out that this is the beginning of real effectiveness.

The other benefit of being fully present-minded is getting back the simple joy of life, because sadness and worry must necessarily come from thoughts about the past or the future. In *The Way of the Peaceful Warrior*, the Dan character makes a great discovery: "There are no ordinary moments!"

Perceiving beyond duality

Every spiritual traveler eventually has an experience of "nonduality," or the appreciation of an essential oneness to the universe that goes beyond worldly opposites such as good and evil, praise and blame, and happiness and sadness. We make endless distinctions in order to maintain the perception that the world is a collection of discrete objects and ideas, but behind all that we can detect an unchanging unity. If there is a God that created the universe, we realize, it follows that God contains all things—even those things that seem opposed to God.

We mistakenly believe that each of us is a sole entity journeying through life, but most of the world's mythologies and religions allude to the soul as simply a splinter of consciousness broken free from a larger Mind. We can seek to maintain the illusion of separateness, but the pain and fragmentation it causes are the very things that may eventually drive us to see the universe in a more holistic way.

There are two clear results of a greater appreciation of oneness. The first is more compassion for all living things, because we realize that we are all simply expressions of the same life force: what you do to another person, at another level you are really doing to yourself. The second result is increased equanimity. Our normal predicament is to swing between pleasure and pain, gain and loss, but as long as we are in this pendulum there can be no real peace. Equanimity is having a mind that does not instantly divide everything into good or bad, like or dislike, but sees that things simply "are." This is the opposite of how most people live. These realizations of oneness are usually only fleeting; however, such glimpses of nonduality, were they to become more common and longer, would transform our lives.

There is a Persian proverb: "Seek truth in meditation, not in moldy books. Look in the sky to find the moon, not in the pond." The commentaries that follow are more of a look in the pond than a direct experience of the moon, but I hope they can provide some motivation for you to gaze on the real thing.

50 Spiritual
Classics

The Road to Mecca

"There are many more beautiful landscapes in the world, but none, I think, that can shape man's spirit in so sovereign a way... The desert is bare and clean and knows no compromise. It sweeps out of the heart of man all the lovely fantasies that could be used as a masquerade for wishful thinking, and thus makes him free to surrender himself to an Absolute that has no image: the farthest of all that is far and yet the nearest of all that is near."

In a nutshell

An evocation of the beauty of the Islamic faith and its role in humanity's spiritual evolution.

In a similar vein

Ghazzali *The Alchemy of Happiness* (p. 90)
Kahlil Gibran *The Prophet* (p. 96)
Malcolm X *The Autobiography of Malcolm X* (p. 160)

CHAPTER 1

Muhammad Asad

When Muhammad Asad traveled to New York in 1952 as Pakistan's envoy to the United Nations, he had been away from the West for 25 years. He had been born Leopold Weiss, a central European Jew who converted to Islam at the age of 26 and effectively turned his back on western culture.

The Road to Mecca is now surprisingly little known, but remains one of the twentieth century's great accounts of spiritual transformation. In no way a full story of Asad's life, it covers only the years he spent in Arabia as a young man, and specifically a 23-day journey to Mecca in the summer of 1932. In the book, which is much more than a travelogue or memoir, Asad recounts the story of his initial attraction to Islam and his eventual marriage to the faith. The beauty of his writing means that few readers will come away from this book without a changed perception of the religion, and this was his purpose in writing it.

Asad was a precociously gifted young correspondent for the prestigious *Frankfurter Zeitung* newspaper, and made hundreds of trips within Arabia, Palestine, Egypt, Syria, Iran, Iraq, and Afghanistan to cover his stories. His adventures are enough reason to get the book, but in this commentary we focus on the rationale for his conversion and the thoughts that led to his Muslim beliefs.

First taste

Asad was born in 1900, the second of three children. His father was a barrister and the family was comfortably off. Though his parents were not strict Jews, he was tutored in Hebrew and the Bible, and at an early age Asad took issue with the idea of Jews being a chosen people, as this seemed to exclude all others. At the University of Vienna he studied history of art and philosophy, and enjoyed mixing with Vienna's intellectual élite. Psychoanalysis was all the rage, but he saw it as "spiritual nihilism" and observed an emptiness in the European soul.

In 1920, without saying goodbye to his father, Asad traveled to Berlin where, after a period as a penniless bohemian, he managed to get work as a journalist. However, the job was not interesting enough, and when Asad received an invitation from an uncle living in Jerusalem to come and join him, he leapt at the chance. He admitted to having had the usual "orientalist" stereotypes: vague ideas of the romance of the Arabian Nights and the exoticism of Islamic culture, and the typical European's view that Islam was of only marginal interest compared to Christianity and Judaism.

Despite being a Jew, in Palestine Asad did not care for the Zionist cause, believing that an influx of European Jews into a land that had not been theirs for 2,000 years was an artificial solution and destined to cause problems. He noticed that the Europeans saw the local Arabs like colonial powers saw Africans—as a backward people of little consequence—and he crossed swords on the issue with one of Israel's founding fathers, Chaim Weizmann. The Zionists in turn could not understand this Jewish man's sympathy for, and interest in, the Arabs.

Conversion and immersion

As the weeks grew into months, Asad began to see European culture from a different perspective, particularly in relation to its emotional insecurity and moral ambiguity. In contrast, he noticed the sense of brotherhood and unity of thought and action that Muslims seemed to enjoy. He realized that Europe too had once enjoyed this spiritual wholeness, expressed, for instance, in the music of Bach, the art of Rembrandt, and the Gothic cathedrals, but that this had given way to a materialism that had fragmented the continent's collective psyche. The aim of "progress" had come to represent European culture, but this focus on material improvements had not actually led to greater happiness. Christianity had lost its force in western society and become a mere convention, politely observed. In Asad's mind, Europeans no longer had the awareness that the universe was "an expression of one Planning Mind and thus formed one organic whole." Instead of faith, the West had put science and technology at the center of life, with the result that legitimacy was only given to things that could be physically proven; there was no longer any room for God in its intellectual system.

Asad was determined to stay in the Muslim world, and fortunately his appointment as a correspondent was extended, allowing him to travel all over the Middle East. In the years to follow he provided hundreds of penetrating analyses of the region's people and issues. He became a Muslim in 1926, and for six years was based in the court of Ibn Saud, the father of modern Saudi Arabia. When they first met, Asad was in the depths of grief following the death of his European wife Elsa, who had died of a tropical disease while they were on their first pilgrimage to Mecca. Normally, a westerner would have been viewed with suspicion, but Asad's commitment to Islam was total, and the connection to Ibn Saud enabled him to visit places that would ordinarily have been off limits. For instance, hardly any foreigners had been allowed to visit the Nadj region of central Arabia, but Asad journeyed there at Saud's invitation, taking two months to arrive. His immersion in Muslim life was complete when he married an Arab woman in Medina and had a son.

Crusader against misperception

Asad notes that westerners could not really comprehend his conversion to Islam because they took it for granted that Muslim culture was inferior to western civilization. History, to Europeans or Americans, was the account of the rise of Occidental civilization, and took in non-western cultures only as they affected the emergence of Europe and America as the leaders of the world. This distorted vision, he comments, began with the Greeks and Romans, who identified themselves as "civilized" and the rest of the world as "barbarian." The western mind could contemplate Hinduism or Buddhism with interest and equanimity because they seem so alien, but Islam—because it had come from the same tradition as Judeo-Christian theology—was feared as a competitor. This antipathy was expressed in the Crusades, which in providing a common enemy for "Christendom" brought Europe together. According to Asad, the Crusades were the beginning of "a poisoning of the Western mind against the Muslim world through a deliberate misrepresentation of the teachings and ideals of Islam."

Asad's intention in writing an autobiography was not to chronicle his adventures in the exotic East for westerners, but to dispel some of these erroneous views. He realized that he was in the unique position of having fully known both cultural hemispheres: "I was a Muslim—but I was also of Western origin: and thus I could speak the intellectual languages of both Islam and the West." He was careful to point out that it was not the Muslim peoples that made him convert to Islam, but rather his love of Islam that encouraged him to stay living in Muslim countries.

The promise of Islam

Asad adored Islam's pared-down love of the Absolute, and the simplicity and beauty of the Koran, which did not require official interpreters of its wisdom. In contrast to the individualism that western faiths seemed to inspire, he reveled in the sense of community that Islam bestowed on its believers. Because Islam had no notion of "original sin," everyone was assumed to be a person of God until proven otherwise; this outlook was expressed in courtly and reverential forms of Muslim greeting, which emphasized "thou" rather than "you." There are many passages in the book in which Asad tries to convey his feelings for the Arabs and Islam. The following quote ends with a line from the Koran that captures the Muslim feeling for the closeness of God:

"They were a people that had grown up in silence and solitude between a hard sky and a hard earth; hard was their life in the midst of these austere, endless spaces; and so they could not escape the longing after a Power that would encompass all existence with unerring justice and kindness, severity and wisdom: God the Absolute. He dwells in infinity and radiates into infinity—but because you are within His working, He is closer to you than the vein in your neck..."

The prophet Muhammed originally found it difficult to get his view of an absolute God accepted in the tribal societies of Arabia, which wanted to maintain the division between private faith and the world realms of business, social custom, and daily habit. Asad argues that only when Islam (which literally means surrender to God) was allowed to shape institutions and customs was the promise of the Arab world fulfilled.

Corruption of the faith

As a scholar of Muslim history and culture, Asad notes that Islamic learning had led the world during the centuries after Muhammad's death, and the reason was simple: This new religion was a profoundly rational one that exhorted believers to marvel at and understand God's creation, unlike, as Asad notes, the "world-hating" theologies of Christian church fathers St. Paul and Augustine. The Prophet had said: "Striving after knowledge is a most sacred duty for every Muslim man and woman." A natural connection was made between knowledge and worship, and science advanced with this inspiration.

Nevertheless, Asad was not blind to the intellectual and material decay in many Muslim societies, which had led them to become scientific and economic backwaters. According to Asad, when this deep faith and day-to-day accordance with Muhammad's teachings waned, so did the creative impulse and ingenuity that had made Islamic civilization great. In total opposition to the western view that adherence to Islam was responsible for the decline, he notes: "It was not the Muslims that had made Islam great: it was Islam that had made the Muslims great."

Final comments

The Road to Mecca sits easily among the world's best travel and adventure writing, providing unforgettable descriptions of black, starry nights in the desert, oases, bustling bazaars, Mecca and Medina, the idiosyncrasies of pampered kings, and the customs of the Bedouin. It provides unique insights into the history of the house of Saud and the politics of colonialism and Arab self-determination, as you would expect from a newspaper correspondent. But the book becomes a work of literature in its description of a man's slow realization that his heart belongs to a religion in which he was not brought up. If you have never really understood Islam and the faith that it inspires, this book will be a great teacher.

Asad wrote his book half a century ago, but there is plenty of evidence that the gap in understanding between the West and the Muslim world has grown wider, which makes perspectives like his all the more valuable. He was a spiritual purist, and regretted people's failure to live up to Islam's high ideals, but this criticism could easily be applied to Judaism and Christianity as well. Late in the book Asad introduces the reader to the Islamic mythological figure Dajjal, who was blind in one eye but possessed powers to see and hear to the far corners of the Earth. Asad saw this figure as representing the power of humanity to control the world through technology, yet the semi-blindness symbolized a mind closed off to God. Every culture has this weakness for worshipping material progress, he noticed, but it can never fill the place reserved in every one of us for a connection to the divine.

Confessions

"I came to Carthage where a whole frying-pan of wicked loves sputtered all around me. I was not yet in love, but I was in love with love, and with a deep-seated want. I hated myself for wanting too little... I hated safety and a path without snares, because I had a hunger within—for that food of the inner man, yourself, my God. Yet that hunger did not make me feel hungry. I was without appetite for incorruptible food, not because I was sated with it, but with less hunger in proportion to my emptiness. And so my soul was sick."

In a nutshell

Religious faith can bring peace and order to a troubled mind.

In a similar vein
Malcolm X *The Autobiography of Malcolm X* (p. 160)
Teresa of Avila *Interior Castle* (p. 252)

CHAPTER 2

St. Augustine

Most of us experience tensions between who we want to be and who we are. The more divided our self is, the greater the torment, but this in itself provides a strong motivation to be healed. Augustine's bitter inner struggles lasted well into his 30s and although he lived over 1,500 years ago, the story of his inner victories is still very relevant.

In the first decades of his life, Augustine coasted on his high native intelligence and was a success professionally, but he found that his brains and wide learning did not make him happy or at peace. His red-blooded enjoyment of life's pleasures delivered only emptiness.

In contrast, after his conversion to Christianity, Augustine became one of the founding fathers of the Church, author of the famous *De Civitate Dei* ("The City of God") and originator of the Augustinian religious order.

Yet the voice that speaks in *The Confessions* is not that of a "great man." Intimate and honest, it charts Augustine's gradual move away from selfish concerns and toward a life with God. With a good translation (here we use E. M. Blaiklock's*) you may feel like you are reading the diaries of a friend, struggling to improve themselves and live a more spiritual life. The *Confessions* is one of the very earliest autobiographies and a seminal work in European literature, and is perhaps the classic book on how spiritual awakening (or being "born again") can radically change a life.

Early years

Augustine was born in 354 in the last years of the Roman Empire in the North African province of Numidia (now Tunisia). His father, Patricius, was a minor local official and followed the conventional paganism of the empire. His mother, Monica, was a Christian convert.

Augustine did not like school, yet was considered a bright student, reading Cicero, Virgil, Plato, and Aristotle. In the *Confessions*, he complains that elegant speech and writing skills were at the time held to be more important than moral teaching, and he had these in abundance. To further his education he was sent to another school of grammar and rhetoric 20 miles from home and graduated at the top of his class.

At 16, Augustine came back to his parents' home for a year. He was growing up, and amusingly recalls that while bathing one day his father noticed his burgeoning "maturity." This year of freedom, he ruefully recounts, was a painful mistake, consumed as he was by lustful thoughts and actions. Sin, he says, "oozed out of him like a secretion out of fat." He suspects that the only reason his parents did not try to channel his energies into marriage was that a wife might have restricted his ambition.

Ever the tormented and guilt-ridden soul, Augustine writes with pain about what to many would seem trifling youthful incidents. There is a famous confession of how he and his friends shook the pears down from a pear tree and made off with them, not because they were hungry but for fun. For Augustine, the incident becomes a personal symbol of the depravity of life without a conscience.

Cauldron of temptation

Augustine's life takes on some direction again with a move to Carthage, a center of learning where he continues his studies. But it is also a port city (across the Mediterranean from Sicily), with all its temptations, "where there sang all around me in my ears a cauldron of unholy loves." He lives only to satisfy his desires, even committing an "act of lust" inside a church. At night he ventures to the theater, particularly to see plays about extreme grief or lewdness. Yet the more pleasures he enjoys, the more meaningless his life becomes.

Nevertheless, he remains a voracious reader, and one book in particular, Cicero's *Hortensius*, increases his liking for philosophy and awakens a search for truth. He also tries reading the Bible, but admits he did not then possess the humility required to understand its message. Augustine's natural spiritual leanings are channeled into the Manichean sect, an offshoot of Christianity that mixes Gnostic gospel, Zoroastrianism, and Buddhism; to his mother's despair, he holds on to the Manichean faith for nine years. He also delves into astrology.

Professionally, Augustine becomes a teacher of rhetoric, which he ashamedly calls "the sale of loquacity," and works in both Carthage and his native Tagaste. That his chosen work emphasizes style over content is just another basis for Augustine's malaise. He turns into an expert cynic, yet enjoys no wellspring of truth in his own mind. This is how he sums up life in his 20s:

"For this space of nine years (from my nineteenth year to my eight-and-twentieth) we lived seduced and seducing, deceived and deceiving, in divers lusts; openly, by sciences which they call liberal; secretly, with a false-named religion; here proud, there superstitious, every where vain.
Here, hunting after the emptiness of popular praise, down even to theatrical applauses, and poetic prizes, and strifes for grassy garlands, and the follies of shows, and the intemperance of desires."

Augustine begins living with a girl out of wedlock and they have a child together, Adeodatus. Because of his guilt he describes the relationship as unholy and conceived in lust, although he concedes that she loves him and they love the child. Later, pressure from his mother makes them split up.

Something else spins Augustine into a dark night of the soul: the death of a friend. The depth of his grief shocks him, until he realizes that his bitterness and misery are underlying, deeper than any specific event. He tries to find peace in quiet places, in books, in eating and drinking, and in sex, but it continues to elude him.

Augustine emerges from his 20s with two realizations: that learning and intelligence have not led him to any sense of the truth (they have only taught him how to question and doubt); and that his long pursuit of pleasure has made him miserable.

He concludes that intelligence must be "enlightened by another light"; that is, God. However, he is not ready to believe that God can accept and transform his misery.

Slow and painful discovery

In 383, escaping his mother, Augustine moves to Rome. The following year, with the help of Manichean friends, he gets a post teaching rhetoric in Milan, where he enjoys going to watch the famous Bishop of Ambrose preach, not for religious insight but to study his skill as an orator. Ambrose becomes something of a mentor, and gradually the bishop's Christian message seeps through to Augustine's thoughts. At first he thinks of the Bible as full of "absurd stories," although he cannot discount other parts of it.

Augustine admits to being "worn out by anxieties and fears," the familiar complaint of someone who lives for external things yet has no inner peace. Prosperity, he says, always eludes him just as he is about to grab it. People are continually saying that what matters is the source of a person's happiness, but his source, he remarks to his friends in characteristic honesty, is pride and glory in himself.

Yet Augustine comes to the realization that it may not be the lot of human beings always to be suffering. With the greater perspective we gain from being closer to God, miseries and torments can be washed away: "For whithersoever the soul of man turns itself, unless toward Thee, it is riveted upon sorrows."

Epiphany

Without God, Augustine reflects, he is nothing but a "guide to his own downfall." However, he continues a painful process of reasoning about his faith, and after still more questioning about who God really is, he hears a voice say to him, simply, "I am that I am."

This does not calm his thoughts for long. His main worry is that if he were to become a priest he would not be able to resist the pleasures of the flesh. The denouement of his struggle comes when he and his friend Alypius are staying at a house in the country. Full of his usual desperation, Augustine throws himself down beneath a fig tree and weeps for his miserable faithless self. How long does he need to wait, he cries out, before he is saved and healed?

Then comes the climax of the *Confessions*: he hears a child's voice coming over a wall, playing some kind of game with the words "Pick it up and read it." Taking this as a sign, Augustine rushes back to where his friend is sitting and grabs the Bible he has been reading before, opening it at random. The passage his eyes fall on says this: The path to God is not in the ways of lust, gluttony and competition, but through Jesus.

Augustine hands in his resignation as a teacher, returns to Africa, and is ordained as a priest. In 396 he becomes the Bishop of Hippo (modern-day Annaba in Algeria), a post he will hold until his death. He becomes a passionate critic of various heresies, including his old Manichean faith, and makes himself the great defender of the orthodox Catholic Church.

Final comments

If your misery is great enough, there is a chance that you will arrive at an equally great sense of peace and purpose that less intense people will never experience. The *Confessions* is one of the best pieces of writing on how a divided, tormented person can be healed through religion.

Yet Augustine is not really an inspirational character in the way that St. Francis of Assisi was, and in many respects his dogmatism and guilt about sex and the enjoyment of life shaped the Church for the worse. Translator E. M. Blaiklock has bluntly noted the elements of weakness in Augustine's personality, which included deception, lust, and the inability to make commitments, and most readers will wince at his treatment of his *de facto* wife. It also might be said that the younger Augustine, with his close friends, lively nature, and wide interests, would surely have been a more enjoyable character to have around than the older, doctrinaire bishop that he became.

However, you will not find many figures in history who more fully expressed their potential to the maximum. From his inauspicious Roman backwater childhood and fast-living student days, it is remarkable that Augustine became (along with Aquinas) the major intellectual figure in the Christian West for the next 1,000 years. His huge work, *The City of God* (426), which took 13 years to write, became a theological foundation stone for the emergent Christian religion. All this from a black man born into the fringes of a white empire.

Augustine died in the year 430, just as the Vandals were closing in to sack and pillage his city. It is said that many of his parishioners were killed. The *Confessions* therefore form an important historical record of the places and customs of a world that was soon to change forever.

These facts are nevertheless not as interesting as the book's description of an inner revolution. Augustine discovered the spiritual secret that is the basis for all religions—that faith can bring peace and order to a tortured mind.

*St. Augustine (1986) *The Confessions of Saint Augustine,* trans. and preface by E. M. Blaiklock, London: Hodder & Stoughton.

Jonathan Livingston Seagull

"He spoke of very simple things—that it is right for a gull to fly, that freedom is the very nature of his being, that whatever stands against that freedom must be set aside, be it ritual or superstition or limitation in any form."

"Jonathan Seagull discovered that boredom and fear and anger are the reasons that a gull's life is so short, and with these gone from his thought, he lived a long fine life indeed."

In a nutshell

The purpose of live is not simply to survive, but to seek perfection in yourself.

In a similar vein
Michael Newton *Journey of Souls* (p. 186)
Paramahansa Yogananda *Autobiography of a Yogi* (p. 300)
Gary Zukav *The Seat of the Soul* (p. 306)

CHAPTER 3

Richard Bach

Like *Starsky and Hutch*, *Jaws*, and flared jeans, *Jonathan Livingston Seagull* was an icon of the 1970s. It was even made into a movie. But what exactly is this book, and is it still worth reading?

Bach's bestseller is an uplifting fable about a seagull, Jonathan, who decides that he is much more than just a seagull and wants something else out of life. It consists of fewer than 100 pages, including many dreamy photographs of gulls in action.

The book is now a symbol of the alternative or New Age spirituality that emerged at this time—yet, as many have noted, Jonathan's experience in the story is an allegory of the life of Jesus.

Flying into the unknown

Jonathan is different to other birds in his flock: "For most gulls, it is not flying that matters, but eating. For this gull, though, it was not eating that mattered, but flight." His father tells him that "the reason you fly is to eat" and that you don't fly for flying's sake.

Still, Jonathan spends his days experimenting with high-speed dives and flying very low over the water. He wants to push his limits, to find out what is possible. Often, his attempts end in dismal failure.

One time he is flying faster than ever before toward the water but cannot pull up in time; he hits the water like a wall at 90 miles an hour. He tells himself: "I am a seagull. I am limited by my nature... If I were meant to fly at speed, I'd have a falcon's short wings, and live on mice instead of fish."

He resigns himself to just being part of the flock, doing things the way they had always been done. Then it comes to him: If he could fly with his wings pulled tighter into his body, he would have wings as good as a falcon, made for tiny changes in direction while flying at great speed. He tries a dive and is able to accelerate to 140 miles per hour, "a gray cannonball under the moon." The next day he goes even beyond this, over 200 miles per hour, the fastest a gull has ever flown.

In his celebration Jonathan flies down from the heights and right through his own flock, luckily not killing anyone. He realizes he has taken his species to a new level. Once he teaches them what he knows, he thinks, they will no longer have a tired life of going from one fishing boat to another, picking up fish heads merely to survive. He will show them a higher level of existence.

Genius banished

Yet the next day, Jonathan is summoned to stand before the gull council. For his "reckless irresponsibility" he is shamed and banished from the flock. He is told that he does not understand the purpose of gull life: to eat to stay alive as long as possible.

Out at the Far Cliffs, Jonathan spends his days alone, sad not so much for himself but for the possibilities the flock has spurned. All the time he is finding new ways to do things. From his flying experiments he discovers that a controlled high-speed dive into the water can get the better-tasting fish that swim some distance below the surface. Ironically, his love of flying itself has led to an abundance of food.

Jonathan later meets a group of more advanced gulls, gulls like him who fly for the sake of it. They take him into another dimension, a sort of heaven for gulls, and he is told that he is a one-in-a-million gull, because he has learned the lesson of life: that it is not just to get through but to seek your own perfection in some way. Most gulls have to go through 1,000 lives before they realize this. He is told: "We choose our next world through what we learn in this one. Learn nothing, and the next world is the same as this one, all the same limitations and lead weights to overcome." We must seek our own perfection—this is the reason for living.

A gull of God

Jonathan meets an older gull who has achieved such perfection that he can travel without moving. He merely thinks of a place and he is there. Jonathan is amazed.

Jonathan himself gets to the point where he knows he is not just "bone and feather" but "a perfect idea of freedom and flight, limited by nothing at all." The remarkable bird is not the one who does things differently, but the one who sees themselves differently. The way to fly better was always there, it only awaited discovery. If you never depart from how you see yourself, you will never see that you have other possibilities. Learning how to fly brilliantly, Jonathan realizes, is a step to expressing a gull's real nature—as a spark of God.

When Bach talks of the "Great Gull," the allegory with Jesus is clear. Jonathan becomes a teacher and tells an aspiring gull that he should not complain when his flock makes him an outcast. He should forgive them, and one day they will appreciate the path he has taken and learn from him. When you are different you either get categorized as a devil or a god, Jonathan tells his pupil, but either way, you know that choosing love and forgiveness is the highest lesson to be learned.

Final comments

These are the bare bones of the book, but if you want to be inspired you should read the full story. It might take only 40 minutes, but it can clear your mind and lift your sights, like a walk on the beach.

It is easy now, over 30 years on, to overlook the originality of the book's concept. Though some people find it rather naïve, in fact it expresses timeless ideas about human potential.

When you go to the seaside you may see gulls squabbling over a single hot chip or a bread crust and think they are squabbling over nothing. Yet this book shows us that most people are like the gulls in Jonathan's flock: If they could only escape their narrow mindsets they would realize what riches awaited them. If you are pondering big changes in your life, this book may inspire the confidence you need.

Richard Bach

Born in Illinois in 1936, Richard Bach went to Long Beach State College. He became an airline pilot and also had stints as an US air force fighter pilot, movie stunt pilot, flight instructor, and aviation technical writer. With his first wife he had six children, and he met his second wife Leslie in connection with the film Jonathan Livingston Seagull *(1973).*

Bach's other books include Illusions, Bridge Across Forever, One, Flying, *and* The Ferret Chronicles *series.*

Black Elk Speaks

"*It is the story of all life that is holy and is good to tell, and of us two-leggeds sharing in it with the four-leggeds and the wings of the air and all green things; for these are children of one mother and their father is one spirit.*"

"*And now when I look about me upon my people in despair, I feel like crying and I wish and wish my vision could have been given to a man more worthy. I wonder why it came to me, a pitiful old man who can do nothing. Men and women and children I have cured of sickness with the power the vision gave me; but my nation I could not help. If a man or woman or child dies, it does not matter long, for the nation lives on. It was the nation that was dying, and the vision was for the nation; but I have done nothing with it.*"

In a nutshell

Consider the whole of life as one, the seen and the unseen, spirit and matter.

In a similar vein
Starhawk *The Spiral Dance* (p. 234)
Emanuel Swedenborg *Heaven and Hell* (p. 246)

CHAPTER 4

Black Elk

I n August 1930, John Neihardt was traveling around Nebraska to
gather information for an epic narrative poem on the history of the
American West. Moving through the reservation of the Oglala Sioux
people (also known as the Lakota), he met an elderly Indian holy man,
almost blind, by the name of Black Elk. Though they had not previously had any contact, Black Elk "knew" that Neihardt would come,
and planned to tell him his story.

Neihardt set about recording the man's memories, which became
Black Elk Speaks. Though critically praised, the book was only saved
from obscurity by a dedicated following of readers both in America
and overseas, who loved its eloquent and poetic language. In the 1960s
there was a surge of interest in Native American religion and the book
finally became a bestseller, assisted by psychologist Carl Jung's interest
in Black Elk's story.

What is the book's enduring attraction? More than a simple record of
historical events, it describes a series of detailed visions that Black Elk
had about the dark future of his people under European civilization, and
the spiritual burden he felt as a result. As a proud warrior of an ancient
people—his cousin was the famous Lakota leader Crazy Horse—the
thought of this emasculated future would have driven most people to
chemical oblivion or suicide, but the book charts Black Elk's attempts to
adapt to the modern, white world and to understand cultures beyond
his own. From his part in the battle at Wounded Knee to his meeting
with Queen Victoria, Black Elk's life is one of those bizarre bridgings of
cultures that could only have happened in the twentieth century.

The book can be read as a work of comparative religion or anthropology, but it is Black Elk's mystical powers and the very spiritual
worldview of his people that we focus on here.

First vision
Black Elk's visions are the heart of the book. The visions were
clearly of a sacred nature, which makes their sharing with Neihardt

31

all the more valuable. Black Elk was only five when he first began hearing voices, but was afraid to tell anyone about them. They continued through his childhood, the most significant being when he was nine.

In this vision, which caused him to be physically sick, he came before his people's Six Grandfathers (spirit lords) who took him on a tour of the universe, revealing great mysteries. The purpose, it seems, was to provide Black Elk with a big picture of his place in the world and his duty in relation to his people. During the vision he learned powerful sacred songs and dances, which later became important to that duty. Black Elk reflected that at the time he was too young to grasp anything of what he saw, and it was years before he began to work out the meaning of the vision. A relative, Standing Bear, had commented that after the visions Black Elk became a different child, and as time passed it grew clear that the vision had somehow bestowed psychic and healing powers on him.

Powers

After the death of Black Elk's famous cousin Crazy Horse, the encroaching Wasichus (white people) ordered the Lakota to move into reserves. A few, including Black Elk, broke off from the group with a view to traveling to "Grandmother's Land," or Canada, where they felt they would be safe from the soldiers. However, the extreme cold brought them to the brink of starvation, and they were only saved when Black Elk had psychic guidance that food in the form of bison would be coming to them.

To the teenage Black Elk the burden of his powers was almost too much to bear. Birds and animals began "speaking" to him, telling him "It's time, it's time," but time for what he did not know. Eventually, Black Elk told an elderly medicine man about his visions, and the man immediately organized for an enactment of the "horse dance" that Black Elk had seen. In a time of war with the Wasichus, the dance succeeded in empowering his people and brought about some physical healing, but Black Elk remained tortured by his inability to really help his people. He continuously questioned why he had been burdened in this way, when others must be more worthy; he felt he had failed his people, that his strength was not sufficient to overcome the troubles that came with the American occupation.

Though many of the visions displayed dazzling beauty and gave Black Elk a realization of the oneness of the universe and the interconnectedness within nature, they also revealed a dark future of brutal oppression, with the Sioux living in "square gray houses" and the bison population decimated. Unfortunately, Black Elk would see some of the more disturbing aspects of his visions come true.

Warrior

The book contains some amazing descriptions of key battles between the Sioux and the Wasichus. Many readers will have heard of the notorious massacre of Wounded Knee, but Black Elk's account is profoundly moving in its detached tone, describing one of the most brutal episodes of American history. On learning that 500 soldiers had assembled at Wounded Knee, he sensed the night before the battle that something terrible was imminent. The next day, dressed in his sacred "ghost shirt" with its protective power, he painted his face and rode out toward the battle scene, armed only with his sacred bow.

This notorious event began because of a simple misunderstanding, which had resulted in a white officer being shot during the collection of ammunition. The Lakota were attacked by armed soldiers but, having handed over all their guns before the attack, had only their bare hands to protect themselves. Among the many gory scenes, Black Elk described the heaps of murdered babies, children, and women whom the American soldiers had shot at as they were trying to run away. The Lakota actually had some successes on the battlefield, and Black Elk told how he himself killed and scalped white soldiers, but did not seem to regret those acts on the basis that it was the Native Americans' land and as warriors they were defending it.

World traveler

Black Elk Speaks is full of anecdotes and descriptions that paint a rich picture of Native American culture, particularly the deep feeling for animal life and nature. The affinity with birds, four-legged animals, the sky, and plants is expressed in such a way that we cannot imagine Black Elk's life without these elements. The language is peppered with native words and terms that refer to nature, such as the months of the year. September, for instance, is "Moon When the Calves Grow Hair," and December "Moon of the Popping Trees."

Nevertheless, his people could not live in isolation, and Black Elk wanted to see for himself whether the Wasichu way of life was better than his own society. At the age of 23 he traveled "across the big water" to Europe, hoping also to educate whites about his people. Although terribly homesick, he spent six months performing in London as a curiosity in Buffalo Bill's famous Wild West show. During this demeaning experience the visions began to fade from his daily life and he felt his spirit weakening.

On a lighter note, he met Queen Victoria and was subsequently invited to Buckingham Palace. Among her comments that Black Elk relates were that he and his fellow Lakotas were the best-looking men she had ever seen, and: "If you belonged to me, I would not let them take you around in a show like this." Black Elk went on to spend several months in Manchester and then in Paris, all the while thinking of his people, but he could not afford the passage back to America. In Paris he had another significant vision, in which his spirit journeyed back home without his body. This is a very moving section of the book, particularly to anyone who has ever spent long periods away from their loved ones.

Final comments

Though it is not a spiritual classic in terms of being a statement of a set of beliefs, *Black Elk Speaks* is a superb record of a people who understood the world to be infused with spiritual meaning and saw all nature as holy, in contrast to the western separation of spirit and matter.

There is some debate over how much of the book is Black Elk and how much is Neihardt. We can be sure, however, that without Neihardt's work to turn the raw material of Black Elk's memories into a book, it would have remained a pile of notes and would not have become a work of literature. Clearly there was a deep bond between the two men and a shared sense of greater purpose about making the visions known outside the Lakota, so that they would belong to humanity.

While Black Elk continually described his despair that he had not fulfilled his duty to his people or led the life that was truly meant for him, by sharing his visions he ensured a legacy of greater understanding. Were he alive today he would be both surprised and pleased at the lasting impact his words and life had within his own people and the broader world. He could not read or write, but as Neihardt suggests, Black Elk was a highly educated man in the full sense of the word. Though it came at considerable cost, he arrived at a deep awareness of things that the average person will never know.

Cosmic Consciousness

"While its true nature has been (and necessarily so) entirely apprehended, the fact of cosmic consciousness has long been recognized both in the Eastern and Western worlds, and the great majority of civilized men and women in all countries today bow down before teachers who possessed the cosmic sense... all uninspired teachers derive the lessons which they transmit directly or indirectly from the few who have been illumined."

In a nutshell

The experience of "cosmic consciousness," or enlightenment, is part of human evolution.

In a similar vein

William James *The Varieties of Religious Experience* (p. 130)
James Redfield *The Celestine Prophecy* (p. 210)
Ken Wilber *A Theory of Everything* (p. 294)
Gary Zukav *The Seat of the Soul* (p. 306)

CHAPTER 5

Richard Maurice Bucke

Richard Maurice Bucke was a highly respected Canadian psychiatrist who in his spare time immersed himself in poetry and literature, sometimes spending whole evenings with friends reciting the work of Whitman, Wordsworth, Shelley, Keats, and Browning. After one such evening on a visit to England, while on a long journey in his horse and buggy and feeling particularly inspired by Whitman's poetry, Bucke had a great illumination, a flash of what he called "cosmic consciousness." In that single moment, he realized that the cosmos is not dead matter but fully alive; that humans have a soul and are immortal; that the universe is built so that all things work toward the good, with everyone's eventual happiness a certainty; and that love is the basic principle in the universe.

Bucke learned more in that moment, he admitted, than in years of study. Yet it was only a glimpse of true enlightenment, and he recognized that there had been a select group of people throughout history who had achieved the state permanently, and who had naturally influenced the rest of humanity in hugely greater proportion than their small number. Some of them—Jesus, Muhammed, Buddha—had inspired great religions, because they offered a new understanding of what it meant to be human. It was part of our evolution to grow in consciousness, Bucke believed, and these figures heralded the adoption of new traits of being and awareness that were not yet available to the general population.

What is cosmic consciousness?

Bucke distinguished between different levels of consciousness. "Simple consciousness" is the awareness that most animals have of their bodies and the environment around them. As Bucke puts it: "The animal is, as it were, immersed in his consciousness as a fish in the sea; he cannot, even in imagination, get outside of it for one moment so as to realize it." "Self-consciousness," on the other hand, is unique to humans and gives us a very different awareness of ourselves: we can think about the fact that we think. Self-consciousness, along with having language to express it and make use of it, makes *homo sapiens* human.

Cosmic consciousness, in turn, puts some humans way above others. Bucke describes it as an acute awareness of the true "life and order of the universe" in which a person experiences oneness with God or universal energy. This intellectual awareness, or the apprehension of truth, brings with it an astounding joyousness, because all the misperceptions of normal self-consciousness are lifted. If people see that the nature of the universe is love, and that we are all part of an undying conscious life force, they can no longer experience fear or doubt.

Implications for humanity

In a time of cosmic consciousness, Bucke says, religion would not exist, as there would be no need to profess belief or unbelief—everyone would have first-hand awareness of God and the perfect spiritual nature of the universe. The difference between that world and the one we know now would be like that between the dawn of humanity and the present.

A leap in evolution of this magnitude sounds far-fetched, but Bucke points out that all new human traits or abilities began first with one person and in time became universal. The apprehension of color, for instance, came relatively late to humans. There is no mention in the Bible of the sky being blue, and the ancient Greeks perceived no more than three or four colors. Bucke's point was that as time has gone on, man has been able to perceive things that weren't previously considered to exist.

Darwin noted that newer traits in species had a tendency to disappear—the principle of reversion. Animals that have been highly bred are more susceptible to disease and have poorer faculties. Their traits are unstable. The flipside of this is that the longer a trait stays with a species or race, the more stable it becomes. How does this relate to cosmic consciousness? Simply that the first instances inevitably seemed like bizarre anomalies, but as more cases have appeared we have become more accepting of the possibility that some people can transcend normal self-consciousness, and we recognize such people as our natural superiors. They are literally more evolved.

Characteristics of illumination

Bucke came up with a list of historical figures who in his view had clearly achieved cosmic consciousness: Jesus, Buddha, Muhammed, St. Paul, Francis Bacon, Jacob Boehme, John Yepes (John of the Cross), Bartolomé Las Casas, Plotinus, Dante Alighieri, Honoré de Balzac, Walt Whitman, and Edward Carpenter. His list of "lesser lights," those he was not sure about, included Moses, Socrates, Blaise Pascal, Emanuel Swedenborg, William Blake, Ralph Waldo Emerson, and Sri Ramakrishna, and a number of his contemporaries identified only by their initials. In this secondary list were four women, including the medieval mystic Madame Guyon.

Bucke's discussions of these cases makes fascinating reading and forms the body of the book. He saw the following as characteristic of people who had achieved cosmic consciousness:

❖ Average age at illumination 35.
❖ History of earnest spiritual seeking, e.g., love of scriptures or meditation.
❖ Good physical health.
❖ Enjoyment of solitude (many on the list never married).
❖ Generally well liked or loved.
❖ Little interest in money.

The features or indicators of cosmic consciousness include:

❖ Initially, seeing an extremely bright light.
❖ Appreciation of separateness as an illusion, i.e., everything in the universe is one.
❖ Appreciation of eternal life as a fact.
❖ After illumination, subjects exist in permanent happiness. They actually look different, and have a joyous expression.
❖ No sense of death, fear, or sin—Whitman, for instance, moved among dangerous people in New York but no one ever touched him.
❖ Those who have experienced illumination recognize others who have, yet find it difficult to express what they have seen.

Bucke made some other interesting points:

❖ Most experiences of cosmic consciousness happen in spring or summer.
❖ The level of education is not a factor—some of the illuminati were highly educated, others had little schooling.
❖ Illumined people generally had parents of opposing temperaments, e.g., a sanguine mother, a melancholy father.

Final comments

Cosmic Consciousness is far from a perfect book. Be warned that Bucke states his beliefs in the superiority of white civilization; the eventual triumph of socialism; and the theory that Francis Bacon wrote the works of Shakespeare. Many readers will take issue with his list of the cosmically conscious, since he fails to mention, among others, Teresa of Avila, Julian of Norwich, and St. Francis of Assisi.

Given what he knew and the time in which he wrote, however, these aspects can be forgiven. In making a convincing case for commonality in the experience of cosmic consciousness Bucke blazed a trail, and his effort has rightly made the book a classic. *Cosmic Consciousness* is not rigorous in a scientific sense, but its goal of objectively mapping out mystical experience came years before William James produced *The Varieties of Religious Experience* (which heaps praise on Bucke's book) and a full decade before Evelyn Underhill's influential *Mysticism*. Bucke's theme that cases of cosmic consciousness are on the rise has also found echoes in modern writers such as Abraham Maslow (his idea of a growing number of "self-actualized" people) and Marilyn Ferguson (*The Aquarian Conspiracy*).

The idea of cosmic consciousness may seem naïve—we are, after all, still walking around with prehistoric humans' instinctive reflexes—yet it is supported by the fact that personal enlightenment as a concept is now an accepted part of our culture. It is appreciated as a noble goal, an alternative to life bound by self-consciousness. We like to know that there are a sprinkling of people who exist in permanent joy and happiness, because they remind us that even within our bodies we can be spiritual beings.

Richard Maurice Bucke

Born in 1837 in Norfolk, England, Bucke was the seventh child of an English family who later settled in Ontario, Canada. His father was a well-read Church of England minister who gave up the cloth for farming. Bucke's mother died when he was 7, and his stepmother when he was 17, at which point he decided to leave home. For the next several years he traveled the United States working as a gardener, steamboat deckhand, and finally wagon train driver. This last job took him into uncharted territory beyond Salt Lake City into the Rockies, where he was attacked by Native Americans, worked as a gold miner, and had a foot amputated after a freezing foray into the wilderness looking for silver.

After inheriting some money, Bucke put himself through medical school, did postgraduate work in England, and became what was then called an "alienist" (psychiatrist). He headed two insane asylums in Hamilton and London in Ontario, and in 1882 was made a Professor of Mental and Nervous Diseases at Western University, Ontario. In 1890 he was elected to the presidency of the American Medico-Psychological Association.

Bucke first met Walt Whitman in 1877 and he dedicated his first book, Man's Moral Nature *(1879), to his friend.*

Cosmic Consciousness *began life in 1894 as a paper presented at the American Medico-Psychological Association's annual meeting. The book was dedicated to his son Maurice, who died in an accident a year before its publication. Bucke himself died less than a year after its release (1902), after slipping on patch of ice outside his home.*

The Tao of Physics

"We shall see how the two foundations of twentieth-century physics—quantum theory and relativity theory—both force us to see the world very much in the way a Hindu, Buddhist or Taoist sees it, and how this similarity strengthens when we look at the recent attempts to combine these two theories in order to describe the phenomena of the submicroscopic world… Here the parallels between modern physics and Eastern mysticism are most striking, and we shall often encounter statements where it is almost impossible to say whether they have been made by physicists or by Eastern mystics."

In a nutshell

Physics and spirituality are two sides of the same coin.

In a similar vein
Aldous Huxley *The Doors of Perception* (p. 124)

CHAPTER 6

Fritjof Capra

What has physics got to do with spirituality? Fritjof Capra asked this question when, while working as a researcher in particle physics, he became interested in eastern religion. The descriptions of matter and reality in the two domains struck him as being remarkably similar, yet no one seemed to have drawn the connection. It was not regular classical physics but the relatively new quantum science that prompted his comparison, which seemed to recall a way of understanding the world that—to conventional eyes—could only be described as mystical.

The Tao of Physics: An Exploration of the Parallels between Modern Physics and Eastern Mysticism helped to create a new genre of writing that bridged science and spirituality, and is still a benchmark because it carries the excitement of previously unnoticed connections. Published at a time when science and technology seemed to have triumphed, the book was a surprise because it revealed modern science to be grappling with strange physical phenomena that spiritual literature had described and explained centuries ago.

Same universe, different eyes

Capra notes that the universe Isaac Newton imagined in the seventeenth century was mechanical, a great machine made up of moving objects that, if you knew its laws, was fully predictable. Everything happening within this universe had a definite cause, and every event had a certain effect. Time and space were separate, and if one were to look closely enough, all matter could be broken down to its basic building blocks.

The Newtonian model clearly does apply to the workings of our daily world, in which a grain of salt falls onto a plate, a ball flies through the air, a planet travels through its solar system. The theory makes intuitive sense. Einstein's theory of relativity, however, showed that matter does not possess the solidity that our senses accord it. Things are not "things" but *energy*, which takes on the appearance and feel of form. The nature of the world is not solidity but perpetual motion.

43

The early quantum physicists confirmed this theory by their discovery that matter, when observed at its most minute level, is better understood as a sort of field in which expressions of energy—protons, electrons, etc.—move ceaselessly about. And in contrast to Newton's "billiard ball" universe, in which objects supposedly forced other objects to do certain things, quantum physics found a much more fluid world not tied to exact causalities. Quantum pioneers Werner Heisenberg and Niels Bohr could not quite believe the results and implications of some of their own experiments, such as the following:

* Particles frequently appeared where they did not expect them.
* They could not predict when a certain subatomic event would occur, only note a probability of its occurrence.
* At some times particles would appear to the observer as particles, at other times as wave-like patterns.
* Particles were not objects in the Newtonian sense, but rather the observable indications of reactions and interconnections.
* Particles did not bounce off each other while retaining their essential properties. Instead, they were constantly absorbing each other or exchanging properties.
* Particles could only be understood in term of their environment, not as isolated objects.

In short, these experiments revealed that the basic nature of our physical world was not like a collection of objects, but more like a complex web of interactions in constant motion.

Capra notes that the nucleus of an atom—its "stuff"—is 100,000 times smaller than the whole atom, yet it constitutes nearly all of the atom's physical mass. From this we can begin to understand that what we perceive to be a chair or an apple or a person, while it looks solid, has a structure based mostly on empty space, and what is solid is usually in a state of frenzied vibration.

Yet, to introduce one of the many paradoxes of quantum science, the "empty space" has an almost alive quality and particles can spontaneously appear out of it for no apparent reason. As Capra puts it: "Matter has appeared in these experiments as completely mutable. All particles can be transmuted into other particles; they can be created from energy and can vanish into energy." In these force fields of subatomic particles the distinction between matter and the void around it becomes fuzzy, and the void itself becomes important. It is now under-stood to be alive, and physical forms simply become "transient mani-festations of the underlying Void."

Void as creator

Through his reading into the cosmologies of Hinduism, Taoism, and Buddhism, Capra realized that their descriptions of how the universe operated chimed with the weird findings and apparent paradoxes of quantum mechanics. These religions, so much older than Newtonian physics, had long incorporated the myth of solidity and permanence.

In Buddhism, for instance, the cause of all suffering is *trishna*, cling-ing or grasping, which does not recognize the essentially transitory quality of life, in which the illusion of fixity can only cause problems. This doctrine of impermanence is also found in Chinese religion, which celebrates nature's quality of eternal flow and change. One of the cen-tral books of Chinese thought is the *I-Ching*, the "Book of Changes," which guides the reader toward action that is complementary with the way things are moving at any one moment.

In quantum physics, the creation or destruction of particles often happens for no reason. There is a field out of which they arise, and into which they go back, but they seem to act as if they are beyond cause and effect. However, Capra notes that nothingness is not emptiness, a paradox amply addressed in eastern religions. Hinduism, for instance, has a word for this void, *Brahman*, a field of potentiality from which all things emerge, and the Dance of Shiva expresses the endless process of creation and destruction of matter. In Buddhism, the *Sunyata* is a living void that gives birth to everything physical. Taoism has as its central feature the *Tao*, the empty, formless nature of the universe, which nevertheless is the basic substance of creation.

Capra thus convincingly argues that the paradoxes of solidity and ephemerality and of nothingness and being, which have bewildered quantum scientists, have been part of eastern religion for centuries. Where before such teachings might have been considered, at least in rational western eyes, as mystical mumbo-jumbo, in fact the opposite turns out to be correct: eastern mystics have all along been accu-rately describing (as much as that is possible in words) the fabric of creation, not in mathematical terms but in mythology, art, and poetry.

From many to one

The *yin* and *yang* of Chinese religion represent apparently opposing forces (feminine–masculine, intuitive–rational, light–darkness, etc.), but in fact they are complementary, each needing the other to exist. Capra notes that the goal of eastern mysticism, whether Hinduism, Buddhism, or Taoism, is to finally recognize that the universe is an unbroken whole, despite the appearance of being a multitude of separate objects.

Seventeenth-century French philosopher René Descartes pictured humans as thinking beings, able to assay the universe objectively, and western civilization developed on this distinction between mind and matter. Quantum physics has shattered this notion of neat objectivity, because experiments showed that particles took on different forms depending on how we decided to look at them. In Heisenberg's words, "What we observe is not nature itself, but nature exposed to our method of questioning." That is, the patterns in nature that we observe with supposed objectivity may not be some final true reality, but will reflect how our own minds have developed. We stop being an observer of the atomic world, and actually become a participator in it.

The lesson of quantum physics, and the contention of Hindu and Buddhist philosophy, is that the distinction between the doer, the doing, and the object of the action is artificial. They are all one.

What does all this mean for us personally? Descartes's division between mind and matter leads to us thinking of ourselves as separate egos within individual bodies. But Capra says that this conscious separation of ourselves from the world creates a sense of fragmentation in which we have a multiplicity of beliefs, talents, feelings, and activities. In Buddhism there is a word for this outlook on life in which we make ourselves an isolated ego: *avidya* or "illusion." The Hindu work Bhagavad-Gita says: "All actions take place in time by the interweaving of the forces of nature, but the man lost in selfish delusion thinks that he himself is the actor." And consider this line from the Upanishads: "When the mind is disturbed, the multiplicity of things is produced, but when the mind is quieted, the multiplicity of things disappears."

In other words, the world literally changes when we perceive it differently. It is very Newtonian to see the world as made up of millions of separate things, but this is potentially very fragmenting if we apply it to our sense of self. When we see the world as one, we can heal and unify ourselves; we will not want to hurt others or damage our environment, as it will only be hurting us.

Final comments

If you take only one point from *The Tao of Physics*, let it be that modern science increasingly validates more spiritual or mystical conceptions of the universe.

Capra makes the point that the mystic and the scientist are both observers of nature and both report their findings in the language they know. Given that these languages are worlds apart, the remarkable similarity in their descriptions suggests that we are closer to knowing what moves the universe. *The Tao of Physics* is able to convey that the universe is much weirder than we could have imagined, or at least weirder than conventional physics imagined, while at the same time showing that humanity has long weaved correct knowledge of its patterns into myth, religion, and art. Newtonian physics craved neat causal explanations for everything, but religion has always known that divinity moves in mysterious and seemingly miraculous ways. To put it another way, what is magical to science is, from the spiritual point of view, just the way things are.

It is close to 30 years since *The Tao of Physics* was published, so the science has moved on. However, the basic concepts are still correct, and an old copy from the 1970s may blow your mind just as much as a newer edition. It is a superb introduction to eastern religions, and if you know little in this area that alone justifies reading the book.

Fritjof Capra

Capra received a doctorate in theoretical physics from the University of Vienna in 1966. He has worked as a researcher in particle physics at the University of Paris, the University of California at Santa Cruz, the Stanford Linear Accelerator Center, Imperial College, London, and the Lawrence Berkeley Laboratory at the University of California. He has also taught at the University of California and San Francisco State University.

Capra's other books include The Turning Point, Uncommon Wisdom, The Web of Life, *and* The Hidden Connections. *He lives in California.*

1972

Journey to Ixtlan

"'We're not talking about the same thing,' he said. 'For you the world is weird because if you're not bored with it you're at odds with it. For me the world is weird because it is stupendous, awesome, mysterious, unfathomable; my interest has been to convince you that you must assume responsibility for being here, in this marvelous world, in this marvelous desert, in this marvelous time. I wanted to convince you that you must learn to make every act count, since you are going to be here for only a short while; in fact, too short for witnessing all the marvels of it.'"

In a nutshell

Respect the world by taking responsibility for your own life.

In a similar vein
Black Elk *Black Elk Speaks* (p. 30)
Carl Gustav Jung *Memories, Dreams, Reflections* (p. 136)
Dan Millman *The Way of the Peaceful Warrior* (p. 180)
Miguel Ruiz *The Four Agreements* (p. 216)

CHAPTER 7

Carlos Castaneda

n 1960, Carlos Castaneda was an anthropology student at the University of California at Los Angeles. His chosen area of study was medicinal plants used by the Indian people in the deserts of southwest United States and Mexico. On one of his trips he found himself at a bus station near the border. A colleague introduced him to an old Yaqui Indian man who had extensive knowledge of these plants. The man, don Juan Matus, agreed to tell Castaneda what he knew.

So began a 10-year apprenticeship into the way of a *brujo* (medicine man or sorcerer) that forced Castaneda to ditch the idea that he was a scientist reporting the facts for some dissertation. He later admitted that what began as an objective study evolved more into an autobiography, as under don Juan's direction he himself became the subject.

Castaneda's first account of this experience, *The Teachings of Don Juan*, electrified readers on its release in 1968 because it offered an alternative reality to modern civilization. In tune with the times, the author's initiation was assisted by psychotropic drugs (datura, peyote, and magic mushrooms), experiences also described in the follow-up, *A Separate Reality*.

However, by the publication of *Journey to Ixtlan*, the third book in the series, Castaneda had realized that natural chemicals were only a spur to personal development. More important were the principles that don Juan reveals for becoming a "man of power," and *Journey to Ixtlan* is arguably the clearest expression of his wisdom. The seemingly endless trials and weird experiences that the author goes through also make for gripping reading.

Becoming inaccessible

In the first pages of *Journey to Ixtlan*, don Juan explains that the world we take to be real is only a description of it, a consensually created reality, programmed into us from birth. The ultimate purpose of his training is to be able to "stop the world," to suspend normal perception so that truth can be perceived. Castaneda does not at first understand such strange ideas, but is willing to humor the old man. All the while, though, it is don Juan who is laughing at Castaneda's fixed, narrow understanding of the world.

Don Juan tells Castaneda that "personal history is crap." It is better simply to leave one's past alone and concentrate on being a new person every day, to have the freedom of not being predictable. Don Juan admits that he has created a fog around his life on purpose, because there is great freedom in being anonymous. In contrast, his younger charge is fully known and therefore taken for granted. The thoughts of other people continue to shape his identity, and everything he does he must explain to others.

Don Juan tries to explain the concept of being inaccessible, or removing yourself "from the middle of a trafficked way." He seems to know a lot about Castaneda that the author has never revealed to him, such as the fact that he still regrets the loss of a girlfriend. Don Juan suggests that she left him because he was always available to her, which led to routine and boredom. He needs to adopt the mindset of a hunter, who is never a slave to routine. If hunters know the routines of their prey, they have them cornered. To avoid becoming prey ourselves, we must break our routines, become less easily placed. If we don't do this, don Juan tells Castaneda, "we end up bored to death with ourselves and with the world." In his eyes, the younger man has committed two interrelated sins: he has little appreciation of the mystery of the universe, and consequently he is too obvious a person.

Seeing beyond the self

At the heart of don Juan's wisdom is the idea that people take themselves too seriously. He notices that Castaneda flares up at the slightest provocation and gets "peeved like an old lady." To help Castaneda get rid of his self-importance, don Juan makes him talk to plants—they are, after all, his equals. He wants to break down Castaneda's belief that he is a man in control with a clear agenda.

Don Juan shocks Castaneda by describing him as a "pimp" who hasn't properly engaged with life and who has no precision in his actions. His self-importance has prevented him from really seeing the world: "You are like a horse with blinders," don Juan tells him, "all you see is yourself apart from everything else."

Mood of the warrior

The old man ventures the idea that the other side of self-importance is insecurity. Castaneda admits that he feels like "a leaf at the mercy of the wind," full of lament and longing, easily upset. He has always found flaws in life and in other people, and doesn't really like himself at all. But don Juan tells him that feeling sorry for himself, even if it seems justified, is not the life of a person of knowledge—a warrior. A warrior's power comes precisely from choosing the state of their own mind; the "mood" of the warrior means being defiant of circumstances at all times.

"It is meaningless to complain," don Juan says. "What's important from this point on is the strategy of your life." With a strategy, we are not weakened by "killing time," because every moment has a purpose. Castaneda feels that he has been dragged unwillingly into certain situations in his life, but don Juan correctly sizes him up as a person who doesn't assume responsibility for anything. Because he believes he will live forever, he also believes that there is time to change course, to have doubts. However, life requires us to make decisions.

Castaneda is taken aback when the old man tells him to constantly be aware of death lurking behind him. If he has this awareness, he will live differently. It will cure him of his self-importance; and it will put apparently difficult situations into perspective. Don Juan notes that people who live as if they were immortal lead petty lives. They let themselves have "crappy thoughts and moods."

Out in the desert, put through various trials by his mentor, Castaneda is almost driven mad. But he comes round to the idea that death can be his best adviser, admitting: "The pettiness of being annoyed with him was monstrous in the light of my death." Don Juan teaches him to live as if it were his last day or hour on earth. This will make him love life. Thinking he had plenty of time had turned him into a timid half-man.

Final comments

Journey to Ixtlan brings surprising lessons for a spiritual book: be tough with yourself, be decisive, be fully responsible for your actions. You may have the body of an adult but your mind is not that of a real man or woman. The great sin, don Juan teaches us, is to think that life itself is not good. Whether in failure or success, we must never take our eyes away from the fact that it is an amazing world, and we must rise to its challenges.

Most people expect the world to do something for them. They live amid technology and entertainment, but remain total strangers to power and have no sense of mystery. The idea running through Castaneda's books is that human beings are like signposts to an entity or force much greater than ourselves; we should realize that self-knowledge can only be gained through recognition of this greater force.

There has been a great deal of controversy over whether don Juan was a real person and whether these books were based on real events. Castaneda maintained that they were not fiction, yet because their contents seem so unreal, they could easily be taken as such. It is human nature, it seems, to deny the legitimacy of ideas that are revolutionary.

Carlos Castaneda

Born Carlos Arana in Cajamarca, Peru, in 1925, Castaneda changed his name when he became a US citizen in 1959. As an anthropology student at the University of California, Los Angeles, he received his BA in 1962 and in 1970 was awarded a doctorate for Journey to Ixtlan.

Castaneda's other books include Tales of Power, The Second Ring of Power, The Eagle's Gift, Magical Passes, *and* The Active Side of Infinity, *the latter published after his death in California in 1998.*

St Francis of Assisi

"Lord, make me an instrument of Your peace.
where there is hatred, let me sow love;
where there is injury, pardon;
where there is doubt, faith;
where there is darkness, light;
and where there is sadness, joy."
St. Francis of Assisi

"What gave him his extraordinary personal power was this: that from the Pope to the beggar, from the sultan of Syria in his pavilion to the ragged robbers crawling out of the wood, there was never a man who looked into those brown burning eyes without being certain that Francis Bernadone was really interested in him; in his own inner individual life from the cradle to the grave... Now for this particular moral and religious idea there is no external expression except courtesy."

In a nutshell

Extreme gratitude enables you to see the world afresh.

In a similar vein

Mohandas Gandhi *An Autobiography* (p. 84)
Teresa of Avila *Interior Castle* (p. 252)
Mother Teresa *A Simple Path* (p. 258)

CHAPTER 8

G. K. Chesterton

Francis of Assisi was born Giovanni Bernadone in 1181, coming of age just as the thirteenth century began. Christendom was emerging from the Dark Ages, an inward-looking and defensive era following the collapse of the Roman Empire, but before the glories of the Renaissance. According to G. K. Chesterton, it was a time of spiritual cleansing, reflected in the monastic ethic of self-denial, and Christendom still felt threatened by paganism and barbarian attacks. One result of this quest for purity was the Crusades, but another, more positive aspect was a flowering of culture.

The popular stars of the day were the French Troubadours, romantic poets whose songs of passion especially captured the imagination of the young. While still a boy, Giovanni was nicknamed Francesco or "the little Frenchman" by his friends because of his love of these French poets, and the name stuck. His father, Pietro, was a self-made and fairly wealthy cloth merchant, and when Francis grew into his teens he liked to spend his father's money on fine, colorful outfits in the French style and generally having fun with his friends around town.

Hearing the call

Full of adventurous spirit and seeking military glory, as a young man Francis joined an expedition to fight the neighboring city-state of Perugia, but was captured and imprisoned for a year. This setback did not stop him joining another military foray to the Neapolitan states in the cause of an Assisi nobleman. This time, however, he began to hear inner voices saying that it was his role to help the poor and the sick, not to fight. Probably in some humiliation, he listened to them and turned back.

Not long after, Francis heard another voice telling him to restore the ruined church of St. Damiano on a hill just outside Assisi. To the consternation of his father, he set about doing this with his own hands, and was joined by a ragged crew of equally intense young men.

Funding the work proved a challenge, however, and Francis hit on the idea of selling some of his father's bolts of fabric for cash. When he discovered this, a suitably furious Pietro Bernardone pursued legal channels, which resulted in a bishop ordering the son to give back the money. This Francis did, but onto the pile of money he also cast his clothes, revealing a hair shirt.

Fools for God

In those early days, Francis's group of neophytes was known as the Jongleurs de Dieu, the jesters or jugglers of God. The Franciscans tried to make people see things differently, just as a clown or jester does, earnestly seeking people's awakening to the presence of God. The goal of medieval life was solidity and strength, but the Jongleurs provided a joyful approach to existence that made the "real" world seem leaden. Abandoning all possessions and even a permanent place to live, they represented freedom.

Francis himself had gone through a number of humiliations, from being a failed soldier to being prosecuted by his father, and realized that he was a fool in just about everyone's eyes. But if that were the case, he would be a fool for God. He began attending to beggars and lepers, and although he attracted the support of a wealthy citizen, Bernard of Quintavalle, and other followers, most people thought him insane—he had thrown away a good life for rags and life in a hut next to a leper hospital.

Fools into Franciscans

Yet Francis's passion and wild ways attracted open-minded people. In the town there was a girl called Clare, like Francis the child of wealthy parents. After hearing him preach, Clare decided to leave home and Francis helped her find refuge in a convent of Benedictine nuns.

Biographers have long supposed that the relationship between Clare and Francis was sexual, but Chesterton believes it was platonic. We should accept the possibility, he says, that "a heavenly love can be as real as an earthly love. The moment it is treated as real, like an earthly love, their whole riddle is easily solved." In our secular age it is hard to comprehend people willingly devoting themselves to a life of chastity and poverty. However, if there ever was a romance between the two, it soon became incidental to their higher reverence for God.

When Francis went to Pope Innocent III to beg approval to found his order, his ragged band only contained 11 men and at first he was turned away. But the Pope had a dream in which a man who looked like a peasant was holding up the papal church of St. John Lateran, and when Innocent saw Francis once more (wearing only a coarse brown peasant's tunic held together with a piece of rope) he recognized him as the man from his dream.

The Pope provisionally approved the establishment of the Franciscan order on the condition that it would grow into something substantial. Chesterton notes that only 10 years later, Francis's trademark coarse brown tunic had become the uniform of 10,000 men (it has remained the Franciscan habit ever since). The girl whom Francis helped become a nun was to become St. Clare, founding sister of the Franciscan Poor Clares, whose first monastery was the church of St. Damiano.

One of God's gentlemen

A key to understanding Francis was his gratitude. While many people give thanks to God daily or weekly, he lived in a permanent state of thanks. He particularly thanked God for his suffering, reasoning that if God had created everything, the only thing we could offer back was our suffering.

Yet Chesterton suggests that he was not a "gloomy ascetic"—he simply presented a radical approach to life. We take pleasure in acquiring things, but Francis knew that if you choose to have nothing you are free to see what is really important. "Blessed is he that expects nothing, for he shall enjoy everything," he said. Taking a vow of poverty could be enormously freeing, reminding you continually of your passion for God. By his vows a Franciscan was not more restricted than an ordinary person but actually freer: "obedient but not dependent."

In the spirit of his times, Francis journeyed to the Holy Land to convert infidels. He was taken prisoner by the Saracens and presented to the Sultan, who let him go. Chesterton refers to him as "The Man Who Could Not Get Killed," a good title for someone who would have enjoyed a martyr's death, but was probably deemed too pleasant and charming to be executed.

To Chesterton, Francis was an exemplar of the true meaning of courtesy; that is, demonstrating not merely equality or respect for others, but a warm camaraderie that can make someone feel they are the center of attention. In an age of rank and honor, Chesterton wrote, Francis "treated the whole mob of men as a mob of kings." He did not distinguish between people in terms of value, whether cohort or enemy, beggar or priest.

In love with all creation

Chesterton claims that Francis was not actually a lover of "nature." He did not love all living things in a broad, pantheistic way like we would talk of Mother Earth—he loved the *individual* person, flower, or animal that came his way. This is why he talked of a donkey as his brother, and a sparrow as his sister.

Later in life, when Francis was going blind, he volunteered to have his eyes cauterized by a hot poker, inviting "Brother Fire" to do his work. This personalization of nature may seem childish to us now, but shows an amazing kinship with the natural world. For Francis, if God had deemed a thing to exist, it was therefore wonderful and deserving of love and protection. Miracles attributed to him, along with the usual saintly stories of human healing, include spontaneously prompting a symphony of birdsong, and taming a wolf. Yet these only seem like miracles to us; to someone who had such sympathy with every living thing, they would be natural events.

Final comments

Chesterton likens Francis's impact to the birth of child in a dark house, wiping away its gloom and ushering in a new spirit. For 1,000 years the Church had been on the defensive, storing up its power and entrenching itself. Francis decided that the time had come to move in the opposite way, to do away with possessions and give out a lot of love.

Many iconoclasts change the world yet are hated for it; their extremism becomes counter-productive. Francis's genuine love for people saved him from this fate. Yet today most people are not interested in what he did for the Catholic faith; his legend presents him as a great and generous lover of life, and his story nearly always produces warm reactions, even to non-Christians. There was something simple about him and his message that is still very attractive, and if it can be summed up, it is the notion that love is more important than power.

Were it not for his vocation, Francis of Assisi would no doubt simply have been a product of his time and place, seeking glory in war and the love of a lady. As Chesterton points out, the motivations of the romantic and the saint are essentially the same: they do what they do—be it standing all night under a lover's balcony or building a church by hand in the snow—out of crazy love. And Francis was essentially a lover, whether it was of other people, of animals and plants, or of God.

Although short, Chesterton's book is dense with ideas and insights. He shows off somewhat in the way he makes his points and in his occasionally flowery language, but his study illuminates Francis as a real person. The book is more of a sketch than a full-length portrait, but like a Picasso line drawing it captures the essence of the subject. Written shortly after Chesterton's conversion to Catholicism, it has the enthusiasm of the convert, but that is balanced by the author's famous talent for accurate character analysis.

G. K. Chesterton

Born in London in 1874, Gilbert Keith Chesterton was a poet, novelist, essayist, and critic. In addition to many articles published in periodicals such as the Illustrated London News *and his own* GK's Weekly, *he published short but critically praised biographies of Charles Dickens, Thomas Aquinas, Robert Browning, and Robert Louis Stevenson. His* Orthodoxy (1908) *is considered a spiritual classic, and he also wrote a popular series of "Father Brown" books about a detective priest.*

Chesterton died in 1936.

The Places that Scare You

"*If we feel distress, embarrassment, or anger, we think we've really blown it. Yet feeling emotional upheaval is not a spiritual* faux pas*; it's the place where the warrior learns compassion. It's where we learn to stop struggling with ourselves. It's only when we can dwell in these places that scare us that equanimity becomes unshakable.*"

"*We are ... very much like a blind person who finds a jewel buried in a heap of garbage. Right here in what we'd like to throw away, in what we find repulsive and frightening, we discover the warmth and clarity of* bodhichitta.*"

In a nutshell

We grow by shining a light on the mind's dark places.

In a similar vein

Eckhart Tolle *The Power of Now* (p. 264)
Chögyam Trungpa *Cutting through Spiritual Materialism* (p. 270)
Gary Zukav *The Seat of the Soul* (p. 306)
The Dalai Lama *The Art of Happiness* (50SHC)
The Dhammapada (50SHC)

CHAPTER 9

Pema Chödrön

" **E**verybody loves something, even if it's only tortillas." Pema Chödrön remembers this remark by her teacher Trungpa Rinpoche, who was trying to explain the Buddhist concept of *bodhichitta*. Its literal definition is the open mind or heart, the "soft spot" that all humans have, even if they are apparently bad.

Chödrön, an American who became a Buddhist nun, has sought to bring this ancient idea to a contemporary audience. Her philosophy is that to get by, most people harden themselves to their soft spots and close off feelings of empathy for others. Most of the time we try to stop feeling *bodhichitta*, putting up false barriers such as prejudices or opinions. But the soft spots remain, Chödrön says, "like a crack in the walls." They point to our genuine nature and are therefore available to us at any time.

In the first chapter of *The Places that Scare You: A Guide to Fearlessness in Difficult Times*, Chödrön tells of a woman who wrote to her about an experience in a town in the Middle East. The woman and her friend were jeered and yelled at because they were Americans and thought they were going to be physically attacked. Though petrified, the woman suddenly understood what it was like to be a persecuted, hated minority. She felt a new connection to everyone in history who had been in this position. Normally such an experience would make us lash out or retreat into our shell, but the woman gained something very valuable out of it. According to Chödrön, she had taken the first step in becoming a *bodhisattva*, a warrior who courageously opens themselves up to pain. A warrior is not more aggressive than other people, Chödrön says, but more open.

Admitting emotion

The *bodhichitta* teachings originally came from India and were brought to Tibet in the eleventh century. They were distilled into easy-to-remember slogans such as "Always meditate on whatever provokes resentment." They arm us with the ability to work through our "difficult" personal traits so that we become enlightened, and one way to do this is to remember such slogans whenever we are caught up in the heat of the moment.

Chödrön notes that people often start meditating in the belief that it will allow them to float above the discomfort of everyday life. But the way of *bodhichitta* requires us to go in the opposite direction: we become enlightened only by getting ourselves deeper into daily feelings, good and bad. First-time meditators sometimes find that instead of them becoming peaceful, many strong emotions come out; in admitting that these emotions exist we can start to see them more clearly. If you get a flash of anger about something, really feel it, Chödrön says. By letting it happen, you don't experience the usual accompanying guilt, and so have the beginning of a better view of self.

What we don't like is simply *life*

The great lesson Chödrön learned from the Buddha was that what we struggle against all the time is just ordinary life. She writes: "Life *does* continually go up and down. People and situations *are* unpredictable and so is everything else." What is surprising is that people are terribly disappointed when something happens that they don't want. We feel pain when we don't get things right, but we shouldn't necessarily take a setback or a failure as something personal—it is the very nature of life that we get both what we want and what we don't want.

Nothing we do that is a blind escape from insecurity or uncomfortable feelings can be of lasting value. Life is about experiencing it as it comes, not only the good parts. When, like Chödrön's teacher Trungpa Rinpoche, you can say "I'm OK" on both good days and bad days, you will have made progress; you can have little to fear.

Samsara

"The central question of a warrior's training is not how we avoid uncertainty and fear," Chödrön says, "but how we relate to discomfort." We shape our lives around mental escape. We have a drink or a large meal or think about sex or go shopping to get away from some uncomfortable thought or feeling in the present. This feeling may be as simple as boredom or mild anxiety, but in our unwillingness to experience it fully we lose an opportunity to really get to know ourselves. We may never become aware that we can get more relief from *fully experiencing* a feeling of discomfort than immediately trying to eliminate it. Always wanting to "take the edge off the moment" keeps us in a cycle of dissatisfaction called *samsara*.

Chödrön tells of the time beat poet Jack Kerouac went into the mountains to meet face to face with God. But all that happened was that he came face to face with his own naked self—"ole Hateful Me," as he wrote in a letter to a friend—for once unshielded by booze and drugs. A lot of people go looking for God but end up with themselves. Yet right here, Chödrön says, is the beginning of enlightenment.

Staying in the scary places

Chödrön notes that we expect things to be permanent and stable. We are emotionally attached to the idea of permanence, so when it doesn't happen we feel fragile and insecure. The Buddhist way is to "relax into change," to make the awareness of it part of all our thoughts.

We crave certainty because uncertainty makes us afraid. We accept the myth that, as Chödrön puts it, "if only we could do everything right, we'd be able to find a safe, comfortable, and secure place to spend the rest of our lives." But life is always uncertain, for everyone.

If we go further into that feeling of being afraid, not trying instantly to "fix" it, somehow it loses its potency. We have to ask ourselves: What exactly are we feeling when we feel that we can't handle something? Coming to grips with what we are running from is the key to growth. If we "stay present to the pain of disapproval or betrayal"—or any other painful feeling—Chödrön suggests it has a way of softening us. If we suppress it we only become a brittle person.

You might think it will be terrible to really feel the weight and intensity of a feeling, but Chödrön says it is actually a relief—an act of kindness to ourselves. If we do not allow ourselves to feel, we become more ego driven, believing ourselves to be invulnerable when in fact we are a structurally unsound fortress that can crumble at the slightest provocation. The ego isolates us from everyone else. It tries to protect the illusion of personal territory, but we have to challenge it to have the courage to go to the places that scare us.

Heart-opening practices

Practitioners of Buddhism seek to cultivate four limitless qualities: loving kindness, compassion, joy, and equanimity. Of the many *bodhichitta* practices for acquiring them, one is "aspiration," or wishing well on others. We wish that we can be free of suffering and find the source of happiness, then we wish the same thing for our loved ones. Finally, we can extend the practice to a wider circle of people, including those we dislike and others we have never even met.

Chödrön is aware how difficult it is to wish goodwill on someone you may normally feel like hating, and that is the idea: to work the muscles of the heart so that it becomes larger. If you fail in sending goodwill to someone you don't feel it for, then you can stop. The idea is not to force yourself to be a saint, but to stretch what you are capable of in terms of compassion and loving kindness.

The root of suffering and ignorance is an inability to see the connection between all people, to see that other people are not that different to us. Chödrön likes to practice aspiration in shops and supermarkets, where the opportunity for getting annoyed is high. When you decide to have positive aspirations for the person ahead of you in the queue, for instance, you suddenly have a connection with them and whatever they are doing seems less annoying. Using aspiration, you can handle anyone because now you see them as basically another aspect of yourself.

Another practice to unharden the heart is to rejoice in others' good fortune. Chödrön relates how she heard that someone she knew had sold more copies of their books than she had, and how envious she was. It was only through rejoicing in the other person's success that she realized how much she had resented it!

It is the people we find most difficult, she says, who are our best teachers in life. By pushing all our buttons they are able to get behind the façade we show to the world, to reach the ugly thinking and raw emotion. Righteous indignation, pride, skepticism, resentment—all these can be brought to the light of day and evaporate in the practices of *bodhichitta* awakening.

Final comments

Many Buddhist writings bring a very rational mindset to spirituality— they are *useful*. Most of the practices Chödrön describes are over 1,000 years old and have been refined to work in an almost scientific way. You don't need to have any great interest in Buddhism to be changed by them. If you are a Christian, for instance, simply put compassion in the place of *bodhichitta*.

Chödrön's other books include *Start Where You Are, The Wisdom of No Escape,* and *When Things Fall Apart.* Each discusses life not as we would like it but as it really is. Their clarity and directness would make them excellent works from a traditional eastern Buddhist teacher, but the fact that they come from an American woman who has been through the same struggle with her emotions and material desires as everyone else makes them especially valuable. It is easy to look at a serene spiritual master and think that they have always been that way, but Chödrön notes, "All those smiling enlightened people you see in pictures or in person had to go through the process of encountering their full-blown neurosis." Every human being has plenty of scary places, but what marks one person out from another is their willingness to peer into these corners of the mind.

Every time we have a feeling of dread or fear or sorrow and don't act rashly on it or try to suppress it, we have advanced. The great truth of *The Places that Scare You* is that enlarging our soft spot may appear to be dangerous, but in fact it gives our life more peace because empathy and compassion are what make us really human.

Pema Chödrön

Born in 1936 in New York, Chödrön is a graduate of the University of California. She only grew seriously involved with Buddhism in her mid-thirties, becoming a novice in 1974. In 1981 she was ordained a bhikshuni *or Buddhist nun in the Tibetan tradition. Her main teacher was Chögyam Trungpa (see* Cutting through Spiritual Materialism, *p. 270), whom she studied with from 1973 until his death in 1987.*

Chödrön is currently the director of Gampo Abbey, a Buddhist monastic center in Nova Scotia, Canada. Further books include Be Grateful to Everyone *and* Tonglen.

The Book of Chuang Tzu

"To consider the origin as pure and that which emerges as coarse; to view accumulation as inadequate; to live by oneself in peace and with spiritual clarity, this is what in ancient times was known as the way of the Tao."

"Do not be subject to labels; do not be full of schemes; do not assume you are in charge of affairs; do not be subject to knowledge. Comprehend the infinite, and roam in the traceless."

In a nutshell

The best life is one that is in accord with the unseen universal order, or Tao.

In a similar vein
Tao Te Ching (50 SHC)

CHAPTER 10

Chuang Tzu

China 2,300 years ago was going through a period of upheaval and civil war. Rulers were desperate for an edge and willing to consider any new ideas that could help them defeat their opponents and maintain order. At this time lived a brilliant philosopher, Chuang Tzu. He was asked by one of the kings to become his adviser, but declined the offer because he did not want to be corrupted by statecraft.

The Book of Chuang Tzu became one of the foundational works of Taoism, a companion to the *Tao Te Ching*, which preceded it by 200 years. Chuang Tzu is said to have written the first seven chapters himself, the others were written by followers. They consist of allegories and anecdotes invoking well-known figures in Chinese history, and include imaginary conversations between great thinkers such as Confucius, Lao Tzu, and Lieh Tzu.

Reading the book, it is easy to understand Chuang Tzu's reluctance to work for a ruler, since his philosophy denies the validity of worldly power and praises anonymity instead of grand schemes. He implies that the turmoil of the Warring States period came about because people had lost awareness of the Tao, which had previously allowed for "unity between Heaven and Earth."

What is the Tao? It is the fundamental order of the universe, how things naturally move. The wise or successful person is aware of this force that moves the universe, stays attuned to it, and never forgets that it is the source of everything.

Humility before the Tao

In the chapter "Season of the Autumn Floods," Chuang Tzu offers the following allegory.

When the autumn floods came, the Lord of the Yellow River felt good because now his waters were very wide. He flowed in his majesty

67

through the country, until finally coming to the North Ocean. There, he encountered Jo, the God of the Ocean, and was humbled by his vastness compared to himself. Observing this, the Lord of the Yellow River was reminded of the frog sitting in a well who marveled at the body of water in front of him, but was forever unaware of the expanse of the sea. He recalls the summer insect that, existing only in one season, would never understand what ice is. In the same way, he notes, a scholar wrapped up in his teachings could not begin to have real comprehension of the Tao. Having some knowledge of Taoism, he may think himself superior, but this is not the same as being attuned to the Tao.

The average person is unwilling or unable to put their small achievements into perspective. They are concerned with their own lifespan, not realizing the aeons that came before them or the vastness of the universe. They make much of little things, which only injects worry and confusion into the world. The story implies that we should forget thinking of ourselves as a mighty river, and remember that we are more like a drop in the ocean.

Knowing the totality

To a normal person there are great distinctions between rich and poor, small and big, right and wrong, useful and useless, but from the perspective of the Tao it is all the same, all one. This is why the advanced person will not go through life making judgments and distinctions, but instead keep their mind on the whole.

Attunement with the Tao allows you to recognize the totality of life, not just the parts you would prefer. This is why an attuned person will seem a bit detached: they are not attached to a particular aspect of life to the detriment of others. To have this attachment would be to deny life's reality. Others, knowing the world only through the fog of their own thoughts and ideas, never comprehend the greatness of the Tao.

People who comprehend the Tao are free from worry about the cycle of birth and death, good fortune or bad. They can live without too much investment in seeking great things or avoiding bad things, their happiness coming from perfect calmness and detachment. They see everything as part of the whole. They cannot be offended or have their reputation ruined, because their eyes are on larger things.

Happiness beyond opposites

In Chuang Tzu's thinking, we should not actually seek happiness. Most people's idea of happiness is pursuing things they desire, and in doing so they are in a constant state of action. With their mind on the future and abstract things, they forget to take care of their body.

But someone in attunement with the Tao does not seek this "happiness." Their genuine happiness comes from not having the normal burden of humans, which is perpetually to swing between joy and sadness, glory and failure. But we can be beyond these extremes and live in a state of "actionless action"; that is, our actions proceed in accordance with the Tao, not in pursuit of our own proclivities and desires.

Most people can say "I am now content" or "I am feeling happy," but someone in attune with the Tao has the type of contentment that has forgotten what contentment is, and does not know what it is like not to be happy. Happiness therefore goes beyond achieving a "state" of happiness. It is to be found in going beyond the normal poles of human thought, desire, and emotion, achieving perfect equanimity.

Choosing anonymity

The great person doesn't make a show of giving and does not seek to strive for gain. They do not look down on people who serve them, nor make anything of the fact that they do not. Although self-reliant, they do not condemn the greedy or the mean. They are selfless, not in a saintly way, but in the sense that their life does not make waves. In contrast, the person who is protective of their reputation, or wants to be famous or rich, does make waves.

In conversation with Confucius, the Grand Duke Jen commented: "The straight tree is the first to be chopped down; the well of sweet water is the first to run dry." He suggests to Confucius that his learning makes him stand out: it draws attention to him because it highlights the contrast between his knowledge and others' ignorance. His point is that a person who spends their time maintaining their image of being "remarkable" ceases to be so; they only stir things up. Someone who is in attunement with the Tao, on the other hand, reflects the nature of the Tao—they don't look or sound like anything special, but they nevertheless have a certain power. Grand Duke Jen adds that real strength is being one element in a larger whole, like a bird in a flock.

Chuang Tzu's idea of the perfect person is someone who does not try to be their own source of light for the world: they act as a clean channel of that light whenever and wherever it is appropriate for it to shine. This requires total humility, being "empty and plain." A person with this quality does not want power and is not interested in criticism, and as a consequence is not criticized themselves. Simply put, they do not let themselves get in the way of life. People think they are crazy because they seek anonymity, but they know that this is the way of real contentment.

The simple life is best

A Chinese ruler once tried to abdicate and attempted to hand the baton to a man called Shan Chuan. This was a time when rulers were called "Sons of Heaven" and being a ruler was held in the highest esteem. But Shan Chuan said, "Why would I want to rule a country?" He had a simple life of working his farm and enjoying the changing seasons. He could see no point in power or honors. Once someone had them, they spent all their time trying to cling to them, which was no life.

Chuang Tzu's point is that a person in tune with the Tao always chooses a life of peace over one of power. Ironically, it is the person who values power least who makes the best ruler, but such kings and ministers are rare. Similarly, the Tao-attuned person does not spend their time chasing profit. They are happy with who they are and do not hunger for more. They forget the reason they are doing their work, becoming one with the task, with no ego or thought of reward getting in the way. Paradoxically, this makes the fruit of their work excellent.

Characteristics of the Tao

The following summarizes the characteristics of a Tao-attuned person, gleaned from Chuang Tzu's stories and commentary:

❖ A person in attunement with the Tao does not have grand plans, but responds to things as they arise.
❖ They let their own self get out of the way of things, because they know that only this allows them to see other people clearly.
❖ Most people try to find fulfillment, but the wise person seeks to be empty, a channel for the Tao.

❖ A Tao-attuned person has a child's delight in life combined with the wisdom of a sage.
❖ They are beyond conventional morality. If someone has to think about virtues, they are not living naturally.
❖ An attuned person puts "knowledge" into perspective. They have a wisdom that comes from awareness of the totality of life, beyond the knowledge of the scholar.

Because they think differently and act differently than the norm, an attuned person can seem a little crazy, but from their perspective it is other people who seem absurd in the way they live.

Final comments

The door Chuang Tzu opens into ancient China is fascinating in itself and may pique your interest in the development of Taoism. It is clear that he had a great sense of humor, always poking fun at the rigidity of Chinese custom and hierarchy. However, what makes this work timeless is Chuang Tzu's brilliant insights into the human condition.

For instance, in our time people are concerned with "life purpose," but Chuang Tzu invites us to consider that instead of actually seeking fulfillment, it is better to cultivate emptiness of mind through contemplation and meditation so that we can see the world more clearly. In this way we will naturally find scope for action that is appropriate to who we are and what needs doing in the world. When we become aware of the concept of the Tao, it gives us a chance to reconnect with an intelligence that is much greater than our own.

The Book of Chuang Tzu is a work to keep with you over a lifetime, to be consulted when you are in need of guidance or enlightenment. As with all allegories some interpretation is needed, and good translations have made the work more accessible than ever before. Two excellent modern versions are those by Martin Palmer and Elizabeth Breuilly, and by Jonathan Cleary.

Be Here Now

"I had an apartment in Cambridge that was filled with antiques and I gave very charming dinner parties. I had a Mercedes-Benz and a Triumph 500 cc motorcycle and a Cessna 172 airplane and an MG sports car and a sailboat and a bicycle. I vacationed in the Caribbean where I did scuba-diving. I was living the way a successful bachelor professor is supposed to live in the American world of 'he who makes it.' I wasn't a genuine scholar, but I had gone through the whole academic trip. I had gotten my Ph.D; I was writing books... But what all this boils down to is that I was really a very good game player."

In a nutshell

Are you genuinely seeking greater truth in life, or merely playing the game of recognition and success?

In a similar vein
Hermann Hesse *Siddartha* (p. 118)
Aldous Huxley *The Doors of Perception* (p. 124)
Eckhart Tolle *The Power of Now* (p. 264)
Chögyam Trungpa *Cutting through Spiritual Materialism* (p. 270)
Paramahansa Yogananda *Autobiography of a Yogi* (p. 300)

CHAPTER 11

Ram Dass

The young psychology professor Dr. Richard Alpert was doing well. As 1961 got under way, he held appointments across four departments at Harvard University, and had research contracts at Stanford and Yale. With the status and money that came with these positions, he had little to complain about.

Yet he felt that there was something missing in his world, though he couldn't put his finger on what it was. The theories of achievement, motivation, and anxiety that he was teaching students seemed to be no more than surface scratchings on the mystery of life; he and his contemporaries had studied all there was to know about the human mind, but had little grasp of the human condition. Their own lives lacked integrity and fulfillment, and Alpert himself had little to show for the five years he had spent in psychoanalysis. His lecture notes, he says, were "the ideas of other men, subtly presented," and his research was not really pushing any new frontiers. Everyone around him was so smart, but there was little wisdom: "I could sit in a doctoral exam, ask very sophisticated questions and look terribly wise. It was a hustle."

New worlds

The cracks in Alpert's life began to widen when the legendary Timothy Leary (then a Harvard psychologist, later a prophet of the 1960s counterculture) became a colleague and drinking buddy. Leary had discovered Tioananctyl, or magic mushrooms, in Mexico, and Alpert was struck by his comment that consuming them had taught him more than all his years as a psychologist. Later, Leary and Aldous Huxley (then a visiting scholar at Massachusetts Institute of Technology) acquired a synthetic form of magic mushroom called Psylocybin, which Alpert was invited to try with them.

The drug prompted visions in which Alpert could see his life as the fêted professor with some objectivity. He experienced the presence of an "I" behind the façade of his knowledge, the I of wisdom and timeless awareness. This was just what he had been looking for.

The group went on researching altered states, testing the drug on other people but also taking it frequently themselves. They realized that it was useless to remain objective about an opening up of consciousness that was changing the way they saw the world, because there was simply nothing in academic psychology that could explain their experiences. Alpert writes of the sensation that everything around him was appreciated as an undifferentiated, vibrating pattern of energy, essentially light, not the objects we normally perceive. In such states he would see his life as a professor as somewhat untruthful and restrictive, and he "came down" with regret. The more he took psychedelic drugs, the more annoyed he got that he had to return from these wonderful astral worlds to mundane reality.

Alpert, Leary, and cohorts must have seemed very strange to their colleagues, and they began to be marginalized. Things came to a head when Alpert was sacked from his academic posts, beginning a wilderness period in which he no longer felt connected to the academic establishment and could not find a way to maintain the states of consciousness he had experienced.

No turning back

When a wealthy acquaintance invited Alpert to go on a journey to India, he leapt at the opportunity. The idea was to travel around in a Land Rover and seek out holy men, but when it was combined with smoking hashish and dropping acid, Alpert felt increasingly depressed. He had been searching for a person who "knew"—who knew secrets of the internal life and was unaffected by what troubles normal people— but he had become no more than a spiritual tourist, like thousands of others.

There is a saying: "When the student is ready, the teacher will appear." At his wits' end, Alpert was sitting in a hippie café in northern India when in walked in a tall westerner with long hair and beads. Alpert instantly felt that this man, called Bhagwan Dass and seen by the locals as a guru, "knew." He had come thousands of miles only to have a young Californian as his teacher!

Following him across the country, learning holy songs and mantras, neither of them with any money, Alpert came to understand what it meant to truly live in the present, to get away from the idea that the events of our life story are that important. When asked how long he thought they would continue to travel around, Bhagwan Dass replied, "Don't think about the future. Just be here now."

From personality to consciousness

As Richard Alpert metamorphosed into Ram Dass (a name that means "servant of God"), what insights did he gain? Perhaps unsurprisingly, he had a realization about the nature of identity itself. Who we are changes from moment to moment, he observed. There are many "you"s and each is a mark of your identification with a particular thought or desire. Our thoughts become our personality, and we identify our personality at any one time as who we are. But the more we are able to see these different selves from a step back in consciousness, the more likely they are to seem illusory.

Dass learned that one way to be aware of our different selves is to adopt the role of unjudgmental witness, watching all the selves in action. This allows us to carry out our roles in life with some detachment. Witnessing our thoughts also allows us to see their impermanence and the fact that there is a part of us that is not our thoughts. The purpose of meditation, he found, is to be free from the thoughts that we normally take to be ourselves, thoughts that perpetuate our suffering. In meditation we disconnect from our ego and our senses. If we do have thoughts during meditation, ultimately they will come only as intuition or guidance, not sabotaging thoughts.

Beyond rationality

Dass observed that the rational, thinking mind works through separating the world into objects; that is, the knower is separate from the known. While many of the achievements of civilization could not have occurred without this level of thinking, it has its limitations. Einstein, for instance, famously said that you couldn't solve the problems of today by using the same type of thinking that created them. Dass noted that the rational mind finds it difficult to handle paradoxical or illogical information, and that the accounts of great breakthroughs in knowledge of the universe usually mention that it was some flash of intuition or picture of truth that led to a discovery, not an analytic frame of mind. Einstein actually admitted: "I didn't arrive at my understanding of the fundamental laws of the universe through my rational mind."

Having lived most of his life in a culture that worshiped the rational mind, Ram Dass was liberated by the idea that we are not simply the sum of our thoughts. With this knowledge, it was no longer possible for him to continue studying consciousness as an objective, scientific observer; rather, he was now able to look on science and psychology as constructs within the larger consciousness that he was beginning to experience.

Final comments

Be Here Now is a classic work of hippie spirituality, but it can take its place as one of the outstanding works of spiritual transformation from any era. Dass's journey from Harvard academic to guru is told beautifully, and in his shaking off of an old, somewhat meaningless life, like a dead skin, Alpert reminds us of St. Augustine in his *Confessions*.

Older copies of the book from the 1970s are a piece of social history. Printed by Dass's own Hanuman Foundation, there are no page numbers until about two-thirds in, and much of the text is in blue or brown ink. While the first section is a relatively straightforward account of Alpert's life, written from a western, chronological perspective, the central section is the voice of a neophyte who has discovered spiritual truths and wants to tell the world. Arranged in a centerfold style with mantras and quotes, and with wild and often beautiful illustrations, the book may be too groovy for some readers, but don't be put off by the frequent use of words such as "love" and "guru" and drawings of Hindu deities. This is actually the core of the book and if you are in the right frame of mind it can take you on a powerful "trip."

The final part of *Be Here Now*, "Cookbook for a sacred life," represents the maturation of Dass's experiments with *sadhana*, or spiritual practice, and goes through every possible means of awakening, from meditation to fasting to drugs.* In discussing the highs and lows of *sadhana*, Dass notes that after an awakening you may feel despair at going back to what feels like your old self—a case of one step forward, two steps back. But as you become lighter spiritually, your greater purity will bring your "grosser" aspects to the surface. Most people on the spiritual path start off by giving a certain amount of time or energy to spiritual matters, but then realize that all of life is a spiritual matter—there is nothing that is not. Dass's other conclusion is to avoid taking yourself too seriously: as you get higher up the consciousness food chain, the true size of your ego is revealed and you have to be able to laugh at your own vanities.

*Ram Dass quotes a guru by the name of Hari Dass Baba, who believed that LSD was God's way of getting Americans to embark on a more spiritual path and open their minds to non-materialistic ways. Ram Dass's own conclusion was that drugs were only one door into higher knowledge, pointing out: "The goal of the path is to BE high, not GET high."

Enchiridion

"Seek not that the things which happen should happen as you wish; but wish the things which happen to be as they are, and you will have a tranquil flow of life."

"Remember that thou art an actor in a play, of such a kind as the teacher [author] may choose; if short, of a short one; if long, of a long one: if he wishes you to act the part of a poor man, see that you act the part naturally; if the part of a lame man, of a magistrate, of a private person [do the same]. For this is your duty, to act well the part that is given to you; but to select the part, belongs to another."

"Men are disturbed not by the things which happen, but by the opinion about the things."

In a nutshell

Appreciate the world as it is, not how you would like it to be.

In a similar vein
Marcus Aurelius *Meditations* (50 SHC)

Epictetus

Epictetus was a Roman slave whose master, Epaphroditus, was an officer of Emperor Nero's personal guard. After his master was put to death by Nero's successor Domitian, Epictetus was given his freedom.

Epictetus might have had an unremarkable life except that, while still a slave, he was allowed to attend philosophy lectures, and as an adult freedman he became a distinguished philosopher in the Stoic tradition. From slave to philosopher is an astonishing leap, and clearly gave Epictetus unusual insight into the human condition.

Epictetus himself did not write any books. His pupil Arrian (later the biographer of Alexander the Great) took down his thoughts to create the eight-volume *Discourses*, of which only four volumes survived. The essence of the *Discourses* was distilled into a much shorter *Enchiridion*, Greek for handbook or manual, which with a good translation (here George Long's is used) is very accessible to today's reader.

What is Stoicism? As a body of thought it originated in Greece around 300 BCE, but became a major influence in ancient Rome. Its intellectual and spiritual features include submission to providence or universal law, independence of mind, restraint in living and emotion, and fearlessness of loss and death. This commentary discusses Epictetus's expression of the Stoic way.

Acceptance

> "Lead me, O Zeus, and thou O Destiny,
> The way that I am bid by you to go:
> To follow I am ready. If I choose not,
> I make myself a wretch, and still must follow."

This verse appears at the end of the *Enchiridion* and sums up the Stoic philosophy of acceptance. By submission to Zeus (the creator in Greek mythology), a person could gain a rare equanimity in the knowledge that they were acting in accord with the universe. As everyone had a certain role to play in life, the choice to fight what was clearly our destiny could only bring misery. Another great Stoic, Marcus Aurelius, put it this way: "Love nothing but that which comes to you woven in the pattern of your destiny. For what could more aptly fit your needs?" It is when we refuse to accept that an event has happened, Epictetus taught, that pain is the most extreme.

Under the heading "How a man on every occasion can maintain his proper character," Epictetus points out that whatever seems "intolerable" can be made tolerable if it is seen to be rational. Events themselves are not necessarily painful; what really causes grief is the feeling that there is no reason behind what we are going through. Yet if we can accept that the workings of God are rational, we can feel safe in the knowledge that all things happen for a reason—even if with our limited vision we cannot see it.

Epictetus mentions the willingness with which Socrates went to his imprisonment and death. Why did he not struggle? Because in his quiet acknowledgment of his fate, he could mentally remain free. Epictetus tells the story of Agrippinus, who when told that the Roman Senate had begun a trial against him (which would probably end with his death or exile), continued with his daily habits of exercise and bathing. When later a messenger came to him with the news that he had been condemned, he did not let out an anguished cry, but calmly inquired whether he was to be put to death or banished. When told the sentence of banishment, he immediately began making arrangements for the move.

Agrippinus is said to have remarked: "I am not a hindrance to myself." He meant that no wild emotions could overtake his inner peace or resolve; full acceptance of his fate provided equanimity, which he prized above all honors or possessions.

The greater gifts

Epictetus observed that although we are animals to the extent that we eat and drink and copulate and sleep, the task of humans is to make sense of the world and understand our place in it. In this contemplation, we are led to an appreciation of the intelligence behind the workings of the universe, and enjoy some detachment from things and events. Our gifts are not just physical, but include the power to endure anything and to develop greatness of soul. These gifts, Epictetus believed, are as much a part of us as hearing or sight.

Epictetus likened difficulties to a "rough young man" whom we are made to wrestle with in the ring. God's purpose is not that we are defeated, but that the fight turns us into an Olympian. If we are tempted by lust, make it an opportunity to develop self-control; if we are physically pained, it is a golden chance to learn endurance; if someone starts yelling at us, what better occasion to practice patience? Having been a slave, Epictetus enjoyed using domestic examples. The master of a house, he counseled, had to forgive the spilling of a bit of oil or the theft of some wine, because at "such price is sold freedom from perturbation." When we get annoyed with anyone, we should remember that the other person, like us, is the "offspring of Zeus"; in attacking them, we undermine ourselves and forget our common humanity.

Epictetus usefully pointed out that it is not actual events that are terrible, but the interpretation we give to them. He noted, "Lameness is an impediment to the leg, but not to the will." Though it may stop us from walking, could a bad leg really be made the cause of our unhappiness? In Epictetus's thinking, no event ever required one particular reaction.

Furthermore, all the discomforts and pains of life had to be weighed against being a witness to the sheer spectacle of the world. To retain this sense of perspective amid the tumult of life was worth everything.

A larger view of life and death

Some things are in our power, others are not, Epictetus said. We have no control over how the dice of life are cast; what we *do* control is the hand we play once they are thrown. The failure to observe this distinction leads to unlimited anxiety.

If we try to avoid disease, death, and poverty, we will live in misery, because none of them, particularly death, is ever under our control. Happiness can emerge only from attention to things we do have command over: our thoughts, actions, and reactions. Peace comes from living a simple life in which we have disciplined our thinking and trimmed our desires and aversions to a minimum.

The twenty-first point of the *Enchiridion* reads:

"Let death and exile and every other thing which appears dreadful be daily before your eyes; but most of all death: and you will never think of anything mean nor will you desire anything extravagantly."

The phrase "These things happen" is often used to put a misfortune into perspective, particularly when it happens to someone else. But when someone close to us dies, Epictetus observed, we cry "Woe is me" and ask "How could this happen?" Suddenly there is one standard for our neighbor and another for ourselves. However, the advanced person is able to apply the remark "These things happen" to their *own* life events, in the acknowledgment that the event is in full conformity with nature, however unfortunate.

Given that most people's greatest fear is the sudden loss of a spouse or child, it is unlikely that many of us could be this stoical. But Epictetus suggested a thought that may help in taking the larger view. We should try to get to the essence or nature of things and people, instead of all the emotionality we normally attach to them. He said:

"If you are kissing your child or wife, say that it is a human being whom you are kissing, for when the wife or child dies you will not be disturbed."

This particular expression of the universal life force—this person—may leave you, but if you can identify with life itself the loss will not seem so horrible and irrational, remembering that it is the irrational that humans cannot bear.

Final comments

The Stoic view is almost the opposite of the "I can do anything" mindset that we see so much of in modern personal development literature. With its emphasis on accepting things as they are, Stoic philosophy can seem fatalistic. In the contemporary world we avoid any type of "mustn't grumble" ethos, and instead are in love with the idea of changing the world.

Yet the common reaction to reading Epictetus and other Stoic philosophers is that they are not pessimistic. In fact, their goal of *eudaimonia*, or happiness, is a type of happiness that comes from being in accordance with divine intelligence, not fighting the world or judging it but doing what we can to increase the store of rationality and wisdom in the particular slice of the world we live in.

Stoic philosophy is spiritual but in a profoundly practical way, recognizing a life lived according to the will of God or providence as the perfect one. While associated with hardness, in fact Stoic literature celebrates the mystery and wonder of the world, and the unique role that each person plays in its unfolding. The equanimity of the Stoic mind comes from an appreciation that nothing that happens to us is not in our destiny, and therefore everything should be embraced willingly. Such courage, so eloquently expressed in *The Enchiridion*, raises the spirit and justifies the privilege of existence.

Epictetus

Epictetus was born in the year 55 CE in Hieropolis in Phrygia (modern-day Pamukkale, in southwestern Turkey). As a boy he came to Rome as a slave of Epaphroditus, a rich and powerful freedman who had himself been a slave of the Emperor Nero. While still a slave, Epictetus studied with the Stoic teacher Musonius Rufus.

In about 89, along with other philosophers in Rome, Epictetus was banished by the Emperor Domitian. He went to Nicopolis in Epirus (northwestern Greece), where he opened his own school. He was a popular teacher and his school attracted many upper-class Romans. One of his students was Flavius Arrian (c. 86–160), who would compose the Discourses *and the* Enchiridion, *and who later served in public office under the Emperor Hadrian and became a historian. Epictetus did not marry or have any children. He lived to a comparatively late age, dying in 135.*

An Autobiography

"What I want to achieve—what I have been striving and pining to achieve these thirty years—is self-realization, to see God face to face, to attain Moksha. I live and move and have my being in pursuit of this goal. All that I do by way of speaking and writing, and all my ventures in the political field, are directed to this same end. But as I have all along believed that what is possible for one is possible for all, my experiments have not been conducted in the closet, but in the open."

"The seeker after truth should be humbler than dust. The world crushes the dust under its feet, but the seeker after truth should so humble himself that even the dust could crush him. Only then, and not till then, will he have a glimpse of truth."

In a nutshell

Life is not a series of events but a series of revelations about truth.

In a similar vein
Nelson Mandela *Long Walk to Freedom* (50SC)

CHAPTER 13

Mohandas Gandhi

hat first strikes you about this book is the strange wording of the title—*An Autobiography: The Story of My Experiments with Truth*. If it had been a mere political life story, the subtitle would have read something like "How I Liberated India from British Rule." But right from the beginning, Gandhi is at pains to point out that it is not simply a description of events (although it does provide this), but a recording of his efforts to isolate "truth" amid the chaos of normal existence.

What makes the book doubly interesting is that it was written before he became a famous world figure. He did not, after all, return to live in India until 1915, when he was in his mid-forties, and he was not then the white-robed figure we think of today but a lawyer in a suit with a family. The salutary term Mahatma ("great soul") had yet to stick, and he was still able to travel around India without being mobbed. Whereas biographical dictionaries devote most of their entries to Gandhi's political work in India, three-quarters of the *Autobiography* is devoted to his youth and the 21 years of his adult life that he spent working for the rights of Indians in South Africa.

Wherever he was, though, the constants in Gandhi's life were his various experiments: vegetarianism, celibacy, non-violence, and simple living. Each was an expression of larger philosophical/spiritual concepts that he drew from Hinduism: *brahmacharya*, *ahimsa*, and *aparigraha*. No understanding of Gandhi is possible without at least having some awareness of these terms and what they meant to him.

Written originally in his native Gurjarati, the book did not appear in English until 1957. Though rather long, it is broken up into short, clearly titled chapters on the essential episodes in Gandhi's life, and is one of the most gripping life stories you are likely to read.

Vegetarianism

Mohandas Gandhi was born in 1869 in Porbandar on the northeastern coast of India. His father, Kaba, was a local politician who married four times, each wife having died. Mohandas was the youngest child of his fourth wife. As the family belonged to the vegetarian Bania caste, one of the defining episodes in Gandhi's boyhood was falling under the spell of a meat-eating friend. This boy convinced him that the reason Indians were controlled by the British was that they had been weakened by not eating meat; the British, conversely, were strong because they were meat eaters. Gandhi felt this to be a good argument, and in secret tried hard to enjoy cooked flesh, but guilt soon made him abandon the experiment.

Clearly a bright student, in his teens Gandhi hatched the idea of going to London to study law. His caste elders forbid him to go on the grounds that he would be corrupted by western living (he was literally pronounced "out caste"), but his mother was willing to let him go on the condition that he vowed not to touch meat, women, or alcohol.

Gandhi amusingly recalls his efforts once in London to become an "English gentleman," and although he was homesick and missing his wife and child, on the positive side he was able to cement his love and respect for English legal principles. His great difficulty was finding vegetarian meals, and he virtually starved for the sake of his vow. Luckily he stumbled on a couple of vegetarian restaurants and fell in with the Vegetarian Society, an organization that crucially provided the first public speaking opportunities for a painfully shy young man.

Gandhi's vegetarianism went from being a commitment to his family to becoming a moral mission. He firmed up his belief that sexual and dietary restrictions are important in humans becoming free of animal drives and base concerns. Personally, his celibacy and vegetarianism paralleled the emergence of his religious consciousness.

Later, Gandhi's beliefs were put to the test in separate episodes of dire illness. The family doctor advised that his son Manilal, with a fever and at death's door, must be given milk to strengthen him. By this point the family had committed to living without any animal products, so they refused. The child not only lived but, as Gandhi notes, became "the healthiest of my boys." When his wife Kasturbai fell seriously ill, a doctor was adamant that she would die if she was not given beef tea. Again, the family refused this cure and she was nursed back to strong health.

Gandhi took these incidents as a salutary lesson on sticking to his principles, and they must have confirmed in his mind the idea that "going without" provided a certain moral force that always put the universe on his side. Though inconvenient, the practice of *brahmacharya* also cut out the fluff from his life and strengthened his purpose.

Brahmacharya

Brahmacharya means "control of the senses in thought, word and deed," particularly sexually. It is self-purifying conduct that leads a person to God.

A little-known fact about Gandhi is that he was married at the age of 13. His wife was illiterate and uneducated. In the India of his upbringing this arranged coupling was nothing out of the ordinary, and the two remained together and had several children.

Looking back, Gandhi was quite ashamed of having such an early marriage, a feeling compounded by his admitted lust for his wife. He came to believe that sexual union was not for the fulfillment of lust but to beget children. In his mid-thirties, and with his wife's agreement, Gandhi took the vow of *brahmacharya* to cover his sexual life. He believed this vow of celibacy to be the beginning of his flowering as a human being.

Though he found it very difficult at first, he noted: "Every day revealed a fresh beauty in it." There was a point where lust no longer had control over his thinking, and instead of being like hard penance, he could appreciate the vow's purpose to protect a person's body, mind, and soul.

Ahimsa and satyagraha

The other concept guiding Gandhi's life was *ahimsa*. In Hindi, *himsa* means the perpetual destruction and pain of normal existence: the way of the world. We can, however, adopt an outlook of compassion—*ahimsa*—which requires us to do all we can to avoid the recurrence of suffering and aggression.

Gandhi believed *ahimsa* to be central to a quest for truth, because any effort to achieve an aim is ultimately self-defeating if it involves mental or physical injury to our fellow sentient beings. Attacking another person, for instance, is like attacking our own selves, since we are all simply representations of the Creator. But how exactly was this concept translated into Gandhi's famous political activism?

He discovered the principle of *satyagraha*—non-cooperation or non-violent struggle—which represents the way of getting things done in the world within the understanding of *ahimsa*. Unlike normal conflict, in which we are inflamed by emotion, the action of *satyagraha* is based on a detached stubbornness that gains strength from the quality of its principles.

Gandhi first practiced it in his various battles for the rights of Indians in South Africa, and his success inspired a young African freedom fighter by the name of Nelson Mandela. Later, the principle was used in the civil disobedience and non-cooperation campaigns against British rule in India, when military might gave way to unstoppable moral force.

Aparigraha

Gandhi was passionate about the virtue of simple living and, despite being quite well off in his barrister days, made a point of cutting his own hair and doing his own laundry. He could never get his head around the idea of servants and, when his ashram or spiritual retreat was established near Ahmadabad, caused considerable controversy by getting everyone involved in cleaning the latrines. This was a time when only "untouchables" did this work.

When the family were leaving South Africa to return to India, they were showered with gifts of jewelry in thanks for Gandhi's legal and political efforts in the Indian community. Though his wife naturally wanted to wear the jewelry, such ostentation was against Gandhi's principles, and he instead put the pieces into a trust. Over the years the interest from this deposit was used to assist various community needs, and his wife later saw the value of the act.

This simple living philosophy was inspired by the principle of *aparigraha*, or non-possession. It incorporated the idea of trusteeship, or wisely utilizing goods for the benefit all. Though he had needed to set up two or three houses for his family, Gandhi came to believe that possessions only created the illusion of security and certainty, which in reality could not be provided by anything or anyone except God. He relates the time he was charmed by a life insurance salesman and took out a policy to protect his family in the event of his death. He later cancelled the policy, believing it to be a moral mistake. His reasoning gives an insight into his broader personal religion:

"I think it is wrong to expect certainties in this world, where all else but God that is Truth is an uncertainty. All that appears and happens about and around us is uncertain, transient. But there is a Supreme Being hidden therein as a Certainty, and one would be blessed if one could catch a glimpse of that Certainty and hitch one's wagon to it. The quest for that Truth is the summum bonum of life."

Spiritual influences

Many of the early chapters concern Gandhi's search for religious truth. In London and South Africa he flirted with Christianity, but could never bring himself to believe that Jesus was the son of God. He was, however, much inspired by the New Testament, not surprisingly those parts mentioning Jesus not fighting back but "turning the other cheek."

Gandhi also got involved in the Theosophical Society, whose members were hungry for his personal experience of Hinduism. Realizing his ignorance of his own native religion, he read the teachings of Patanjali and Vivekananda, and began his love affair with the Bhagavad-Gita, which he described as a "dictionary of conduct" that led him to most of his principles. He also made a point of reading the Koran, and among secular authors found life-changing ideas in Leo Tolstoy's *The Kingdom of God Is Within You* and John Ruskin's *Unto This Last*.

Gandhi's spirituality was of the classic self-made variety, with each idea and faith carefully weighed in a search for truth. It was clearly his belief that all religious traditions were expressions of the one God, and his last struggles in India revolved around the unifying of Muslim and Hindu points of view, an effort that would cost him his life.

Final comments

Gandhi did not like the title Mahatma, as he did not think of himself as a great man. Far from being a trumpet-blowing exercise, his autobiography was designed to detail objectively his discoveries and failures in relation to right principles and spiritual truth, and he never claimed to have been perfect.

His morality was so refined that he was prepared to die for his cause, but such high principles did not always make for a neat reality. He was criticized for the discord and sometimes violence that came as a consequence of non-cooperation. Yet ultimately, Gandhi's *satyagraha* policy was a triumphant success, and what began as a personal experiment had enduring consequences for the whole peace movement.

Our choice today is to look on him as a singular individual whose like we may never see again, or to take the trail he blazed as our own. Either way, what Gandhi achieved in his experiments is now the spiritual heritage of all of us.

The Alchemy of Happiness

"*Any one who will look into the matter will see that happiness is necessarily linked with the knowledge of God. Each faculty of ours delights in that for which it was created: lust delights in accomplishing desire, anger in taking vengeance, the eye in seeing beautiful objects, and the ear in hearing harmonious sounds. The highest function of the soul of man is the perception of truth; in this accordingly it finds its special delight.*"

"*Man was not created in jest or at random, but marvelously made and for some great end. Although he is not form everlasting, yet he lives for ever; and though his body is mean and earthly, yet his spirit is lofty and divine.*"

In a nutshell

We exist to learn the higher truths about our relationship to God.

In a similar vein

Muhammad Asad *The Road to Mecca* (p. 14)
Kahlil Gibran *The Prophet* (p. 96)
Michael Newton *Journey of Souls* (p. 186)
Idries Shah *The Way of the Sufi* (p. 228)
Emanuel Swedenborg *Heaven and Hell* (p. 246)
Rick Warren *The Purpose-Driven Life* (p. 282)

CHAPTER 14

Ghazzali

Abu Hamid Muhammad ibn Muhammad al-Ghazzali (also known simply as Ghazzali) was born in 1058 in Tus, in what is now northern Iran. Considered one of the leading minds of his day, by his early thirties he had been appointed to a prestigious position as a professor of Islamic jurisprudence at Baghdad's Nizamiyyah College.

All his life he had aimed to know the "deep reality of things" and his mental powers had led him to eminence. But at the very peak of his career he began to have doubts that his powers of reasoning had really led him to truth. As he told in his autobiography, *The Deliverance from Error*, Ghazzali had a kind of spiritual crisis in which he was no longer sure of what he knew.

Dark night and epiphany

In this period of doubt, Ghazzali observed that the evidence of our senses can often be wrong, overtaken by some higher order of truth. Although, for instance, a star in the sky appears tiny, mathematics proves that it is in fact much larger than the Earth. Similarly, during a dream we can see and feel fantastic things, but on waking we realize they have no basis in reality. He wondered whether the reasoning we use to structure and explain our day-to-day reality might also seem like an illusion seen from some higher state of wakefulness. Ghazzali remembered that Sufi mystics claimed that their higher states of consciousness made reasoning worthless, and recalled also Muhammad's statement, "Men are asleep; in dying they awaken." That is, it is only on death and the leaving behind of the reasoning mind that the veil of illusion is lifted and we see truth for the first time.

In the midst of these ponderings, Ghazzali had an epiphany. A blaze of light seemed to pierce through to his heart, and in an instant the "well-ordered arguments" that had been his basis in reality thus far became insignificant next to his direct experience of divine truth.

Finding the proof of God

This experience on its own was alone not enough to sustain him, however, and he began an exhaustive program of private reading and study to discover the school of philosophy, religion, or mysticism that would best correspond to the truth to which he had been witness. This study evolved into his monumental work *The Revival of the Religious Sciences*, which progressively debunked every school of philosophical learning except for Sufism, which in his eyes provided the route to direct experience of God of which Islam had lost sight.

The intensity of the work led Ghazzali to a nervous breakdown and left him with a speech problem that made him unable to continue lecturing. Leaving behind his family and colleagues, he resigned his post and began over a decade as a wandering mystic in Syria, returning to teaching only many years later.

The Alchemy of Happiness

In time, Ghazzali's attempt to revive his religion was fully recognized, and he was given the peculiar title Hujjat-el-Islam, or "The Proof of Islam." Given that as a Sufi mystic he was outside the mainstream of Islam, this was quite an accolade. What Aquinas was for medieval Christendom, so Ghazzali was to the Muslim world of the early Middle Ages, except that his ideas were also influential in Europe, where he was known as Algazel.

Though he was a theological heavyweight, one of his wiser acts was to make an abridgment of *The Revival of Religious Sciences* that could reach a wider audience. The result was *The Alchemy of Happiness* (in Arabic *Kimiya'-yi sa'adat*). The first four chapters follow the *hadiths*, or sayings of Muhammad, in making a case for the impossibility of true happiness without a close relationship to God. Though now relatively obscure in the West, the book has for nine centuries remained one of the great inspirational tracts of Islam.

Ghazzali begins by stating the four elements in the metamorphosis that turns an average person "from an animal into an angel."

❖ Knowledge of self.
❖ Knowledge of God.
❖ Knowledge of the world as it really is.
❖ Knowledge of the next world as it really is.

Knowledge of self

Ghazzali drew attention to the simple fact that until we know something about ourselves we cannot fulfill our potential as human beings. The key to knowledge of the self is the heart—not the physical heart but the one given us by God, which "has come into this world as a traveler visits a foreign country... and will presently return to its native land."

To lose our heart in the things and concerns of this world is to forget our real origins, whereas knowledge of the heart as given by God provides a true awareness of who we are and why we are here. When people allow their passions to take over, Ghazzali said, it is as if "one should hand over an angel to the power of a dog." In another analogy, he suggested that just as polishing iron can turn it into a mirror, so a mind conditioned by discipline can eliminate its mental and spiritual rust and be shined up to truly reflect divine light.

Humans delight in using the faculties they have been given, Ghazzali pointed out: anger delights in taking vengeance, the eye delights in seeing beauty, and the ear glories in hearing music. If the highest faculty of human beings is the location of truth, then we must delight in its discovery. The lustful and the gluttonous think they are getting the most enjoyment out of life by satisfying their appetites, but they cannot know the much greater delights that come with knowledge of the self and of God. Saints and mystics are ecstatic for a reason.

While all bodily appetites are forgotten as soon as we die, whatever knowledge we have gained of God in life does not die; it becomes part of our soul and stays with us for eternity. A person who gives little attention to their soul is a loser both in this world and the next. In contrast, a person who can lift themselves from the level of an animal to a higher awareness engages in a process of personal alchemy that will bring them happiness. This is difficult, Ghazzali admitted, because we tend to be attracted to things that are not good for us, whereas those things that are best for us "are not to be obtained without toil and trouble."

Knowledge of God

Ghazzali referred to a line in the Koran: "Does it not occur to man that there was a time when he was nothing?" Many people refuse to look for the real cause that brought them into creation. He likened a physicist to an ant crawling across a piece of paper who, seeing letters being written on to it, believes they are the work of a pen alone. A person suffering from depression will be told a different cause for their ailment depend-

93

ing on who they see, a doctor or an astrologer. It does not occur to them that God may have given them the illness for a reason and caused the conditions that led to their dissatisfaction with the normal pleasures of life, in the hope that it would draw them closer to God. There is always a real cause behind the apparent one, and that real cause is God's.

Many people do not care for the idea that every person is called to account when they die, but Ghazzali says these people are like those who do not take their medicine because they believe the doctor does not care whether they do or not. The issue is not the doctor's concern, but the fact that the person will self-destruct through their disobedience. In the same way, God appreciates our worship, but if we do not worship often it does not mean that God will waste away, but that we will forget who we are; that is, spiritual beings who have been asked to take on a human life.

Knowledge of this world
Ghazzali likened the body to a horse or camel that the soul uses in its journey through life. The soul has to take care of its body in the same way that a pilgrim on a journey to Mecca needs to look after the camel they are riding. Yet if the pilgrim spends too much time attending to the animal itself, feeding and adorning it, they will both die in the desert instead of reaching their goal.

Ghazzali observed that most people do not take a big decision to remove themselves from the path to God. They begin with trifles, but these small things grow and in the end swallow the person whole:

"Those who have indulged without limit in the pleasures of the world, at the time of death will be like a man who has gorged himself to repletion on delicious viands and then vomits them up. The deliciousness has gone, but the disgrace remains."

In contrast, a person who keeps their eyes on eternity is like a guest who "eats as much as is sufficient for him, smells the perfumes, thanks his host, and departs."

Knowledge of the next world
According to the Koran, souls were sent down to earth against their wishes in order to acquire greater knowledge and experience. They were told not to fear or panic, but to wait for God's instructions about how to live. Those who did not take this advice would find life on

Earth a sort of hell, hence the Koranic phrase, "hell surrounds the unbelievers."

Ghazzali noted that neither animals on earth nor angels in heaven can change their appointed rank or place—but human beings have the choice to descend to the level of animals through their actions, or by the same token soar to angelic heights. This extreme free will is the human burden, meaning that we have to think about how we live instead of existing in an automatic sense.

Final comments

Though he was a hard-core mystic who experienced spiritual mysteries at first hand, Ghazzali's influence came from his ability to make a case for the existence of God employing reason alone. While he may have been called "The Proof of Islam," his writing in fact built a watertight case for the truth of any religion, and as a tool for winning over a doubter or lapsed believer, *The Alchemy of Happiness* is hard to beat.

There are other factors that make this 900-year-old book influential still: a title that carries a great promise; the book's basis in the authority of Muhammad's sayings in the Koran; and its short length, compared to the weighty tome from which it was abridged. As Claud Field noted in his classic 1909 translation (the one we use here), the power of Ghazzali's writing lay in his ability to create pictures in the mind that illustrate subtle spiritual or philosophical points. This was recognized by the great Sufi poet Rumi, who in the famous *Masnavi* borrowed several allegories from *The Revival of Religious Sciences*.

What is Ghazzali's legacy? He felt that Islamic culture had lost its way, with people merely going through the motions of worship and not really seeking to transform themselves. His effort to restore the faith had deep consequences, as it contributed to a disenchantment with secular philosophy in the Muslim world. While western Europe slowly moved toward a separation between church and state, the revival of Islamic spirituality led to a further indivisibility between Muslim belief and societal institutions.

But the larger message of *The Alchemy of Happiness*, whether you are Muslim or not, is that genuine happiness comes from the knowledge that we are creations of God, and have therefore been made for a purpose. Peace comes from knowing that we are merely "travelers in a foreign land" and will before long return to the eternal non-physical realm from which all things emanate.

The Prophet

"You are not enclosed within your bodies, nor confined to houses or fields.
That which is you dwells above the mountain and roves with the wind.
It is not a thing that crawls into the sun for warmth or digs holes into darkness for safety,
But a thing free, a spirit that envelops the earth and moves in the ether."

In a nutshell

Take a broader view of your life and recognize that you are a spiritual being having a human experience.

In a similar vein

Richard Bach *Jonathan Livingston Seagull* (p. 26)
Ghazzali *The Alchemy of Happiness* (p. 90)
Michael Newton *Journey of Souls* (p. 186)

CHAPTER 15

Kahlil Gibran

*T*he *Prophet* is a book of prose poetry that made its Lebanese-American author famous. Commonly found in gift shops and frequently quoted at weddings or any occasion where uplifting "spiritual" thoughts are required, the work has never been a favorite of intellectuals and to some readers it may seem a little twee or pompous, yet its author was a genuine artist and scholar whose wisdom was hard-earned.

The book begins with a man named Almustafa living on an island called Orphalese. Locals consider him something of a sage, but he is from elsewhere and has waited 12 years for the right ship to take him home. From a hill above the town, he sees his ship coming into the harbor, and realizes his sadness at leaving the people he has got to know. The elders of the city ask him not to leave. A priestess steps forward and asks Almustafa to tell them his philosophy of life before he goes, to speak his truth to the crowds gathered. What he has to say forms the basis of the book.

The Prophet provides timeless spiritual wisdom on a range of subjects, including giving, eating and drinking, clothes, buying and selling, crime and punishment, laws, teaching, time, pleasure, religion, death, beauty, and friendship. Corresponding to each chapter are evocative drawings by Gibran himself.

Here we look at a handful of the themes; however, this is a work that asks to be read in full.

Love and marriage

Foolish is the person, the prophet says, who "would seek only love's peace and love's pleasure," since wishing this leads to less of a person, who has seen less pain but also less pure joy. The prophet says:

> *"When love beckons to you, follow him*
> *Though his ways are hard and steep."*

We cannot wish for love to reach only a certain measure, or to presume that we can direct its course, "for love, if it finds you worthy, directs your course." As much as love allows for our growth, it also acts to prune us so that we grow straight and tall.

When questioned about marriage, the prophet departs from the conventional wisdom that it involves two people becoming one. A true marriage gives both people space to develop their individuality, in the same way that "the oak tree and the cypress grow not in each other's shadow." His rule for a good partnership: "Fill each other's cup but drink not from one cup."

Work

Why do the unemployed feel so wretched? Is it just the lack of money? The answer can be found in the prophet's explanation of the real meaning of work:

"You work that you may keep pace with the earth and the soul of the earth. For to be idle is to become a stranger unto the seasons, and to step out of life's procession."

It is not merely the loss of a wage or even status that is so disheartening, but the feeling that you have been left out of normal life.

Neither is it enough just to work for money alone. People think of work as a curse, the prophet says, but in doing your work "you fulfill a part of earth's furthest dream, assigned to you when that dream was born." Through work you express your love for whoever will benefit from it, and satisfy your own need to create. Those who enjoy their work know that it is a secret to fulfillment, that we can be saved through what we do.

Sorrow and pain

Sorrow carves out our being, says the prophet, but the space it makes provides room for more joy in another season of life. In one of his outstanding lines, he remarks, "Your pain is the breaking of the shell that encloses your understanding." Try to marvel at your pain as another experience of precious life. If you can do this, you can be more serene about your emotions, like the passing of the seasons.

Few realize, the prophet says, that suffering is the means to heal ourselves, "the bitter potion by which the physician within you heals your sick self." The next time you feel sorrow, consider that it may have been self-chosen at some level of your being, to bring about an enlargement of your self. Without struggles we would learn nothing about life.

Property

Guard against the love of houses and things, the prophet warns, for these comforts erode the strength of the soul. If you attach yourself too much to the domestic luxuries of life, "You house shall not be an anchor but a mast." You will be tied to it when the ship sinks.

Freedom

The longing for freedom is itself a kind of slavery. When people speak about wanting to be free, often it is aspects of themselves they are trying to escape.

Good and evil

There is no such thing as evil. Evil is simply good that has gone hungry and thirsty, and can find satisfaction for its needs nowhere else but dark places. There is light, and there is the absence of light, which is evil. Shine a light on evil and it will disappear.

Prayer

You cannot ask for anything in prayer, because God already knows your deepest needs. As God is our main need, so we should not pray for other things, but should ask for more of God.

The divided self

The prophet likens the soul to a battlefield, in which our reason and passion seem eternally opposed. Yet it does not do much good to fight either: you have to be a peacemaker, loving all your warring elements, before you can heal yourself.

The boundless self

The prophet tries to convey to those gathered that the lives we lead on Earth represent only a fraction of our larger selves. We all have "giant selves" inside us, but we first have to recognize that they may exist. "In your longing for your giant self lies your goodness," the prophet says. In pursuit of self-knowledge, therefore, we are looking for the best in ourselves.

Final comments

Taken as a whole, Gibran's book is a metaphor for the mystery of life: we come into the world and go back to where we came from. As the prophet readies himself to board his ship, it is clear that his words refer not to his journey across the seas but to the world he came from before he was born. His life now seems to him like a short dream.

The book suggests that we should be glad of any experience of life, even if it seems full of pain, because after death we will see that life had a pattern and a purpose, and that what seems to us now as "good" and "bad" will be appreciated without judgment as good for our souls. The prophet tells the crowd waiting his departure—probably to their bafflement—that soon "another woman shall bear me." He promises to return, no doubt as some advanced soul able to lift up those who trudge through life having forgotten their heavenly origin.

Yet the reader understands that the "me" of whom the prophet speaks is an illusion, that the separation we feel from other people and all forms of life while on Earth is not real. We are merely expressions of a greater unity now forgotten. As he looks forward to his journey, Almustafa likens himself to "a boundless drop in a boundless ocean." To feel yourself to be a temporary manifestation of an infinite source is greatly comforting, and perhaps accounts for the feeling of peace and liberation that many people experience on reading *The Prophet*.

Kahlil Gibran

*Born in 1883 in northern Ottoman Lebanon, Gibran received no
schooling, but was given informal religious and language lessons by a
priest. His father's gambling brought the family to financial ruin, which
prompted his mother to emigrate with her children (and without
Gibran Sr.) to the United States. A registration error on arrival in
Boston created the name "Kahlil" instead of the correct Khalil.*

*At school, Kahlil showed talent at drawing and found a mentor
in the artist and photographer Fred Holland Day, but he returned to
Lebanon to complete his secondary schooling. At 19 he went back to
Boston, but his mother, brother, and one of his sisters tragically died
from tuberculosis. He found another mentor in Mary Haskell, a
headmistress with an interest in orphans who supported Gibran's painting career, and he began to have his prose poetry, short stories, and
essays published in Arabic.*

*In 1908 Gibran began a two-year stay in Paris, studying art,
and in 1912 he moved permanently to New York, where he was able to
exhibit his paintings and have more work published, including* Al-
Ajniha Al-Mutakassirah *("The Broken Wings") and* The Madman. *In
1920 he established a society of Arab writers, and continued his writing
in Arabic in support of Lebanon and Syria's emancipation from
Ottoman rule.*

The Prophet, *published in 1923, received largely unfavorable
reviews, but word of mouth made it a bestseller. After Gibran's death in
1931, associates completed and published the two sequels he had
begun:* The Garden of the Prophet *and* Death of the Prophet.

Meetings with Remarkable Men

"From my point of view, he can be called a remarkable man who stands out from those around him by the resourcefulness of his mind, and who knows how to be restrained in the manifestations which proceed from his nature, at the same time conducting himself justly and tolerantly towards the weaknesses of others."

In a nutshell

Most people sleepwalk through life. Reject convention and become your own person

In a similar vein
Carlos Castaneda *Journey to Ixtlan* (p. 48)
Aldous Huxley *The Doors of Perception* (p. 124)
James Redfield *The Celestine Prophecy* (p. 210)
Idries Shah *The Way of the Sufi* (p. 228)

CHAPTER 16

G. I. Gurdjieff

In any age you can find individuals who follow their interests and live on their own terms. Georgi Ivanovitch Gurdjieff, perhaps the original New Age guru, led a life that was one long snub to convention. A constant traveler and relentless spiritual seeker, he was also the most practical of people, a good example of the challenge that we face in needing to make a living while wanting to pursue spiritual interests.

Shoe shining, manufacturing plaster ornaments, guiding tourists, holding seances, and fixing household goods were among the many things he cheerfully did to support himself, in line with his belief that we should live very much part of the world yet not get bogged down in mind-deadening routine. While later in life he became more settled, with groups of followers in European and American cities, Gurdjieff maintained the view that an external environment of change was good for developing inner fixity of purpose. He believed that most people sleepwalk through life, and that our true individuality can only be fulfilled when we challenge habitual ways of thinking.

All and Everything, or Beelzebub's Tales to His Grandson, is Gurdjieff's 1,300-page *magnum opus*, but *Meetings with Remarkable Men* contains the elements of his philosophy while also being a fascinating read. Consisting mainly of character sketches, the title of the book is somewhat misleading, as the "remarkable men" are the mentors of his boyhood, his close friends, and anyone who shaped his view of the world. The descriptions are not simply tributes but show how each person brought out a different aspect of Gurdjieff's self. Let us briefly look at some of these characters and why they were influential to his thinking.

Gurdjieff Sr.

Gurdjieff's father was Greek but had settled in Armenia, in Alexandropol and later Kars. He was an amateur *asokh*, a poet, singer,

103

and storyteller who immersed his son and three daughters in folklore, sayings, and music.

The family had originally been well off, owning large herds of cattle and also managing livestock for others. However, a cattle plague wiped out virtually all the animals, leaving the family with almost nothing, and despite attempts at various businesses they did not regain their prosperity. Looking back, Gurdjieff surmises that his father did not do well in business because he was not willing to capitalize on others' naïveté or bad luck. Gurdjieff's own knack for making a buck was perhaps a compensation for this trait of his father's.

Yet Gurdjieff Sr. was remarkable for his ability to remain calm and detached despite these seesawing fortunes. His great enjoyment was gazing at the stars at night, a pastime guaranteed to put small worries into perspective. He told his son to cultivate a space within his mind that was always free, and to develop an attitude of indifference to everything that normally disgusts or repels others. For instance, Gurdjieff would find a mouse or a non-poisonous snake in his bed, put there by his father, yet be expected to react calmly. This teaching, to observe without judgment and not be a slave to his reactions, was to be highly useful in his later life of perpetual travel and change.

Early teachers

Despite his straitened circumstances, Gurdjieff's father enjoyed the company of cultured friends. One of them was a man named Borsh, the dean of the local Kars Military Cathedral. The two of them decided that the young Gurdjieff was better off being home educated, and Borsh arranged a top-class education for him for such a small provincial town. As the two men talked into the night on deep and important issues, the boy soaked up the conversation, sowing the seeds for his life of questioning and philosophizing.

Another person to influence Gurdjieff in his youth was the deacon at Kars Cathedral, Bogachevsky. His mentor would eventually become Father Evlissi of the Essene Brotherhood monastery on the Dead Sea. This brotherhood, Gurdjieff noted, was formed over 1,000 years before Christ, and Jesus was initiated into its mysteries.

Bogachevsky told Gurdjieff that there are two moralities: objective morality, which has evolved over millennia and represents the basis for goodness as given by God; and subjective morality, that evolved in cultures as represented by intellectual and social conventions, which tends to distort truth.

The priest's legacy to Gurdjieff was his warning not to adopt the conventions of the people around him. He should live only according to his conscience, or objective morality. This alone he could carry with him wherever he went.

Prince Yuri Lubovedsky

This friend of Gurdjieff's was a rich Russian prince. His young wife had tragically died, and in his grief he became a recluse, drawn into the world of occult science and spiritualism. Lubovedsky spent most of the rest of his life on expeditions to exotic corners of the world. Gurdjieff first met him at the Pyramids in Egypt, where the former was acting as guide to an archaeologist, Professor Skridlov. Lubovedsky knew the professor, and the three became life-long friends. The prince traveled with Gurdjieff to many places, including India, Tibet, and Central Asia. Their last meeting, so well described, happened by chance at a remote monastery in Tibet.

The lesson of the prince's life for Gurdjieff was that unfocused curiosity, hopping from one excitement to another, can work against us. Lubovedsky became depressed, and recounted a meeting with a Hindu man who pointed out that his enthusiasms had outbalanced the attention he should have paid to his inner life. Gurdjieff's friend represented to him the dangers of being too tied up with our emotions; instead, as his father's example provided, an evolved person always had a certain detachment, at ease with themselves no matter what the circumstances.

Lubovedsky also demonstrated Gurdjieff's view that an advanced person would be able to balance thought, instinct, and feeling within themselves. Some people were too intellectual, at the expense of their powers of intuition, while others never achieved the civility that comes from development of the mind. Balance and integration of our various aspects are the goals of living.

The world according to Gurdjieff

Meetings with Remarkable Men is an unusual mixture of travelogue, snippets of wisdom, and character portraits.

Gurdjieff mentions more than once the western world's ignorance of all matters Asian, but the circumstances of his upbringing enabled him easily to bridge East and West. Sandwiched between Turkey, Russia, and Iran, his homeland of Armenia had always been a place of many influences, and his Christian heritage was spiced with folk beliefs and stories of the Near East. In the course of his journeys he would learn many languages and build up a significant knowledge of Islam, Hinduism and Buddhism. His way of seeing the world was strongly influenced by Sufism, and he counted whirling dervishes among his friends. His fame is based partly on the belief that he discovered and carried with him ancient esoteric secrets. Whether this is true or not, it is safe to say he had seen things most people had not, and this air of the exotic must have been attractive to his early followers in the West.

Gurdjieff's mistrust of established sources of knowledge went back to his childhood, when he realized that science could not explain the apparent miracles he witnessed. His later motivation for travel was to experience things at first hand, and a plank of Gurdjieffian philosophy was the insistence on experiential learning—if something is true for you, then it is true. You become your own authority on life. Gurdjieff had little time for newspapers, which he believed engineered automatic reactions such as shock or pride in the reader. A journalistic culture turned people into pallid reflections of the mindsets of the day. While the average person constructed a world for themselves that seemed "real," it was actually based on the filtering out of true reality. The awake person, in contrast, was able to look at everything as if it were brand new.

Gurdjieff referred to an ancient saying: "Only he will deserve the name of man and can count upon anything prepared for him from Above, who has already acquired corresponding data for being able to preserve intact both the wolf and the sheep confided to his care." The wolf and the sheep represent our instincts and feelings, which we have to control and balance before emerging whole. He was dismissive of modern European literature, because he felt that the European mind had become dominated by thinking at the expense of instinct and feeling. When Gurdjieff came to formalize his philosophy into self-teaching centers, they were called Institutes for the Harmonious Development of Man; that is, for the balancing of all mental and physical elements in a human being.

Final comments

Was Gurdjieff one of the twentieth century's more significant philosophers or, as *The Skeptic's Dictionary* would have it, a charlatan?

Such was the power of his personality that he attracted a number of famous followers, including the Hollywood actress Kathryn Mansfield, architect Frank Lloyd Wright, and P. L. Travers, author of the Mary Poppins books. But his most important follower turned out to be mathematician Pyotr Ouspenky, whose *In Search of the Miraculous* brought his ideas to a wide audience. Some thought Gurdjieff arrogant and uncompromising, but in fact he generally shunned publicity. He did seek donations to keep his organization going, but unlike some of today's personal development gurus, never sought to create an industry around himself.

Gurdjieff's system of personal development, "the Work," sought to bring people out of their normal sleepy state into higher awareness via self-questioning, group encounter, and sacred dance. It was an important influence in the counterculture of the 1960s, seen, for instance, in the Gurdjieffian methods adopted by the pathbreaking Esalen center in California. His philosophy of first-hand spiritual truth and knowledge became central to the New Age movement.

Gurdjieff recognized the malaise of the modern person as being that they could be one person one day and another the next, and his psychology aimed for the integration of our many selves. A remarkable person was simply one who could escape the pressures of automatic reaction and cultural conditioning to be "all of a piece." Without this unity of self and purpose we could not really lead an authentic life.

Georgi Ivanovitch Gurdjieff

Gurdjieff was born in 1877 in Alexandropol, Armenia. After many years of travel he arrived in Russia in 1913, just before the Bolshevik revolution, and for the next few years divided his time between Moscow and St. Petersburg.

In 1917 he returned to Alexandropol, and then lived in camps on the Black Sea coast of southern Russia, working with his pupils. He lived for a year in Constantinople from 1920, and then toured European cities giving talks and presentations. In 1922 he established the Institute for the Harmonious Development of Man in Fontainebleau, south of Paris. After a near fatal car accident he began writing All and Everything, or Beelzebub's Tales to His Grandson. *During the Second World War Gurdjieff lived in Paris, and he died in Neuilly, France in 1949.*

1963

Markings

"Success—for the glory of God or for your own, for the peace of mankind or for your own? Upon the answer to this question depends the result of your actions."

"Be grateful as your deeds become less and less associated with your name, as your feet ever more lightly tread the earth."

"So, once again, you chose for yourself—and opened the door to chaos. The chaos you become whenever God's hand does not rest upon your head."

In a nutshell

Don't allow your vanities to sabotage your life purpose.

In a similar vein
J. Krishnamurti *Think on These Things* (p. 148)
John O'Donohue *Anam Cara* (p. 198)
Chögyam Trungpa *Cutting through Spiritual Materialism* (p. 270)

CHAPTER 17

Dag Hammarskjöld

A Swedish economist and statesman, Dag Hammarskjöld was Secretary-General of the United Nations from 1953 to 1961. Among his achievements were the negotiation of the release of US airmen captured in the Korean War, diffusing the Suez Canal crisis of 1956, and establishing the United Nations Emergency Force. He worked continually for peace in the Middle East, and it was in the midst of negotiations during the Congo crisis in 1961 that he was killed in a plane crash in Zambia.

After his death, a manuscript titled *Vägmärken* was found in his house in New York, together with an undated letter to a friend, fellow UN official Leif Belfrage. In this letter, Hammarskjöld described the work as "a sort of 'White Book' concerning my negotiations with myself—and with God." While it is essentially a collection of personal notes, not intended for an audience, he left it up to his friend to decide whether it should be published.

The original Swedish edition of the book was followed by an English translation by Leif Sjöberg and the poet W. H. Auden. In his Foreword, Auden noted the absence of an exact equal phrase for Vägmärken, but the translators settled on "Markings," meaning the signs you might see on a trail.

The book consists of thoughts, quotes, fragments of text resembling short stories, and poems, beginning in 1925 and ending only a month before Hammarskjöld's death. They span the naïve teenage ambitions and the wizened but still idealistic observations of a person who has seen raw power and politics in action. *Markings* is very similar to the *Meditations* of Roman emperor Marcus Aurelius and, like the concise musings within Aurelius's famous work, Hammarskjöld's beautifully crafted entries were probably made at the end of long, pressured days.

Hammarskjöld was heavily influenced by the Christian mystics, particularly Meister Eckhart (whom he quotes freely), and his tortured thoughts about the value of his life will not appeal to many readers. However, this earnestness is balanced by many beautiful passages on the mystery of existence, and poems inspired by Japanese *haiku*.

Genuine success

Hammarskjöld was very much a success in worldly terms, the type of person envied for their apparently easy accomplishments at a relatively young age: top student at his university, assistant professor while still in his twenties, chairman of the Bank of Sweden at 35, followed by a glittering career as a foreign minister and UN head.

Yet the conclusion from *Markings* is that success and achievement do not mean anything if they are willed into being. Whatever you do must be consecrated to some higher purpose, one that discovers you rather than one you intentionally create. From his youth Hammarskjöld had been seen as a leader or future leader, but he constantly worried whether he was going through the motions of success without actually achieving anything. Was it his desire for regard that motivated him, or a real purpose? In the book he employs an image from Herman Melville's classic *Moby Dick* of Captain Ahab, in pursuit of a whale, "being driven... over the oceans of his fleeing goal." An achievement orientation tends to make us live in and for the future—it depends on time for its fulfillment—whereas living according to a deeply felt purpose enables us to live fully in the present.

The lesson Hammarskjöld drew from being a VIP was not to believe in his own publicity, even though he had helped to nurse the legend into being. The paradox of the successful person is that although they have got where they have through self-control, genuine success will only emerge when they let go of self-regard and just became a tool of God. We can only perfect ourselves through effacing our selves. Yet this is difficult in practice. In one of the earlier entries, Hammarskjöld recognized the contortions that the ego gets us into: "Praise nauseates you—but woe betide him who does not recognize your worth."

Hammarskjöld notes that we can either take the "strait road" or the "broad." On the first we live for the good of others, and we cannot exult because we know our work is not about us. The second road is the way of self-esteem, on which we are always thinking about "posterity," or what would be thought of our actions.

In a culture that glorifies success, the deadening effect of its pursuit is hardly talked about, but *Markings* provides the perfect antidote to vainglory. Hammarskjöld wrote: "How dead a man can be behind a façade of great ability, loyalty—and ambition! Bless your uneasiness as a sign that there is still life in you." His conclusion was that genuine achievements are possible as long as we are able to keep vanity out of the equation.

The one before the many

Hammarskjöld once joked that being the UN Secretary-General was like being a secular Pope. The position required him to be impartial and above politics, but also allowed the use of considerable power.

With his earnest desire always to do the best thing, the weight of this responsibility must have been very tough. His great insight was that it was easier to voice commitment to great causes than it was actually to make a difference to an individual human being. Laboring for the masses meant that you also did not have to pay much attention to improving yourself or paying attention to those around you. Hammarskjöld clearly felt he could go this way if he was not careful—his job of trying to bring about world peace was a big-picture task in anyone's language—yet he realized that any agreements or rapprochements would only work if those involved felt valued and depended on.

In *Markings* he observes that the ego doesn't like commitment or opening itself up to vulnerability, but only in doing so is real progress—personal and professional—made.

Final comments

Would *Markings* be considered a spiritual classic if it had not been written by a UN Secretary-General who died tragically early? Possibly not, but it is our knowledge of the author's outward life as a public figure that makes his inner one so fascinating. Famous or not, we all come to the issue of life's meaning. Hammarskjöld's conclusion was that just by existing we have a debt to repay, and we do so by being fully alive in each moment, not worried about past or future. One side of life is to observe and appreciate beauty; the other is to work tirelessly for others without self-congratulation.

Markings contains many thoughts too profound to gloss over here, and will reward quiet bedtime reading or meditation. It is sometimes obscure, as you would expect from a work never properly edited by the author, but the entries should be seen as the title suggests, as signs or markings on a path that took Hammarskjöld closer to the mystery of why he existed and therefore why anyone exists.

Hammarskjöld loved poetry, painting, and music, and was a keen skier and mountaineer. He was posthumously awarded the Nobel Peace Prize.

The Sabbath

"Six days a week we wrestle with the world, wringing profit from the earth; on the Sabbath we especially care for the seed of eternity planted in the soul. The world has our hands, but our soul belongs to Someone Else. Six days a week we seek to dominate the world, on the seventh day we try to dominate the self."

"The Sabbath, thus, is more than an armistice, more than an interlude; it is a profound conscious harmony of man and the world, a sympathy for all things and a participation in the spirit that unites what is below and what is above."

In a nutshell

Set aside time in your life to honor God and all that has been created.

In a similar vein
Daniel C. Matt *The Essential Kabbalah* (p. 168)
Rick Warren *The Purpose-Drive Life* (p. 282)

CHAPTER 18

Abraham Joshua Heschel

Throughout history, humans have sought power through manipulating and transforming things in space; that is, the world of matter. We have conquered nature, created advanced machines, and built cities, but as philosopher and theologian Abraham Heschel argued, this has been at the expense of our sense of time. When life becomes only about doing and acquiring, we lose our grip on what is really important.

Because we work in order to have the physical things we feel we need, and that work takes time, time generally has a negative quality for the modern person, Heschel says. Easily lost, it appears as the enemy and we have little of it for ourselves. But the idea of the Sabbath is to have a break from the anxious worries of work—of survival or gaining status. Many will feel that in their work they virtually sell their soul, but the Sabbath is a chance to get the soul back.

At first glance, a whole book about the Sabbath may seem somewhat obscure. But *The Sabbath: Its Meaning for Modern Man*, at only 100 pages, is an eloquent education in the Sabbath as the heart of Judaism. Although written over 50 years ago, the beautiful prose of Heschel's work can make you ponder over what may be missing in your busy life.

Sacred time

Before Judaism, humans found God in nature, in sacred places, and in things such as mountains, springs, trees, and stones. Religious festivals had always been based on the seasons and the movements of sun and moon. Gods, to be made present, had to be represented in a figure or a totem or a shrine. The great leap of Hebrew cosmology was to go beyond space and physicality and put time at the center of spiritual understanding. By having a specific day for worship, the Jews had a reminder that God was beyond matter, and that humans could transcend the material too.

The God of Israel, Heschel suggested, became the God of history, its great events being the freeing of the Jews from slavery in Egypt and the revelation of the Torah. In place of the idol of the golden calf, Jews were given a golden day, a holy time in which they could renew their divine link.

In biblical Hebrew, Heschel observed, there was no word for "thing." In later Hebrew there was a word, *davar*, which came to mean this, but even then it referred to things like a message, a tiding, a story, a manner, a promise. The Sabbath is therefore a reminder of living no longer within a human sense of time and morality, but a divine one.

Honoring a holy guest

The word Sabbath comes from the Hebrew *Shabbat*. The Friday evening service is called *kabbalat Shabbat*, roughly meaning the obligation to accept the presence of God in the Sabbath. The candles that are lit on Friday evening mimic God's statement "Let there be light" at the dawn of creation.

Traditional Jews do not grudgingly observe the Sabbath, Heschel says, they love it. It is to be delighted in, a celebration. The feeling it can give is reminiscent of the absolute love written about in medieval chivalry books, except that the Sabbath "is the love of man for what he and God have in common." This total love is the reason the ancient rabbis created so many rules and restrictions around the Sabbath: to protect its glory.

In the mythology of the Bible, it took God six days to make the world, and on the seventh day He rested, pleased with what had been created. On this day was created *menuha*, in Hebrew stillness and peace. The Sabbath is therefore a place of still waters that soothes the soul; it is a different atmosphere that envelops those who celebrate it.

There is a prayer said on the Sabbath evening: "Embrace us with a tent of thy peace." Heschel notes that old rabbis likened the Sabbath to a bride or a queen, because the day was not merely an allotted space of time but a real presence that came into their lives.

Freed from materialism

With time appearing to be always shrinking, we seek comfort in the realm of space—in things. As Heschel put it, "possessions become the symbols of our repressions." The Sabbath supplies the antidote to consumerist madness. It is designed for us to make friends again with time, to appreciate the "now" when we are not begetting things or worrying or regretting, but simply being in God's presence.

"Thou shalt not covet," Heschel notes, is the only one of the Ten Commandments that is stated twice. It is given this extra importance because God wants us to have inner liberty, not wasting our time on earth hankering after the things of the world. The Sabbath reminds that life is not merely about earning money and creating things, which is why observant Jews do not handle money on the Sabbath.

The rest of the week we spend our time, on the seventh day we *collect* time and in doing so collect ourselves. We turn "from the results of creation to the mystery of creation," Heschel writes. We are given a regular opportunity to ponder eternity.

Living in matter creates the sensation of constant change, of time moving. But in truth, Heschel notes, time is the constant and it is the things of this world that are turning over continually:

"Things perish within time; time itself does not change. We should not speak of the flow or passage of time but of the flow or passage of space through time."

It is difficult to appreciate time because we live in a world of things. But it is possible to become friends with time and see the greater reality behind matter.

Final comments

The idea of a day of rest from the working week now seems a little old-fashioned. Shops trade seven days a week and are open late into the night, and it is a badge of honor for many people to have to work through the weekend. Why should we stop for anything?

Heschel's book is potentially more significant now than when it was written, because there is even greater pressure on us always to be doing something. A whole day set aside for contemplating our connection to God may seem like an impossible luxury, yet bringing it back would lend quality to the rest of our week.

Heschel's book will open the eyes of any reader who does not know much about the importance of the Sabbath within Judaism, but perhaps one of the reasons it is a classic is because it goes beyond a single religion. Jews celebrate the Sabbath on a Saturday, Christians on a Sunday, and Muslims make Friday special, which suggests a basic human need to regain a still mind on a regular basis, to have a time for meditation or contemplation even as the world continues to rush on. Without this window into eternity we can become economic robots, so tied up with getting ahead on this Earth that we forget our place in the cosmic scheme of things.

Abraham Joshua Heschel

Born in Warsaw, Poland in 1907, Heschel received a classical Jewish education and later gained a doctorate from the Central Organization for Adult Jewish Education in Berlin, where he also taught. After the Nazis came to power he was deported to Poland, teaching in Warsaw and London, before moving to the United States in 1940. He joined the faculty at the Hebrew Union College in Cincinnati, and in 1945 was appointed professor of Jewish ethics and philosophy at the Jewish Theological Seminary in New York. He would remain in this position until his death in 1972.

Heschel's many books include Man Is Not Alone: A Philosophy of Religion, God in Search of Man: A Philosophy of Judaism, The Insecurity of Freedom, *the two-volume* Theology of Ancient Judaism, Maimonides *on the Jewish philosopher,* Israel: An Echo of Eternity, *and* A Passion for Truth.

Siddartha

"Too much knowledge had held him back, too many sacred verses, too many ritual rules, too much denial, too much doing and striving. He had been full of arrogance—always the smartest, always the most industrious, always a step ahead of everybody, always wise and spiritual, always the priest or sage. Into this priesthood, into this high-mindedness, into this spirituality, his ego had crept."

"Most people, Kamala, are like fallen leaves that blow and whirl about in the air, then dip and fall to earth. But others, only a few, are like stars, which move on a fixed course where no wind reaches them; they have their law and their course within them."

In a nutshell

Instead of striving for great spiritual heights, gain peace and power from the acceptance of life as it is.

In a similar vein
Ram Dass *Be Here Now* (p. 72)
The Bhagavad-Gita (50SHC)
The Dhammapada (50SHC)

CHAPTER 19

Hermann Hesse

efore he was Hermann Hesse, the great writer, Hesse was
struggling to bring up three sons with a wife suffering from
schizophrenia. When the illness became too much to bear, she
was put into an institution and the boys were fostered out to friends.
Hesse moved into a large and enchanting house, Casa Camuzzi, near
Lake Lugano in Switzerland, and found some peace. He meditated
during the day and wrote during the evening, and was fond of walks
and painting watercolors of the landscape. *Siddartha*, a novella set in
India at the time when Buddha was alive, was written here.

Both Hesse's father and grandfather were Christian missionaries, but
his grandfather also spoke nine Indian languages and was able to give
Hermann an appreciation of eastern spiritual literature. When the
author's rebellious and non-conformist nature is taken into account (he
dropped out of school at 13, and was later a strident pacifist), it is not
surprising that he would produce a book like *Siddartha*, a synthesis of
Buddhist, Hindu, Taoist, and Christian concepts that nevertheless ends
up rejecting conventional religion in favor of a very personal and
individual form of spirituality. But what is the story of Siddartha and
why has it captured spiritual imaginations for the last 80 years?

The quest

In strong echoes of his own life, Hesse introduces the character of
Siddartha as the son of a high-caste Brahmin scholar, immersed at an
early age in the discussions and practices of the Hindu religion.

As the book begins, Siddartha is restless. He has grown up with so
much knowledge, but there is something lacking: everyone talks of God
and the great unity of all that exists, but he wonders who has actually
experienced it. With the quest for purity characteristic of some young
men, and against his father's wishes, Siddartha decides to go off and
join the *shramanas*, the wandering holy men with their harsh existence.
Joined by his friend Govinda, from now on Siddartha owns nothing
but a loincloth, and fasts for weeks at a time. In this ascetic life he aims

to shed all his desires and rid himself of his ego, and in this quest hunger, thirst, fatigue, and pain are happily endured.

Meeting the Buddha

After three years the two friends begin hearing about a legendary figure by the name of Gotama, a buddha with a "radiant countenance" who has attained *nirvana* and now suffers none of the usual pain of living. They journey to visit Gotama, and Siddartha is taken by his perfect explanation of the universe as an unbroken and eternal chain of causes and their effects.

Yet Siddartha does not become a follower of Gotama, believing that liberation from suffering can happen not through teachers or teachings but only through taking our own, direct path. Now alone, he has an epiphany. Whereas before he despised the physical world as *maya* (illusion), now he looks at the trees, the sun, the moon, the rivers as if for the first time, without "thinking" about them. He realizes that his relentless work to find inner wisdom has blinded him to the beauty of the world.

Coming down to earth

The story continues with Siddartha emerging from the forest and entering a city. He sees a beautiful woman being carried aloft by servants, with a mouth "like a fig freshly broken open." He feels the stirrings of love and attraction, but the woman, Kamala, finds it amusing that a bedraggled ascetic from the forest thinks he can befriend her, with her fine clothes and shiny hair. He wants to learn from her the ways of love, but when she asks him what he can do in return, all he can say is that he can "think, fast, wait, and compose poetry." She likes his poetry, but tells him he will need to have clothes and look good before things can go further.

Siddartha begins working as an assistant to a businessman, quickly learning the ways of the business and proving invaluable to his employer. He is a success because, unlike his boss, he is detached from his dealings, carrying them out without fear of loss or skewed by greed, able to live in the world of striving and suffering without being too much a part of it. To him, people worry and fight over things that are really of little consequence: money, pleasures, recognition. These are merely *samsara*, the game of life, rather than life itself. Since he has the mind of a *shramana*, these things do not move him.

Yet Siddartha begins to lose his detachment and is pulled more into the selfish concerns of normal human existence, of property and money and pride. He becomes fond of gambling and drinking, and realizes that he is becoming one of the "child people" whom he once looked down on. In fact, after a night of wine and dancing girls, he realizes that he is worse than most.

Merchant to ferryman

In his misery, Siddartha flees into the forest, ready to die. Falling asleep by a river, he awakens to find his old friend Govinda, who provides a sounding board to reflect on his life and to find within himself the germ of the purer spirit he once was. It dawns on Siddartha that, being who he is, he had to go through the stage of lust and love of worldly things in order to see that they did not satisfy him. Only in disgust of what he had become could he be reborn, and not as the wandering ascetic he had been, but as someone who was part of the world but not seduced by it.

He becomes a helper to a ferryman, learning how to use the oar to take people across the river, and living in a hut. It is a simple life, but the river speaks to him in a way that a teacher never could, and he finds peace.

One day a woman and her small son are traveling to see the Buddha, who was said to be near the end of his life. The two are not far from the ferry crossing when the mother is bitten by a snake. Their cries are heard by the ferrymen, who comes to see what is happening. Siddartha quickly recognizes the woman; it is Kamala, his former love, and the boy is his son.

Joining up the circle

What happens next can be left up to the reader, but Siddartha learns the simple but powerful love a parent has for their child; he no longer looks down on those whose attachments run deep. He realizes that it has not been constant spiritual striving that has led him to a degree of peace and enlightenment, nor was it throwing himself into worldly pleasures and status. Offered in a conversation with his old companion Govinda, Siddartha's conclusion is this:

"The only thing of importance to me is being able to love the world, without looking down on it, without hating it and myself—being able to regard it and myself and all beings with love, admiration and reverence."

It is the river that helps him to arrive at this awareness. He listens to the "thousandfold song of the river," which sounds like life in its unceasing movement toward goals, its strivings, sufferings, and pleasures, yet which also moves as one. Existence, though it may seem a bewildering and fearful tumult of separate people, places, events, and feelings, is like the river in that it is really all one current. And in its oneness it is perfect.

Final comments

The message of *Siddartha* is that we should not try to withdraw from life to have a superior feeling of holiness, but throw ourselves into things. Filled with events, thoughts, and relationships, life often seems terribly fragmented, but from the perspective of the bank it is one, smooth-flowing river of experience. If you can appreciate this unity, you become less wrapped up in yourself and identify with the larger flow of life.

The book also suggests that neither a hard existence of going without, nor one of sensuality and "things," nor even a life of the mind and knowledge can result in the spiritual development we crave. What Siddartha finds is that it is only when he gives up finding *nirvana* that a degree of enlightenment comes to him.

Though the book was published in German in the 1920s, the first English translation of *Siddartha* did not appear until 1951, and it was only in 1960s America, with the explosion of interest in eastern philosophy and religion, that it became an influential bestseller. As translator Sherab Chödzin Kohn notes, the work chimed perfectly with the free-spirited non-conformity of the times, but its theme of a life beyond materialism has remained attractive. The book's timelessness also comes from the simple prose, and Hesse's descriptions of the healing power of the river are quite beautiful.

Siddartha was the fruit of Hesse's own grueling spiritual journey (in Sanskrit the name means "he who has found the goal"), but thankfully you do not have to be such a tortured soul to make use of the insights he reveals in the book.

Hermann Hesse

Born in 1877 in Calw, Germany, at 18 Hesse went to live in Basel, Switzerland, working as a bookseller. His early novels include Peter Camenzind *(1904),* Beneath the Wheel *(1906), and* Gertrud *(1910). In 1911 he traveled to India, and in 1914 he published* Rosshale. *His first real literary success was* Demian *(1919). In the same year Hesse took up residence in Montagnola, in the Ticino region of Switzerland. There he wrote* Klein and Wagner, Klingsor's Last Summer, Siddartha, Steppenwolf *(1927),* Narcissus and Goldmund *(1930),* Journey to the East *(1932), and* The Glass Bead Game *(1943).*

Hesse wrote the first part of Siddartha *easily, but stopped for over a year due to depression. The book was finished in May 1922 and published in October of that year, and was translated into a number of Asian languages.*

In 1923 Hesse became a Swiss citizen. Throughout his life he was a pacifist and in wartime a conscientious objector. In 1946 he won the Nobel Prize for Literature. He died in 1962.

1954

The Doors of Perception

"To be shaken out of the ruts of ordinary perception, to be shown for a few timeless hours the outer and the inner world, not as they appear to an animal obsessed with survival or to a human being obsessed with words and notions, but as they are apprehended, directly and unconditionally, by the Mind at large—this is an experience of inestimable value for everyone."

In a nutshell

Escape the habits of normal perception and see things as if for the first time.

In a similar vein

Fritjof Capra *The Tao of Physics* (p. 42)
Ram Dass *Be Here Now* (p. 72)
G. I. Gurdjieff *Meetings with Remarkable Men* (p. 102)
William James *The Varieties of Religious Experience* (p. 130)
Emanuel Swedenborg *Heaven and Hell* (p. 246)
Eckhart Tolle *The Power of Now* (p. 264)

CHAPTER 20

Aldous Huxley

art of Britain's postwar intellectual élite, Aldous Huxley was educated at Eton College and Oxford University, where because of an eye condition he was diverted away from a scientific career toward the world of literature. The same condition later prompted a move to the sunny dryness of California.

Ironically for a person with eyesight problems, Huxley's great interest was how our ways of seeing could either liberate or imprison us. He is probably best known for *Brave New World*, the dystopian vision of a society in which technology has outstripped morality. Like Orwell's *1984*, it showed that power lay in the ability to make other people accept your view of the world, and that this uniformity of perception killed the human spirit.

One path around perceptional conformity, Huxley noticed, was through mystical or religious states of mind. His book *The Perennial Philosophy* had picked out the common threads in the world's religions, quoting at length from the various saints and mystics that had taken human consciousness to another level. One of these was English visionary William Blake, who had written: "If the doors of perception were cleansed everything would appear to man as it is, infinite."

Taking off the blinkers

That quote appears at the beginning of Huxley's *The Doors of Perception*, an essay that describes his eye-opening experience with the drug mescalin. Though no mystic himself, Huxley wanted at least to have a glimpse of the higher states that the likes of Blake, Emmanuel Swedenborg, and the eastern mystics had described, and in mescalin he found a possible shortcut to open the perceptual doors.

Mescalin is an extract of the root of the Mexican peyotl cactus, which had long been eaten and venerated by the peoples of Mexico and the American Southwest because it prompted visionary experiences. The drug, which was not illegal, inhibited the production of enzymes regulating the supply of glucose to the brain cells. While normally the brain worked as a filtering mechanism, sifting out information not relevant to survival, mescalin effectively took these blinkers off. Those taking it would therefore see the world as if for the first time.

So it was that one spring day in 1953, in the presence of his wife Maria and a friend playing the role of scientific observer, Huxley first tried mescalin in his Los Angeles home. In the first hour of the experiment, he saw no wonderful worlds of the William Blake variety, only a modest dance of lights and moving structures and shapes. Instead, it was the everyday things around him that took on a new significance.

A small vase of flowers including a rose, a carnation, and an iris stood on the table next to him, which he had admired in passing that morning at breakfast. As the drug began to really take effect, the flowers seem to shine with inner light as well as their surface beauty. Huxley wrote: "I was seeing what Adam had seen on the morning of his creation—the miracle, moment by moment, of naked existence."

Seeing beyond the object

Our normal state of mind is continually calculating the relationships between things, measuring and analyzing. But Huxley reported that under the influence of mescalin, place, time, and distance ceased to matter very much.

He looks at his watch, but realizes it exists "in another universe," because he has discovered what it means to live in a perpetual present. For the first time, he grasps directly the idea of "beingness" that he has read about in eastern religion, the bliss of truly living in the moment.

He looks at a table, desk, and chair that are also in the room, but not as discrete objects. They appear to him more like the abstract arrangement of diagonals and shapes of modern art, like a composition by Georges Braque or Juan Gris. He now sees only patterns of light; the part of his brain that normally speaks in terms of "that is the chair where I sit to work at my desk" has been shut off: "The legs, for example of that chair—how miraculous their tubularity, how supernatural their polished smoothness!" He sees the "nature of things" as opposed to their worth as objects—the way a mystic perceives the world.

Huxley marvels at the folds in his trousers, which suddenly appear as "a labyrinth of endlessly significant complexity!"

Taken out of context, these descriptions make the author seem like just another idiot on drugs. But that very opinion would prove his point—that someone in normal reduced consciousness cannot appreciate the world for itself, but only fit things into existing categories or labels. This, he argues, is why artists labor to recreate in stone or in oil paint the intricate details of the fabric of a dress or a curtain, not so much to make it look "correct," but to express the quality of matter itself—the fabric of creation itself.

In discussing the paintings of Dutch master Jan Vermeer, Huxley proposed that the artist was not interested in expressing the personality of his subject, because for him people were just still lives that afforded the chance to express the "is-ness" of matter, for example the skin of a girl, a pearl earring, the folds of a skirt. His paintings glow with something, but it is less the sitter themselves than the mystery behind existence itself, the beauty within.

Fitting reality into language

Huxley explained his experience in terms of the fact that the brain and nervous system are a "reducing valve" that present to us only a small amount of the consciousness of the "Mind at large." Language, he suggests, is simply how we have come to encode this reduced awareness. The positive side of language is that it gives us access to accumulated wisdom and experience; its downside is that it sets ways of seeing the world into concrete. Unless something has been given a name, for instance, it does not really exist.

However, when we are able briefly to shut off our mind, which interprets reality in symbols or speech or words, our perception again takes on the freshness of first discovery. Huxley mentions St. Thomas Aquinas, who had some kind of spiritual experience near the end of his life. Aquinas decided not to go on with his unfinished book, because after what he had experienced, all his verbalized concepts and thoughts on theology and God seemed like a lot of clumsy nonsense.

This mistake of understanding our symbols of things as their actuality is one of the insights that came to Huxley. He saw that language and art, however beautiful, can only ever be a representation of the higher beauty of unseen reality.

Beyond the self

At times the trip got a bit much for Huxley, and he realized why the literature of religious experience talks of horror and fear as much as ecstasy. In higher states there is the fear of being overwhelmed, of your little brain not being able to cope with what you see and experience. He describes this as "the incompatibility between man's egotism and the divine purity."

Huxley explains that mescalin's restriction of sugar to the brain results in the normal activity of the ego becoming weak. There were two people in the room with him, he wrote, "but both belonged to the world from which, for the moment, mescalin had delivered me—the world of selves, of time, or moral judgments and utilitarian considerations, the world (and it was this aspect of human life which I wished, above all else, to forget) of self-assertion, of cocksureness, of over-valued words and idolatrously worshipped notions."

Huxley's insight is echoed by many a saint, mystic, genius, and yogi who has tried to convey what being a human is like when the ego has been transcended. Lost in the direct perception of reality, our ego disappears and we become a "not-self," one with nature or God.

Many mystics have been reluctant, given what they have seen, to be brought back to earth and deal with the problems people bring before them. Yet for Huxley, the experience of loss of a sense of self was liberating. With the ego moved temporarily out of the way, he was allowed to observe the true wonder of existence. He saw that personal feelings are just not that important, that the cheap thoughts and pretensions that normally fill the mind are nothing when brought before that wonder. Further, imagination and creativity did not really emanate from personality, Huxley now understood: they were more the result of a lifting of the veil, allowing him to see *beyond* the self.

Final comments

Huxley's drug experiment showed him that most people live within a very narrow band of perception, and that this narrowness makes for less of a life. If something came along that was an aid to breaking free of these intellectual chains, it was worth investigating. Yet Huxley also acknowledged that a drug-induced opening up of the mind could only ever be temporary; he did not live to see the social and intellectual revolution of the 1960s in which people forgot this essential caveat.

The very literate Californian rock legends The Doors took their name from Huxley's essay, and the term "human potential" arose from a series of lectures given by Huxley at the groundbreaking Esalen Institute, founded in 1962. Though it was by no great design that he ended up there, Huxley's presence in California until the early 1960s was one of the seeds that grew into a flowering of alternative ways of seeing and being.

Huxley's simple observation was that if our great artists, geniuses, and saints had been able to break open the doors to perception, surely this was a path that all humanity might take. While our language and way of perceiving had been shaped by the need for survival, and therefore had admitted only a limited reality, it was also part of being human to try to go beyond the normal sense of self. Perhaps in the future, it would be not only the mystics who could experience the great spiritual mysteries first hand, but anyone who was open to them.

Aldous Huxley

Born in 1894 in Surrey, England, Huxley was the grandson of the distinguished biologist Thomas Henry Huxley, and had writers and poets on his mother's side of the family.

His mother died of cancer when he was only 14. While at Eton, an eye disease almost turned him blind, but he recovered enough to go on to Oxford University. While at Oxford he enjoyed the company of Bertrand Russell, Lytton Strachey, and D. H. Lawrence.

Huxley married in 1919, to the Belgian Maria Nys. They traveled frequently through the 1920s, including trips to India and the United States, and divided their time between England and Italy. In these years Huxley wrote Chrome Yellow *(1921),* Antic Hay *(1923),* Those Barren Leaves *(1925), and* Point Counter Point *(1928).* Brave New World *(1932) was partly inspired by his experience of fascist Italy under Mussolini.*

The Huxleys moved to California in 1937, where Aldous worked as a Hollywood screenwriter. Maria died of breast cancer the year after the publication of The Doors of Perception, *and Huxley married again in 1955 to Laura Archera. The essay* Heaven and Hell *(1956) expanded on the ideas in* The Doors of Perception, *and the utopian novel* Island *(1962) provided a spiritual counterpoint to* Brave New World.

Huxley died in 1963, on the same day as C. S. Lewis and President John F. Kennedy.

The Varieties of Religious Experience

"Were one to characterize the life of religion in the broadest and most general terms possible, one might say that it exists of the belief that there is an unseen order, and that our supreme good lies in harmoniously adjusting ourselves hereto."

"The potentialities of development in human souls are unfathomable. So many who seemed irretrievably hardened have in point of fact been softened, converted, regenerated, in ways that amazed the subjects even more than they surprised the spectators."

In a nutshell

If a person's religion succeeds in making them more whole and providing inspiration, then it works.

CHAPTER 21

William James

The Varieties of Religious Experience was first presented as a series of lectures at the University of Edinburgh in 1901. To prepare for the talks, Harvard psychologist William James read widely in the religious classics, including the personal accounts of various saints and mystics.

His decision to look at spiritual experience from a psychological point of view seemed very new at the time, even blasphemous. Mountains of books were still being churned out on the finer points of dogma and theology, but James was more interested in the universe of *individual* experience. His purpose in writing the book was to convince readers that although religion itself often *seem* absurd, the spiritual impulse is still humanity's most important function. It is what makes us human. James wanted to know why the human is a religious animal, and what *practical* benefits spirituality brings us, assuming that we would not engage in it if it did not do us some good.

His emphasis on the individual, rather than institutions, in spiritual matters paved the way for the whole New Age and personal development ethic, in which it is taken for granted that our beliefs are based on personal meaningfulness and efficacy.

The book's insights are wrapped in prose as elegant and forceful as anything written by his novelist brother Henry James, and it was recognized as a classic virtually from the day of publication. Its great service was to make the religious reader see spiritual matters from a more rational, objective perspective, and to persuade the scientifically minded that religious experience has its value and is a "fact."

The science of spirituality

James wrote *The Varieties of Religious Experience* at the end of a century of scientific advance that reacted against the unthinking faith of earlier times. In this milieu, the Bible was newly appreciated as just a collection of stories, and in the new science of psychology, religious experience could be explained away as a creation of the mind.

Yet James was skeptical of the idea that all religious experience could easily be reduced to states of the brain, what he calls the "Nothing-but" view of spirituality. St. Paul's vision on the road to Damascus, for instance, could be explained away as "a discharging lesion of the occipital cortex" (an episode of epilepsy). And according to this "medical materialism," St. Teresa of Avila (with her uncontrolled ecstatic raptures) was simply a "hysteric."

A physical state can help to produce a mystical experience, James noted, but this does not discredit the revelatory worth of the experience. For centuries, monks and nuns had consciously manipulated their bodies (going without food and sleep, breathing differently etc.) because these physiological states helped them enter higher states of awareness. Religious experience was therefore not "created" by such manipulations—it was there all along for the taking; it was a matter of making ourselves more sensitive to its occurrence.

Yet ultimately, James felt that this question of whether the experience was "in the brain" or a communion with God was irrelevant. The crucial point, it seemed to him, was whether the experience had good effects.

"By their fruits shall ye know them, not by their roots"

James wrote that spiritual ideas should be judged on three criteria: immediate luminousness; philosophical reasonableness; and moral helpfulness. Put simply, do they enlighten us, do they make sense, are they a good guide to living?

He quotes a passage from St. Teresa of Avila's autobiography in which she talks about her visions. At the time some suspected that she was seeing the devil, not God, but she protested that what she saw could not be just the work of the imagination, since it had made her a much better person ("uprooting my vices, and filling me with a masculine courage")—and her confessors confirmed it. Teresa also made a distinction between imaginings and spiritual reality, pointing out that while pure imagination weakens the mind and soul, "genuine heavenly vision" revitalizes and strengthens the subject. In Teresa's case, she felt that her visitations guided her toward the reform of the Carmelite order, of which she was a member.

This was the practical effect of religious experience that James was so fascinated by. These "visitations" may have come from inside a saint's own mind, or they may indeed have been from God. But as cases such as St. Paul's, St. Augustine's, or St. Teresa's demonstrated, what was certain was that they could transform a life.

The motivation of the convert

Both psychology and religion, James observed, agree that a person can be transformed by forces apparently beyond their normal consciousness. But while psychology defines these forces as "unconscious"—that is, within the self—in religion redemption comes from outside the person, a gift from God.

To the rational or scientific frame of mind, the "born-again" person or garden-variety religious convert may seem imbalanced, even a nutcase. Conversion can be sudden, James pointed out, but that does not mean it is pathological. To the onlooker, it may look like patching on a holy outlook to a person's existing life, but to the one experiencing it, it is a total transformation. Suddenly, it is other people who are in the dark.

James recognized a pattern in conversion experiences. They tended to happen when people were so low that they just "gave up," the vacuum of hope providing space for revelation. The religious literature is full of stories along these lines, in which the constrictions and negative aspects of the ego are finally discarded; we begin to live only for others or for some higher goal. The compensation for becoming dependent on God is a letting go of fear, and it is this that makes conversion such a liberating experience. It is the fearlessness and sense of absolute security in God that give converts their breathtaking motivation. An apparently perfectly normal person will give up everything and become a missionary in the jungle, or found a monastery in the desert, because of a belief. Yet this invisible thing will drastically change their outward circumstances—which led James to the unavoidable conclusion that for such a person, their conversion or spiritual experience is a *fact*, indeed more real than anything that had so far happened in their life.

Why religion has a transforming power

James offered the idea that religion does not have to be worship of a God. It can be simply a belief in an unseen order, to which our task is to harmoniously adjust ourselves. James noted, "Religion, whatever it is, is a man's total reaction upon life, so why not say that any total reaction upon life is a religion?" Under this appreciation, atheism could be a religion. The fervor with which some atheists attack Christianity, he noted, is religious in nature.

Similarly, the view of life encapsulated by the phrase "Who cares?" is for some a personal religion. Consider also the spiritual philosophy of the Transcendentalists, posturing an unseen and never-erring Law that regulates the universe. People take on religion for personal reasons, James argued, thus it must serve them in some way. He quoted J. H. Leuba, an early psychologist of religion: "God is not known, he is not understood; he is used."

The religious attitude, though, is normally associated with a willingness to leave the self behind in the cause of something greater, for example God or country. This denial of the self is what makes the religious impulse different from all other types of happiness, and so uniquely uplifting. A religious feeling can be distinguished from other feelings because it ennobles the person feeling it, giving them the sense that they live according to larger forces, laws, or designs.

Religions exist, James suggested, to provide a solution to humans' perennial uneasiness, or our sense that there is something wrong. It enables people to see the higher part of them as their real self, and also to leave their lower self behind.

We all want to connect with something "more," whether that is something great inside us or an external higher power, and religion provides a framework for us to experience the better things that come from living by faith instead of our more natural state of fear. "Not God," James stated, "but life, more life, a larger, richer, more satisfying life, is, in the last analysis, the end of religion."

Final comments

Inserted into *The Varieties of Religious Experience* is a mention of a man who managed to save himself from insanity by anchoring his mind to powerful statements from the Bible. It so happens that this person, referred to as a "French correspondent," was James himself.

His conclusion was that a state of faith could transform a life utterly, even though what is believed is invisible to the eye and strictly speaking may not exist. Religion could genuinely heal a person, integrating what before was fragmented. For James, who fell in and out of depression and endured a sense of alienation for many years, this alone justified religious activity. While he admitted to being far from spiritually advanced himself, it was clear to him that belief in the unseen had unleashed in many the great forces of individuality and purpose.

James acknowledged that science will be forever trying to blow away the obscuring mists of religion, but in doing so it will totally miss the point. Science can only ever talk in the abstract, but personal spiritual experience is more powerful precisely because it is subjective. Spirituality is about the emotions and the imagination and the soul— and to a human being these are everything.

William James

James was born in the Astor Hotel in New York in 1842. His grandfather was a strict Presbyterian who had created a fortune in the years following his arrival in America in 1789. William's father, Henry James Sr., embraced the philosophy of the mystic Emanuel Swedenborg (see p. 246) and encouraged his children to be independently minded when it came to religion. The family environment was intellectual and cosmopolitan.

In his late teens James wanted to be a painter, but with his father's encouragement enrolled in courses at Harvard, studying chemistry, anatomy, and later medicine. Though a late starter professionally, in 1872 he gained an appointment in anatomy. A decade later he was made a professor of philosophy, before changing his professorship to psychology.

James's landmark Principles of Psychology, *published in 1890, spans 1,400 pages and took 12 years to write. Other key books include* The Will to Believe *(1897) and* Pragmatism *(1907).*

James was plagued by poor physical health and depression. The Varieties of Religions Experience *was written while he was recuperating from an illness acquired while he was on a trip to the Adirondack mountains in 1898.*

James married Alice Howe Gibbens in 1878, and they had four sons and one daughter.

Memories, Dreams, Reflections

"We are very far from having finished completely with the Middle Ages, classical antiquity, and primitivity, as our modern psyches pretend… But it is precisely the loss of connection with the past, our uprootedness, which has given rise to the 'discontents' of civilization."

"Unfortunately, the mythic side of man is given short shrift nowadays. He can no longer create fables. As a result, a great deal escapes him; for it is important and salutary to speak also of incomprehensible things."

"The more the critical reason dominates, the more impoverished life becomes; but the more of the unconscious, and the more of myth we are capable of making conscious, the more of life we integrate."

In a nutshell

Modern life must be enriched by an awareness of dreams, an appreciation of myth, and a sense of mystery.

In a similar vein

William James *The Varieties of Religious Experience* (p. 130)
James Redfield *The Celestine Prophecy* (p. 210)
Gary Zukav *The Seat of the Soul* (p. 306)
Joseph Campbell (with Bill Moyers) *The Power of Myth* (50SHC)
James Hillman *The Soul's Code* (50SHC)
Thomas Moore *Care of the Soul* (50SHC)

CHAPTER 22

Carl Gustav Jung

Most autobiographies cover the main events of the author's life, with the reader often left with only glimpses of the inner life. Carl Jung's autobiographical *Memories, Dreams, Reflections*, in contrast, focuses on the great psychologist's spiritual and intellectual awakenings. The descriptions of his visions, dreams, and fantasies, which he considered his "greatest wealth," fill the book; this he did not for indulgence's sake, but because he considered them the prism through which he could perceive the collective psyche of humankind.

Memories, Dreams, Reflections is controversial because it was still in manuscript form when Jung died, and required further editing to become the final version. But it found the popular audience that Jung had always hoped for, and inspired many people to become psychoanalysts. Like a Christmas cake, it will be too rich and dense for some; for others it may inspire a life-long interest in Jungian psychology, which aims to reveal the spiritual forces that lie behind the science of the mind and personality.

Jung and God

Other volumes carry Jung's thoughts on mythological and psychological concepts such as the "God-image," but *Memories, Dreams, Reflections*, according to its editor Aniela Jaffe, is Jung's "religious testament" to the world, the only occasion on which he really talked about his personal experience of God.

Both sides of Jung's family had been pastors and theologians, and his father was a rather doctrinaire minister. In this environment Jung naturally grew up dwelling on religious issues. The God he imagined was not personal or enlightening, but simply represented the power of the universe in all its light, darkness, chance, and infiniteness. Through dreams he felt led to the conclusion that God actually wants us to think "bad thoughts," thoughts that go against established morality, so that we can make our way independently back to God. He felt that the truly spiritual person is a free thinker who demands *experience* of God rather that mere faith.

This idea of the divine as not all sweetness and light, and his belief that Christianity had never been able to deal satisfactorily with the question of evil, put Jung at odds with orthodox Christianity. Yet he considered himself a Christian, and in 1952 wrote to a clergyman, "I find that all my thoughts circle around God like the planets around the sun, and are irresistibly attracted by Him."

Everyone has religious ideas in them, Jung believed, feelings about the infinite or intimations of greater meaning. He had observed that those who shut them out often developed neuroses, yet such people would not have been "divided against themselves" if they had lived in an earlier time, in which their lives would have been closely tied to myth, ritual, and nature. Modern people are too objective, he wrote, their spiritual horizons too narrow; many lives are lived almost entirely on the plane of the conscious, rational mind. Were they to close the gap between their ego and unconscious minds, Jung believed, people would return to full mental health.

His experience with psychiatric patients led him to believe that the psyche is by nature religious, and that the spiritual dimension is a basic element in psychology. Though we normally think of him as a psycho-analyst, Jung's larger quest in his work was definitely spiritual, and in a time of scientific materialism this made his ideas resonate. Asked in a television interview whether he believed in God, Jung replied: "I don't believe—I know."

Integrating the self

When Jung was at university in Zurich, he decided to specialize not in internal medicine, his original choice, but psychiatry, then a new and somewhat dubious field. In 1900, he began work as an assistant at the Burhölzli mental hospital in Zurich. At this time, psychiatrists were strangely uninterested in what went through a patient's mind. The emphasis was on symptoms and making a diagnosis. As Jung puts it, "the human personality of the patient, his individuality, did not matter at all." Both Freud and Jung went against scientific opinion by being interested in the whole person, not simply their medical conditions, and

Jung's first book, on the psychology of schizophrenia, aimed to show that delusions and hallucinations were not simply random symptoms of disease but were closely related to the patient's personality.

The goal of what Jung termed "individuation" was the uniting of inner opposites, or recognizing the many contradictions within ourselves. This self-knowledge would allow a sense of unity of purpose about our life and our personality to emerge. Jung recounted that as a boy, he realized that there were two basic aspects to a person's being, which he termed personality No. 1 (what we usually think of as the self) and personality No. 2 (the "other"). His own No. 1 was the boy who did his homework and got into fights, but he also sensed a No. 2 that rested on a "timeless, imperishable stone" of wisdom.

Jung went out of his way to listen to this part of himself because he felt it to be his most valuable, and his lifetime's work in exploring the various sides and dimensions of the self means that today we are not afraid of talking about this No. 2 personality (variously called the "shadow," the "higher self," and the "true self"). We appreciate that its integration is necessary for mental health. Without such integration, we tend to project onto other people or things what we do not recognize in ourselves, with often harmful consequences.

Freud and beyond

At their first meeting in Vienna in 1907, Freud and Jung talked for 13 hours straight. In *Memories, Dreams, Reflections*, Jung describes Freud's *The Interpretation of Dreams* as "epoch making," and states, "By evaluating dreams as the most important source of information concerning the unconscious processes, he [Freud] gave back to mankind a tool that had seemed irretrievably lost."

Their famous split came about because Jung could not accept Freud's belief that most human behavior and any instance of the spiritual in art or in a person was the result of "repressed sexuality." From Jung's point of view Freud, who so abhorred the religious impulse, wanted to turn his scientific ideas into a religion. "When I parted from Freud," Jung writes, "I knew that I was plunging into the unknown. Beyond Freud, after all, I knew nothing; but I had taken the step into the darkness."

In this darkness Jung would develop many of his now famous ideas. Though he coined the psychological terms "complex," "introvert," and "extravert," he went out on more of a limb with his idea of the "collective unconscious," a larger human mind of which every individual is a part, manifested in the images, symbols, dreams, and myths that seemed to emerge in all cultures. He also developed the concept of "archetypes," ways of being or acting that people unthinkingly adopt but that are also patterns in this broader collective psyche.

Another of Jung's famous ideas, "synchronicity" or the occurrence of seemingly meaningful coincidences that go beyond the realms of normal probability, suggested a universe in which the boundaries that humans normally perceive between mind and matter may in some circumstances fell away. Synchronicity is now a key concept in the New Age movement (see James Redfield's *The Celestine Prophecy*, p. 210), but was also given credence by Jung's friend, Nobel physicist Wolfgang Pauli. Jung was equally interested in numerology, particularly the significance in art and mythology of the number four, and became a scholar of alchemy, Gnosticism and the Bible. He understood the real meaning of alchemy not as turning ordinary metals into gold, but as the transformation of the psyche, an awakening.

In 1913, Jung had a powerful vision of all the land between the North Sea and the Alps being flooded. On closer inspection the water was shown to be blood, in which floated the drowned bodies of millions. At first he thought this indicated that a revolution would take place, then it dawned on him that the Great War was about to break out in Europe.

Jung's personal powers of precognition led to his delving into parapsychology, and the credence that he gave, as a scientist, to non-physical causality was met with derision by Freud. Only time will tell whether Jung or Freud was right on these non-traditional areas of science, but it is reasonable to say that Jung's star has risen in the last few decades, while much of Freud's thought has been reassessed.

Final comments

Jung admitted that his "mythologizing" gave life a glamor that, once experienced, was difficult to do without. But then, he asked, why *should* we do without it? To the intellect, matters to do with dreams and the unconscious may seem like a waste of time, but if they enrich our emotional lives and heal a divided mind, surely they are valuable. If we have a purely rational, artless existence, never taking account of our dreams or fantasies, we become one-dimensional. In seeking perfect explanations, we never dwell on the "incomprehensible things," as Jung described the mysteries of time and space; yet that which is mysterious also gives meaning to life.

If you are tired of the shallowness of materialist, consumer culture, this book may be exactly what you need. Jung's account of travels in Africa, America, India, and Italy are fascinating, as is the chapter on the tower house he built at Bollingen on the shores of Lake Zurich to get away from it all. The descriptions of dreams and visions that appear throughout the work will not hold everyone's attention, but for many they will spark a new interest in the unconscious mind as a provider of guidance and wisdom.

Carl Gustav Jung

Jung was born in Kesswil, Switzerland, in 1875, the son of a Protestant minister.

In 1895 he enrolled at the University of Basel to study medicine, and when his father died the following year had to borrow money to remain a student. He began to specialize in psychiatry, and from 1900 worked at the Burhölzli clinic in Zurich under the pioneering psychiatrist Eugen Bleuler. In 1903 he married Emma Rauschenbach, a Swiss heiress. Under Swiss law Jung had access to her fortune, and they built a large house in Kusnacht for their young family.

In 1905 Jung became lecturer in psychiatry at the University of Zurich, and the same year senior lecturer at the Psychiatric Clinic, a post he relinquished in 1909 due to a burgeoning private practice.

Jung was a prolific writer. His books include The Psychology of the Unconscious, Psychology and Religion, Psychology and Alchemy, *and* The Undiscovered Self. *Many writings are included in* The Collected Works of C. G. Jung. *He died in 1961.*

The Book of Margery Kempe

"And so it was twenty years and more from the time this creature had her first feelings and revelations, ere she did any writing. Afterwards, when it pleased Our Lord, He commanded her and charged her that she should get written her feelings and revelations and the form of her living, that His goodness be known to all the world."

In a nutshell

Intense spiritual experience can change the life of even the most unlikely person.

In a similar vein
St. Augustine *Confessions* (p. 20)
Malcolm X *The Autobiography of Malcolm X* (p. 160)
Teresa of Avila *Interior Castle* (p. 252)

CHAPTER 23

Margery Kempe

U ntil the twentieth century, all the world knew of *The Book of Margery Kempe* were brief extracts taken from the original manuscript, which had been lost. Then in 1934, a full copy of the original book came to light in a private English library.*

The book is considered the first autobiography in the English language. As R. W. Chambers notes in his introduction to the book, nearly every document at this time was in Latin or French, Latin because it was the tongue of medieval officialdom, and French at the insistence of Britain's Norman rulers after the conquest of 1066. But away from London, where Kempe lived, even many middle-class people had not been schooled in either official language, and Kempe had not learned to read or write at all. Thus her life story was dictated to a scribe in the only tongue she had ever known—vernacular English.

In two parts totaling 99 chapters, the work is of substantial length. It charts Kempe's transformation from housewife to celebrated mystic, and gives an amazing insight into medieval Britain. No dressed-up "life of a saint," it is an honest account that she clearly hoped would set the record straight and win over her doubters.

Town princess

Born in 1373, Margery was the daughter of John Brunham, a parliamentarian and five-time Mayor of Bishop's Lynne (now King's Lynn) in Norfolk, a port in the east of England. At the age of 20 she married a young merchant, John Kempe, and quickly became pregnant. That child was the first of 14.

After the birth Margery Kempe became mentally ill ("hindered by the devil," as she describes it) and was tied up in her own house for apparently manic behavior involving food. But during one of these episodes she had a vision of Jesus robed in purple silk, and he said to

her: "Daughter, why hast thou forsaken Me, and I forsook never thee?"
The vision, she relates, showed her how close God is even in our deepest tribulations, and brought her back to sanity.

Yet the visitation was not really enough to make her change her ways. She continued to wear flashy dresses so that men might find her attractive, and liked to boast of her "high-born" relatives. In her own words: "She would not take heed of any chastisement, nor be content with the goods that God had sent her, as her husband was, but ever desired more and more." For the sake of "pure covetousness" (i.e., greed) she started a brewery, quite a substantial operation, but after a few years lost much money over it. When later her mill also failed due to the non-cooperation of the horses, Kempe took it as a sign of God's displeasure with her, and vowed to walk the way of the Lord from then on.

Chaste goodwife

While lying in bed with her husband one night, Kempe heard a beautiful, heavenly melody. This celestial music made her wonder why she had ever sinned, and from that point on she would often declaim: "It is full merry in Heaven." The incident had the effect of turning her off sex, and she told her husband that from now on her thoughts and devotion would be only to God. He respected her sentiment, and agreed they should give up their lovemaking—"but not yet." Kempe continued to let him have his way, but her heart was somewhere else. She fasted, wore a hair shirt, and continually wept for her sins, often to the extreme annoyance of people who believed she was just "turning it on" to attract attention. This inevitably lost her the friendship of many who preferred the old Margery.

Things came to a head with her husband when they were walking along a roadside in the heat of the summer. John asks Margery a hypothetical question: If a man came along and threatened to cut off his head unless they returned to their normal sex life, what would she choose? When she replied that she would rather see him slain, he says: "Ye are no good wife." But they strike a bargain in which he agrees not to make advances to her, while she will pay off his debts before heading off on a pilgrimage.

Kempe felt that she had now transcended the vain wants of the world, and that "all fleshly lust had wholly been quenched in her." Though she had some further temptations, God let her know that he was supporting her and she became celibate for good. Some years later her husband finally got the message and also took a vow of chastity.

Tears and travels

Kempe was famous for two things: her fits of weeping and her travels. Yet it was not until she was in her forties, having had 14 children, that she began her roving life of pilgrimage and visits to well-known church figures and mystics. In 1414 she journeyed to the Holy Land and also spent time in Rome for the canonization of her beloved St. Bridget, returning home the following year. In 1417 she sailed for Spain and took a pilgrimage to Santiago de Compostella, and in her later infirm years again crossed seas on pilgrimages to Aachen and Danzig. She also traveled to holy sites and churches within England. These travels were generally undertaken alone and in discomfort, and usually with little money.

She was not able to control her tearful visions of Jesus on the cross, and people naturally thought—given the woman she had been—that her crying fits were either a false display or, worse, the work of the devil. Even now we may think that the outbursts were the work of a drama queen, but as Barry Windeatt** notes, this expression of divine calling was not uncommon in her era. The French mystic Mary of Oignies was a weeper, as were Blessed Angela of Foligno and Dorothea of Montau. The last two, like Kempe, had been mothers and wives.

Proving her case

Kempe was also accused of being a Lollard, a heretic who wanted to reform the church, which at the time was punishable by burning at the stake. She relates a journey to York where she was detained by the Archbishop for fear of her corrupting the townsfolk. Ordered to answer on the articles of faith, she was luckily well versed in Church dogma and was allowed to leave town. Although unlettered, Kempe notes that she could equal "in wit and wisdom" the learned clerks and priests of the time.

Such independence and defiance, at a time when most English women were at home weaving, made Kempe a threat to the established order, and for her pains she was scorned, ridiculed, and threatened. She had to continually prove that she was indeed a woman of God, and her book is filled with the efforts of "this creature," as she describes herself, to win people over. For example:

145

"Afterwards this creature came to Assisi, and there she met with a Friar Minor, an Englishman; and a devout clerk, he was held to be. She told him of her manner of living, of her feelings, of her revelations, and of the grace that God wrought in her soul by holy inspirations and high contemplations, and how our Lord dallied to her soul in a manner of speaking."

While many others thought it very suspect, this particular friar was struck by Kempe's conversational method of prayer and felt that the Lord's "dallying" (at that time meaning talking) to her soul was real.

In reading Kempe's story it is difficult not to think of Teresa of Avila, who a century later had uncontrollable "raptures," or visions of Jesus, and had to defend herself against male church skeptics. Teresa used famously sensual language to describe her love for the Lord, and in her book Kempe reveals a similar sort of love. She recounts a conversation with Jesus in which he apparently says to her:

"My dearworthy daughter, I swear by My Majesty that I shall never forsake thee. And, daughter, the more shame, despite, and reproof that thou sufferest for My love, the better I love thee, for I am like a man that loveth well his wife. The more envy that men have of her, the better he will array her in despite of her enemies. And right so shall I fare with thee."

These comforting words from an invisible presence were all Kempe needed to continue her new Christian life, despite the difficulties.

The Lord's lover

The Book of Margery Kempe does not contain much reflection by the author on her life as a whole, but in simply getting it down on paper she was able to show how a vain and prideful harridan could be turned into a woman of God. She looked back with horror on her former vanities and lax morality.

This objectivity could only have been won, you would think, if she had indeed seen and felt real spiritual truths. Kempe lived at the same time as the famous "anchoress" (saintly recluse) Julian of Norwich, and Kempe records their meeting. Julian wrote the classic meditation *Revelations of Divine Love*, and was clearly Kempe's superior in theological learning and insight, but Kempe's book also contains many subtle theological points that you would not expect from an illiterate woman. There is one beautiful passage, for example, in which God spoke to her on the eternal unity of man and God:

"For daughter, thou art as secure in the love of God, as God is God. Thy soul is more certain of the love of God, than of thine own body, for thy soul shall part from thy body, but God shall never part from thy soul, for they are united together without end."

In Kempe God found not a mindless devotee but one who was clearly prepared to think about her faith and how it had transformed her.

Final comments

At a time when demure piety was the model of a good woman, Kempe was clearly a "handful," and her outspoken nature got in the way of her credibility. Yet the beauty of her story is that spiritual insight can come to anyone, not just the quietly devout, and *The Book of Margery Kempe* is an outstanding account of transformation through religion.

The book is not a modern-style autobiography where everything happens in neat chronological order, so it takes some getting used to. Those who persevere will find it frequently amusing and a unique first-hand view into pre-Shakespearean England. Some editions are written in a more contemporary style, but this has to be weighed against the loss of some of the rich medieval feeling of the original language.

The book ends abruptly with Margery back home in Lynn, where she lived into her sixties. Her husband had become senile and died some time before her.

* The library of my grandfather, Col. William Butler-Bowdon, whose translation of *The Book of Margery Kempe* from the Old English was published in 1936 by Jonathan Cape. Includes R. W. Chambers' Introduction. Quoted material comes from this edition.
** *The Book of Margery Kempe*, Penguin, 1985. Introduction by Barry Windeatt.

Think on These Things

*"Rain on dry land is an extraordinary thing, is it not? It washes the
leaves clean, the earth is refreshed. And I think we all ought to wash
our minds completely clean, as the trees are washed by the rain,
because they are so heavily laden with the dust of many centuries, the
dust of what we call knowledge, experience. If you and I would cleanse
the mind every day, free it of yesterday's reminiscences, each one of us
would then have a fresh mind, a mind capable of dealing with the
many problems of existence."*

In a nutshell

**Become a real revolutionary by learning how to think beyond the
confines of culture.**

In a similar vein

Dag Hammarskjöld *Markings* (p. 108)
Robert M. Pirsig *Zen and the Art of Motorcycle Maintenance* (p. 204)
Shunryu Suzuki *Zen Mind, Beginner's Mind* (p. 240)
Eckhart Tolle *The Power of Now* (p. 264)

CHAPTER 24

J. Krishnamurti

I s your life one big struggle to succeed? Are you afraid of being ordinary? If these questions just about sum you up, take a brief holiday from your striving and read *Think on These Things*. Probably philosopher J. Krishnamurti's most practical work, it arose out of question-and-answer sessions with Indian school students, but has touched hearts and minds universally.

Krishnamurti teaches these students that the real purpose of education is not to prepare us for getting a job, but to "help us understand the whole process of life." Education is about how to love, how to live simply, how to free our mind from prejudice, superstition, and fear. Without this knowledge we will walk through life in an almost mechanical way, instead of becoming the truly creative person we could be. "If the mind does not penetrate beyond its own barriers," Krishnamurti states, "there is misery."

Through its inescapable logic, *Think on These Things* shatters our belief in the salvation of celebrity, money, and success, demonstrating that desire for these things leads only to sorrow. Everyone now wants to be "someone," but Krishnamurti shows how this urge paradoxically churns out mediocre people.

Ambition and success

The book expounds at length on the subject of worldly success. Our culture glorifies ambition and achievement, and consequently we feel we must always be striving for some goal. But Krishnamurti suggests that the desire to become something always ends in disappointment or emptiness. It is not an intelligent way to live because it means you are always unhappy with the present, captured by envy and endless unsatisfied desires. Krishnamurti's statement "We all want to be famous people—and the moment we want to be something, we are no longer free" is the opposite of what you will see in a motivational book, but his comment rings true.

It makes sense that wanting less can make you more content with what you have, but who wants to give up on the fulfillment of their

149

potential? Krishnamurti tells of an alternative way that would not lead to depression or insanity. He suggests that the real purpose of education is to help people identify what they love to do. Doing what you love has a double benefit: not only will you find an uncommon level of contentment in daily life, but your enthusiasm for the work will take care of "success."

Ambition requires us to live constantly in the future, a future that, if it does arrive, may still leave us empty. But a vocation means we can enjoy our work detached from the anxiety of achieving certain results. Nothing lasts forever anyway, so the world is much better served by people who work without the ugliness of desire for gain. At present we have a culture built on competition, but doing work that is unique to us makes competing meaningless. Competition is only necessary when we are all aiming for a single prize, but each person must realize that the treasure is not "out there" but to be found within our own abilities and interests. That is intelligence.

The myth of security

We want to make life permanent, but in doing so we go against nature, and there lies our pain. Only the mind that is always moving, without resting places and fixed ideas, can be in tune with life and therefore joyful. Human beings, Krishnamurti says, "dig a little pool for themselves away from the swift current of life, and in that little pool they stagnate, die; and this stagnation, this decay we call existence."

Harsh words, but could it be true that the life we make for ourselves, a little pool of family, work, fears, ambition, religion, and so on, is an attempt to avoid experiencing larger reality? The more we believe that this place beside the river of life is secure, the less we are aware of the real nature of life—constant change. We cling to the known, Krishnamurti says, but in this clinging we become a person of fear.

All this does not mean that we have to give up the external circumstances of our life, but simply that we need to appreciate that we have created merely a representation of life that suits us. The object of living is to find truth, and if we are not actively engaged in trying to get closer to the heart of things, then we are quickly dying.

Solving problems

The mind can never solve problems when it is occupied with them. "It is only the unoccupied mind that can be fresh to understand a problem," states Krishnamurti. If you can create a space between your thoughts, you will regain a freshness and creativity that the normal mind, weighed down with one thought and worry after another, can never experience.

If the mind that has got us into the current mess is employed to solve it, the solution will not be very good. But in closing off that mind, elegant solutions will appear. We think of the mind as being everything, but it is not. We can enrich our life by tapping into the vast intelligence of the universe that exists beyond our brain. Paradoxically, by stopping the incessant chatter of the mind, we also gain self-knowledge. Thus not thinking, if it is done with purpose, can be the highest form of intelligence.

The creative person

Most of us live as mere technicians, Krishnamurti notes. We study mechanically and pass exams, get jobs; we learn the techniques to succeed in this society. But if we don't pay attention to the real stuff—beauty, love, peace—then we will live in what seems like a hard, fragmented world. So we have the choice of being either a technician or a creator; to be less or more human. Krishnamurti comments:

"You can be creative only when there is abandonment—which means, really, when there is no sense of compulsion, no fear of not being, of not gaining, of not arriving."

A person who has learnt how society works and has "done well" acquires a kind of technical confidence. This leads to arrogance. But there is another type of confidence that comes from thinking outside the system. This confidence is more innocent. If we don't have it, Krishnamurti says, we "are going to be absorbed by the collective and lost in mediocrity." If we try at all costs to remain ourselves, we will know true creativity that is not shaped by what is socially accepted or fashionable. A technician can produce "outcomes," but a creator, by the very nature of their being and their focus on what is important, improves the world around them.

Krishnamurti talks of the need to have a spirit of revolt. In this he does not mean changing society from within, but revolting against existing ways of seeing and thinking. If you rebel against "the system," if you lobby for reforms, is it not a case of the prisoner revolting inside the prison for better conditions? The real revolutionary does not complain about the prison, but looks through its bars in order to see the institution within a larger context.

We need to see our own mind in this way, to watch it at work and understand why it has arrived at its conclusions. For instance, we cannot halt our greed and envy by trying to eliminate them; they will only begin to disappear when we can witness our mind as a whole. When we admit that our mind is full of greed, envy, loathing, and ambition, we create a space to be where we are *not* these things. That is the beginning of a free person who can draw on the wellsprings of creativity that lie outside the thinking mind.

Happiness and love

Because we are people who strive to achieve things, we also believe that happiness is something we can seek. But as Krishnamurti rightly points out, happiness cannot be "found," it is a by-product of meaning and occurs in the absence of fear. It does not result from achievement and ambition; life is in the moments when we are hardly concerned with these things, when we are lost in a task or feel part of the environment around us. To even think or speak of happiness indicates that we are not one with its source.

At root, unhappiness comes from a lack of love, or the distance between ourselves and others. This distance is created by our judgments and criticisms. It is difficult to truly love if we are thinking about ourselves and our goals; to others, this seems shallow. The striver will say, love is fine, but it is a nice dream—in the meantime I must get on in the world. Krishnamurti counters, "Love is the most practical thing in the world." The ambitious seek power, and in their quest are blind to the fact that love is the greatest power known to us. Great love is great intelligence, because it recognizes that ultimately love is the only thing that matters.

Final comments

Krishnamurti's book was written years before it became fashionable to exhort people to do what they love doing, instead of doing a job for security's sake. He also understood our celebrity culture in which everyone wants to be someone else, to be famous, and the resulting misery it causes.

Think on These Things is hardly about spirituality as we conventionally understand it, but about an opening up of the mind. It is about being intelligent, though not in the ways we normally think of intelligence. Everyone assumes that they are a free-thinking, spirited individual, when often nothing could be further from the truth.

This book gets you to ask yourself: Am I just a technician of life, or a creator?

Jiddu Krishnamurti

Krishnamurti was born in Madras (Chennai) in 1895, the son of Brahmin parents. His father worked at the Theosophical Society's base in Adyar. At 15 Krishnamurti was noticed by Theosophist leader Annie Besant and her associate C. W. Leadbeater for apparently having a remarkable "aura." They formally adopted him and he was taken to England to be educated. Held up to be a "World Teacher," in 1911 the Order of the Star in the East was formed around him.

In 1929, Krishnamurti announced that he was no messiah, or even a guru, and parted company with his protectors and the Theosophy movement. He began a life of traveling and speaking, and became known for a philosophy of the independent mind and wariness of set beliefs. He died in 1985, and the Krishnamurti Foundation continues to make his writings available.

The Screwtape Letters

*"My dear Wormwood,
I noted with grave displeasure that your patient has become a
Christian. Do not indulge the hope that you will escape the usual
penalties... In the meantime we must make the best of the situation.
There is no need to despair; hundreds of these adult converts have been
reclaimed after a brief sojourn in the Enemy's camp and are now with
us. All the habits of the patient, both mental and bodily, are still in our
favour."*

In a nutshell

We can only know what is good when we contrast it with what is not.

In a similar vein
Rick Warren *The Purpose-Driven Life* (p. 282)

CHAPTER 25

C. S. Lewis

Screwtape is a senior devil whose job is to increase the store of malice and misery on Earth. He achieves this by carefully targeting humans and then providing them with an array of temptations that can take their minds away from God.

Under Screwtape's charge is his nephew Wormwood, a novice devil. The letters between them record their efforts to turn a young man from his newly adopted Christianity back to "Our Father Below" (Satan). Wormwood receives detailed instructions on how to exploit the man's weaknesses and bring him permanently around to sin.

Both shocking and amusing, C. S. Lewis's satire *The Screwtape Letters* was a bestseller in its day, selling over half a million copies. It was a brilliant riposte to the creeping atheism, existentialism, and materialism of Lewis's time, attracting the smart reader who normally may have dismissed Christianity as a moral guide. Lewis's Screwtape works relentlessly to turn the victim not simply toward sin, but toward a fashionable resignation about the "way of the world" that denies human progress.

The book is quite a challenge to understand, because everything is morally in reverse. You have to remind yourself that the "Enemy" referred to is God, and that the way of life advocated by Screwtape is the exact opposite of being a good Christian. For instance, Screwtape bemoans that that the Enemy has given human beings free will to choose the Good, and that God actually loves "the human vermin." In one letter he writes:

"One must face the fact that all the talk about His love for men and His service being perfect freedom is not (as one would gladly believe) mere propaganda, but an appalling truth. He really does want to fill the universe with a lot of loathsome little replicas of Himself."

Each chapter of the book deals with a different temptation, such as a lack of neighborly love, smugness, or lust, and identifying with non-believers because they are clever and witty.

Beginning the assault

We are made aware that Screwtape and Wormwood's victim is an eligible bachelor, and they work on getting him hitched to various unsavory women. They are horrified when their man falls in love with a Christian woman of good repute and family. At this point they realize that it is no use trying to turn him away from his growing spirituality, so instead attempt to corrupt what spiritual feeling he does have. As the victim moves in intellectual Christian circles, they make him attracted to fashionable ideas, such as that the church is a mere bureaucratic perversion of the original intention of its founder; that Jesus is a mere historical figure and not really divine; and that Christianity on its own is not enough—it has to be allied to social programs to "create a better society." The idea is to make him feel that Christianity on its own is a little "old hat," that to make it really come alive in the greater population it must be made sexier.

This ploy works. The victim is now moving in a fast set of intellectuals who are far in advance of him, and Screwtape succeeds in instilling in the man a certain spiritual pride. The idea is to make him feel that as a Christian he is better than others, and that as an intellectual Christian he is even more special. Screwtape tells Wormwood: "The idea of belonging to an inner ring, of being in a secret, is very sweet to him. Play on that nerve. Teach him... to adopt an air of amusement at the things the unbelievers say."

We'll get him still

The book is set in wartime England, where bombs threaten to rain down and kill. Wormwood is excited at this prospect, but Screwtape tells him not to be so silly—it is better that their victim be kept alive. If he survives the bombs they will have him in the palm of their hand, because with the advancing years he will succumb to the spiritual wasteland of middle age. Routine and the failure of youthful hopes and loves, they are sure, will turn him their way. Screwtape gleefully writes of "the drabness which we create in their lives and the inarticulate resentment with which we teach them to respond to it—all this provides admirable opportunities of wearing out a soul by attrition."

However, if the man is successful and prosperous, Screwtape slyly observes, "our position is even stronger." He explains that prosperity cements a person to worldly concerns by increasing their place in the world. If they become well known and important with many connections, what need will they have of God?

The goal of the dark side is to increase attachment to earthly concerns, and this becomes easier with age. In contrast, the spontaneity and love of life of the young (or young at heart) make it very difficult for Screwtape and his kind to win a human over to their side.

The final assault

Screwtape's larger aim is to prevent the victim from gaining any self-knowledge. The idea is to keep him locked into raw emotions that cancel out any hope of objectivity and reflection. As the bombs fall on London, Wormwood suggests injecting a bit of cowardice into the man, but Screwtape says no—cowardice brings on shame, which can lead to self-evaluation and a desire to be a stronger person.

The diabolical two try to prevent the victim from persevering in anything, attempting to get him to fail in his resolutions, to avoid making commitments, as all such things make a person evolve into something better. They want him to feel that he is the master of his destiny who does not need God's help. In times of adversity, Screwtape observes, "the fun is to make the man yield just when (had he but known it) relief was almost in sight."

When the man sees burning flesh on the wall of a bombed-out house, the devils hope they have succeeded in making him believe that life is just a house of horrors with no meaning. But the man shocks them by seeing beyond the rubble to the miracle of life. He is now well beyond the reach of the devil. Screwtape had described the victim as "This animal, this thing begotten in a bed." Now that animal sees in the same way that God does.

Final comments

When Lewis wrote *The Screwtape Letters*, dedicated to his friend J. R. R. Tolkein, his writing was already known to a huge audience who had listened to his *Ten Minute Talks* on the BBC in the early years of the Second World War. These talks covered his conversion to Christianity, morality, and many other subjects.

The Screwtape Letters may have seemed to represent what was going on in the political world, but the author's real concern was our inner life and the decisions we make every day. The old-fashioned morality that the book espouses still packs a punch, and although Lewis wrote as a Christian, readers can easily substitute their own devils for his Screwtape and Wormwood.

Is painting the world in terms of good and evil too simplistic? Perhaps, but Lewis's quirky presentation of the polarities as real is quite convincing and makes us think about all the rationalizations we use to justify our thoughts and actions. What we can take from this book is a reassurance that there is something in us that is naturally resistant to corruption—and that by being true to ourselves we can succeed in increasing that resistance.

C. S. Lewis

Born in Belfast in 1893, Clive Staples Lewis was the son of a solicitor. He taught English literature at Oxford University from 1925, and stayed there for most of the next three decades. In 1954 he was lured to Cambridge when a new post of Professor of Mediaeval and Renaissance Literature was created.

Lewis wrote more than 30 books, including The Allegory of Love, *a key source on medieval literature; the famous children's books* The Chronicles of Narnia; *science fiction novels* Out of the Silent Planet *(1938) and* Perelandra *(1943); Christian and philosophical works* The Problem of Pain *(1940),* Beyond Personality *(1944), and* Mere Christianity *(1952); and an autobiography,* Surprised by Joy *(1955).*

In 1956 Lewis married for the first time, to Joy Davidman. He died on November 22, 1963, the same day as Aldous Huxley and President John F. Kennedy.

1965

The Autobiography of Malcolm X

"Awareness came surging up in me—how deeply the religion of Islam had reached down into the mud to lift me up, to save me from being what I inevitably would have been: a dead criminal in a grave, or, if still alive, a flint-hard, bitter, thirty-seven-year-old convict in some penitentiary, or insane asylum."

"Mankind's history has proved from one era to another that the true criterion of leadership is spiritual. Men are attracted by spirit. By power, men are forced. Love is engendered by spirit. By power anxieties are created."

In a nutshell

Go beyond color and creed to see the basic unity of humankind.

In a similar vein

Muhammad Asad *The Road to Mecca* (p. 14)
St Augustine *Confessions* (p. 20)
Mohandas Gandhi *An Autobiography* (p. 84)

CHAPTER 26

Malcolm X

Most people have some awareness of Malcolm X as a firebrand campaigner for black America in the 1960s, but what do we know about him as a person? In a far-sighted and fortunate act, Alex Haley, author of *Roots*, persuaded him to get his life story down on paper. Reluctant at first, Malcolm X began pouring out the details of his life, from the poverty of his childhood to his criminality in his teens, and then to his emergence as a national leader and world figure.

As with everything he did, Malcolm X had a sense of urgency about the project, and it was all but completed by the time he was gunned down in 1965. While the book is a superb account of the underside of twentieth-century American life and some of its turbulent events, it is also a *tour de force* as the record of a spiritual and intellectual enlightenment. The reader is never allowed to forget that Malcolm's conversion to Islam was the turning point in his life, transforming his violent despair into a moral purpose.

Black history

The man we know as Malcolm X was born Malcolm Little in 1925 in Omaha, Nebraska. His mother was from the British West Indies but looked white. Young Malcolm was considered lucky by other blacks in that his skin was a lighter color than most, but when he was older he "hated the white rapist's blood that was in me." His father was a Baptist minister and follower of Marcus Garvey, whose Universal Negro Improvement Association raised the banner of black pride for a generation.

The family moved to Lansing, Michigan, where in 1931 Malcolm's father was brutally murdered by the Black Legion, a white supremacist group. When the life insurance policy he had taken out was not paid (the company maintained that the death was suicide because the body had been found on railway tracks), the family slid into dire poverty. Living on food handouts, Mrs. Little became mentally unstable and finally had to be institutionalized, and the children were split up by the state. Malcolm writes: "I truly believe that if ever a state social agency destroyed a family, it destroyed ours. We wanted and tried to stay together. Our home didn't have to be destroyed. But the Welfare, the courts, and their doctor, gave us the one-two-three punch."

From Malcolm's point of view, the white man had killed his father, now the white system had destroyed his mother.

Invisible boy

At the age of 13, Malcolm was expelled from his school for bad behavior and ordered to go to a reform school in another part of Michigan. He was fostered out to a white family who managed to get him sent to a better school, and he entered the seventh grade. One of few black students, Malcolm was a novelty and strangely popular. Academically he excelled, always being in the top three of his class, and was elected class president. He was trying in every way to be white, but full acceptance always eluded him. The most embarrassing times were school dances, when it was made clear that he could not dance with white girls.

He announced to his teacher that he wanted to be a lawyer. At this time, being a waiter or a bootblack was considered a good, respectable profession for a "Negro." Blacks were not even employed in car plants. The teacher said to him: "A lawyer—that's no realistic goal for a nigger. You need to think about something you can be." It was suggested that he go into carpentry. It dawned on Malcolm that to both his foster family and his teachers, he was more like a pet or a mascot: "They didn't give me credit for having the same sensitivity, intellect, and understanding that they would have been ready and willing to recognize in a white boy in my position... Thus they never did really see *me*."

He decided to leave and live with his aunt Ella in Boston.

Harlem hustler

Boston was Little's first introduction to a real city and a large urban community of black Americans, but at the beginning of the Second World War, when he was 17, he moved to New York. He got work as a steward on the trains running between New York and Washington, and immersed himself in Harlem's buzzing music scene.

His detailed description of this time is a highlight of the book and reveals his descent into a world of crime and moral corruption. He remembers whites coming up to the Harlem clubs for the "soul" atmosphere. Drunk, they would hug waiters, saying things to the effect of: "You're just as good as I am—I want you to know that!" Respectable white men came to Harlem to have every kind of sexual proclivity satisfied, including getting whipped by black Amazons, "the blacker the better." Everyone in Harlem played the "numbers," a form of lotto, and the men who ran it were numerically brilliant. Malcolm writes: "If they had lived in another kind of society, their exceptional mathematical talents might have been better used. But they were black."

Along with just about every other "cat" he had a "hustle," and he became a seller and user of marijuana and cocaine. He was known as Detroit Red (for his slightly reddish hair) and lived in a building with prostitutes and other drug dealers. Later he moved into armed robbery and delivering bootleg liquor.

Though the years that Malcolm spent as Detroit Red sound exciting, he is careful to point out the feeling of hopelessness that he and most other people around him felt. There were so few opportunities that people tended to fall into well-worn ruts of criminality. Looking back on this time, Malcolm felt that God was watching over him because, realistically, he should have been killed by some other hustler.

Instead, he got "lucky" in that he went to prison. In 1946, when still 20 years old, Malcolm was given a 10-year sentence. "I had not even started shaving," he remarks.

Steel bar university

While he was in prison, Malcolm's brother Philbert and his other siblings joined a group called The Nation of Islam, led by a Chicago man named Elijah Muhammad, which taught that the position of blacks had been caused by the "white devil" who tried to keep blacks downtrodden. Blacks needed to realize their glorious history and forget about trying to be white, "conking" (straightening) their hair and trying to date white girls. The Nation of Islam taught that Christianity

163

was a white man's religion forced onto Negroes by slave owners to keep them in their place. Islam, in contrast, was the natural religion of the black man and black power. In prison, Malcolm was given the nickname "Satan" because he hated any talk of the Bible or God. But, prompted by his family, he gave up smoking, drugs, and pork, and submitted to what he believed to be Islamic ways. He began to understand the Muslim concept of submission to God, and learned how to pray.

Malcolm did a correspondence course in grammar and another one in Latin, and managed to get transferred to a prison in Norfolk, Massachusetts, which had an emphasis on prisoner rehabilitation and a huge library. With the luxury of his own room, Malcolm began reading for up to 15 hours a day across a range of areas including religion, eastern and western philosophy, and history. He came to the conclusion that history had been written almost exclusively from a white point of view, and was particularly inspired by Mahatma Gandhi's story of his struggle to free India from English rule.

This homemade education opened his eyes to the power of knowledge and language (he would retain a strong interest in etymology, or the science of word derivation), and he admits, "I never had been so truly free in my life." Locked up as a crazed, God-hating criminal, he emerges still angry, but as an educated man with a spiritual and political purpose.

Thorn in the side

Released from prison in 1952, Malcolm took the surname "X" in remembrance of the real African names that slaves had had to relinquish in favor of white surnames. He worked for a time on the assembly lines for Ford Motor Company, but quit to become a minister with his own Nation of Islam temple. As Elijah Muhammad's protégé, he gradually gained a large following and a national reputation for his tirades against the white subjugation of black Americans. Although the Nation of Islam's strict moral code (no smoking, drinking, gambling, going to films, sports, etc.) turned a lot of people away, Malcolm argued that whites actually wanted blacks to live in poverty and moral squalor, thereby making it easier to control them. By this reasoning, African-Americans would only escape their current conditions by being independent, with their own schools, businesses, and so on.

This idea flew in the face of the anti-segregationist ideas of the white liberals and mainstream black leaders of the time (such as Martin Luther King), and thus Malcolm was a thorn in the side of both blacks and whites who wanted to make race less of an issue. Yet most whites could not see their treatment of non-whites objectively, he points out, because it was so much a part of the culture. One of his frequent points was that a white immigrant to the United States had more rights and respect the day he set foot on American soil than did a black person whose family had been around for 400 years. Of the wasted opportunities of his life in the ghetto, he writes:

"All of us, who might have probed space, or cured cancer, or built industries—were, instead, black victims of the white man's American social system."

Enlightened pilgrim

A television documentary on the Nation of Islam, a book, and articles in *Life* and *Playboy* gave Malcolm X a national profile. He helped to establish over 100 mosques across America, and relentlessly criss-crossed the country giving speeches and interviews. But he was devastated when he learned that Elijah Muhammad was not in fact a chaste Muslim but a serial adulterer, and Muhammad in turn became jealous of his protégé's growing fame. Isolated from his own organization, it become clear that thugs had been sent to kill Malcolm.

At about this point, having begun to create a new organization, Malcolm decided to go on a pilgrimage (Hajj) to Mecca. His two chapters on this trip are superb in their description of the sense of brotherhood and oneness he experienced in the heart of the Muslim religion. That people of all colors, rich and poor, came to pray together, eat together. and sleep under the same roof during the Hajj was a revelation. It confirmed his belief that America's racial divide was a tragic illusion, and that he was still not quite free of some false perceptions of himself. He wrote:

"In my thirty-nine years on this earth, the Holy City of Mecca had been the first time I had ever stood before the Creator of All and felt like a complete human being."

At a press conference after the trip, reporters were surprised that the "black supremacist" Malcolm X seemed to have softened his stance a little. He was making statements such as:

"I'm for truth, no matter who tells it. I'm for justice, no matter who it is for or against. I'm a human being first and foremost, and as such I'm for whoever and whatever benefits humanity as a whole."

While the journey to the Holy Land had led him to orthodox Islam (not Elijah Muhammad's version of it), at the same time the importance of religion had actually diminished in his mind. What was important was the sense of brotherhood he had experienced. Whereas before he believed that white civilization was responsible for black misery, now he understood that it was the belief in separation (racism being an expression of this) that was the real cause of human suffering. What he was really fighting, he noted, was "strait-jacketed thinking, and strait-jacketed societies." Ironically for a person considered so divisive, he realized that his life's real purpose had been to appreciate the oneness of humankind before God, and his battles were against the *thinking* that created false distinctions between one person and another.

Final comments

After his death, Malcolm X became a symbol of black power in its most uncompromising form, a sort of bad guy complement to Martin Luther King. While King was the great orator and devout Christian, Malcolm's Muslim faith and fast-talking ex-con demeanor were always going to make him easier to deride. But we have to put ourselves in Malcolm's shoes. If your father had been killed by racist thugs and your mother turned insane by having her family bankrupted by a bad insurance company and then split up by the state, would you be a well-adjusted person? If you were called "nigger" to your face for more than half your life, would you have a feeling of the oneness of humanity?

Amazingly, in Malcolm's case the answer was yes to both questions. His rage motivated him, but his miracle was to take all that was bad in his life and transform it into something good; among other things, he created a successful marriage and family. In many points in his life he could have fallen into the abyss, but he believed that Allah had intervened to protect him on each occasion. Malcolm really had two great awakenings, the first in prison and the second at Mecca. The first may have given him the pride and purpose to fight an external monster—American racism—but the second gave him the courage to throw off his own prejudices.

He clearly saw his life's mission as to empower black Americans, but after Mecca he was able to see this as only one battle in the larger war on closed-mindedness and bigotry. While he had originally embraced Islam as a black person's religion in contrast to white Christian oppression, it was actually through this faith that he grasped the true oneness of humanity beyond any religion. As in the life of Gandhi, his politics would have been empty without his spiritual awareness.

The Essential Kabbalah

"All the troubles of the world, especially spiritual troubles such as impatience, hopelessness, and despair, derive from the failure to see the grandeur of God clearly."
Abraham Isaac Kook

"The purpose of the soul entering this body is to display her powers and actions in this world, for she needs an instrument. By descending to this world, she increases the flow of her power to guide the human being through the world. Thereby she perfects herself above and below, attaining a higher state by being fulfilled in all dimensions. If she is not fulfilled above and below, she is not complete."
Moses de Leon

In a nutshell

Self-fulfillment is only achieved through greater knowledge of God.

In a similar vein
Ghazzali *The Alchemy of Happiness* (p. 90)
Abraham Joshua Heschel *The Sabbath* (p. 112)
Idries Shah *The Way of the Sufi* (p. 228)
Starhawk *The Spiral Dance* (p. 234)

CHAPTER 27

Daniel C. Matt

Every religion seems to give rise to mystical offshoots that provide more intimacy with the divine, compared with the dogma and institutions of the mother faith. These offshoots push the boundaries of devotion, contemplation, and knowledge and can inspire believers and reinvigorate the faith. From Islam, for instance, came Sufism, from Christianity the medieval mystics—and from Judaism Kabbalah.

Like everything else, spirituality has its fashions, and in recent years Kabbalah (which means "receiving") has become a craze that has attracted celebrities. In a mundane secular world there is an air of holy mystery and impenetrability about Kabbalah that is alluring, and many of the popular books on the subject also market it as a tool to solve the reader's problems. The further attraction of Kabbalah is that it brings out the feminine aspect of Judaism.

Daniel Matt's *The Essential Kabbalah: The Heart of Jewish Mysticism* was written before the craze, yet is a modern, accessible introduction to the movement's origins and fundamental ideas, in the same way that Idries Shah's *The Way of the Sufi* is a classic introduction to Sufism. Essentially an anthology of writings by some of the great interpreters of Kabbalah, the book retains the reserve traditionally associated with the subject, but also gives the reader a taste of its wisdom.

A path out of obscurity

Though its roots are ancient, Kabbalah did not really come into being until the 1100s, in a learned Jewish community in southern France. It eventually spread over the Pyrenees into Spain, incorporating elements of Pythagorean, Neoplatonic, and Sufi mysticism along the way.

In 1280, Moses de Leon, a Spanish Jewish mystic, produced a body of writing that he claimed was "channeled." This grew into the huge *Sefer ha-Zohar*, "The Book of Radiance," written in Aramaic. These writings, essentially a commentary on the Torah in fictional form, became the Zohar as we know it today. The Zohar revealed the Torah to be a code that illuminates the mechanics of creation, or how the world emerged from the Infinite (called "Ein Sof").

In 1492 the Jews were expelled from Spain, and many kabbalists went to Palestine, specifically to the village of Safed above the Sea of Galilee. The most famous among its teachers was Moses Cordovero, whose *The Pomegranate Orchard* summarized three centuries of Kabbalah wisdom. His mantle was taken over by Isaac Luria or Ha-Ari ("The Lion"), who wrote nothing but whose ideas became a strong influence on Hasidic Judaism in Eastern Europe.

Interestingly, the Renaissance philosopher Pico della Mirandola read all Latin Kabbalah translations, and defended them as writings that confirmed the divinity of Jesus. This tradition of Kabbalah influence on non-Jewish philosophers continued with, among others, Gottfried Leibniz, Emanuel Swedenborg, and William Blake.

Kabbalah's best-known modern-era exponent was Abraham Isaac Kook at the end of the nineteenth century, but the revival of contemporary interest can be traced to Gershom Scholem, whose classic *Major Trends in Jewish Mysticism* (1961) took Kabbalah out of the shadows and made it accessible to the world.

What is Kabbalah?

The purpose of Kabbalah practice is to take a person back to the "cosmic consciousness" or mystical union that humankind once enjoyed with God at the beginning of creation, before the "fall" into the knowledge of good and evil (symbolized by Adam and Eve).

To achieve this mystical end and still remain within conventional Judaism, Matt notes that the early kabbalists had to stay very observant of traditional teachings and law. They remained committed to the Talmud (the foundational body of Jewish law, story, and custom) and the Bible, which expressed the traditional, masculine values of God, exemplified by the *mitsvot* (Commandments), but sought to complement these with an exploration of the more feminine aspect of the divine (symbolized by the female archetype or goddess, Shekhinah) which they believed was conducive to mystical union.

Enlightenment of this type was not going to be achieved through mere intellectual study, so a system of learning was devised based on the *sefiroth*, a map of consciousness evoking every aspect of creation and personhood.

The ten vessels

Before Kabbalah came into being there was the *Sefer Yetsirah* ("The Book of Creation"), a foundational book in Jewish mysticism. It said that God created the world by speaking it into existence through a combination of sacred letters and numerical entities, the ten *sefirot*. These emerged from Ein Sof, the unknowable divine essence or godly infinity that preceded time and space.

Early kabbalist Isaac Luria attempted to explain the beginnings of the world and the meaning of human existence through his teachings on the *sefirot*. His conception was as follows: Within the emptiness or vacuum of Ein Sof there appeared a light. The light began emanating into spiritual containers or vessels (the *sefirot*). Some of these could not withstand the divine light and so shattered. Most of the light returned to its origin but the shattered remains of the vessels, plus the sparks created, were trapped in material existence. The task of human life is to "raise the sparks" again to their original divinity, which can only be achieved through living a holy life; actions in everyday life are considered either to promote or impede the raising or restoration of the divine sparks.

Another way to explain Ein Sof and the *sefirot* is to imagine the light of God shining through stained-glass windows, with each of the *sefirot* being an archetypal expression or quality of God that can be found in creation generally or humans specifically.

The *sefirot* and their qualities include: Keter (the crown from which the others spring); Hokhmah (wisdom); Binah (understanding); Hesed (love); Gevurah (power); Tif'eret (beauty); Netsah (eternity); Hod (splendor); Yesod (foundation); and Shekhinah (divine presence).

Matt provides a lengthy explanation of the *sefirot* and how they can be guides to character and life. They are potentialities that wait to be activated within us. People can become expressions of particular *sefirot*, he suggests. Abraham was a man of Hesed, Isaac of Gevurah, Joseph a master of Yesod, and so on.

Self-fulfillment

According to Kabbalah, the divine realm needs human action to make the world fulfill its potential. Without us, God is incomplete. In return, it is up to us to ponder the mysteries of God and creation.

Matt quotes Moses de Leon as observing:

"How precious it is to know that God generates all of existence. From one bit of existence, the soul can perceive the existence of God, which has neither beginning nor end."

By frequently thinking of the vastness of God, we are humbled and become merely a vehicle for divine expression.

Dov Baer, an eighteenth-century Hasidic master, said:

"If you think of yourself as something, then God cannot clothe himself in you, for God is infinite."

Kabbalah is about self-fulfillment, but this true fulfillment of all our potentialities can only come about through a "cleaving to God." De Leon held that the soul takes on human form because it is not complete and needs to be fulfilled "in all dimensions." Our lives on Earth are about fulfillment of a purpose that God has intended, and the Kabbalah provides the path to self-knowledge that is required to discover this purpose. The notion of "raising the sparks" means simply to begin recognizing and fulfilling the potentiality that God has endowed us with.

Final comments

Why has there been so much secrecy surrounding Kabbalah learning? Traditionally there were restrictions on who could gain access to kabbalistic teachings, such as that they had to be over 40, married, and in sound heart and mind. While these restrictions have in many cases gone by the wayside, the reasoning behind them is not unsound. Because it deals with the deepest issues of self and God, Kabbalah is apt to spin anyone out of their normal orbits of thinking, and its masters know that mystical knowledge can drive a person mad if they are not able to incorporate it into their understanding of the world. On this point, Matt quotes Isaac of Akko:

"Strive to see supernal light, for I have brought you into a vast ocean. Be careful! Strive to see, yet escape drowning."

Kabbalah teachers have never gone out of their way to find adherents, for the simple reason that there is no point forcing learning on anyone who is not ready to swim in its waters. But for those who are genuine in their desire for spiritual development, Kabbalah is an incredibly rich ground of inspiration and guidance that belongs not merely to Judaism, but to humanity.

There are now many introductions to the field, but *The Essential Kabbalah* remains one of the best because it is not too academic, but nor is it lightweight, the author being a leading scholar in his field and a Zohar translator. If you want greater depth, read Gershom Scholem (*The Origins of the Kabbalah* or *On the Kabbalah and Its Symbolism*), or Moshe Idel (*Kabbalah: New Perspectives*). Better still, read the Zohar itself.

Daniel C. Matt

Matt has a doctorate from Brandeis University and has taught at Stanford University and Jerusalem's Hebrew University. From 1979 to 2000 he was Professor of Jewish mysticism at the Center for Jewish Studies, Graduate Theological Union in Berkeley, California. From this post Matt was asked by the Hyatt hotels heiress Margot Pritzker to produce a new English translation of the Zohar. The first volume was published in 2003.

Matt's other books include Zohar: The Book of Enlightenment *and* God and the Big Bang: Discovering Harmony Between Science and Spirituality. *He is based in Jerusalem.*

The Razor's Edge

"He is without ambition and he has no desire for fame; to become anything of a public figure would be deeply distasteful to him; and so it may be that he is satisfied to lead his chosen life and be no more than just himself. He is too modest to set himself up as an example to others; but it may be he thinks that a few uncertain souls, drawn to him like moths to a candle, will be brought in time to share his own glowing belief that ultimate satisfaction can only be found in the life of the spirit."

In a nutshell

Attain real peace by moving beyond the ego's fears and wants and living a life of the spirit.

In a similar vein

Chuang Tzu *The Book of Chuang Tzu* (p. 66)
Hermann Hesse *Siddartha* (p. 118)

CHAPTER 28

W. Somerset Maugham

*T*he Razor's Edge reads like a novel but was based on Maugham's remembrance of people he knew. Involved himself in the events he relates, he was both the narrator and one of the book's characters.

What does the title mean? Maugham prefaced the work with a line from the Upanishads: "The sharp edge of a razor is difficult to pass over; thus the wise say the path to Salvation is hard." The book is about what people do with their lives, and the difficulty that most of us have in choosing a path that allows us to really develop our spiritual muscles. On one side of the razor is an existence of security seeking, conformity, and accomplishment of social goals; and on the other a losing of the self within a larger quest to find life's meaning. Most of us do not consciously choose this latter path, but Somerset Maugham's fascination with a person who did was the seed for *The Razor's Edge*.

Maugham sold a remarkable 40 million books, but this was his biggest seller. Set in Paris, Chicago, London, and the south of France in the 1920s and 1930s, the story pulls you in from the start and the characters are beautifully drawn. However, it is the book's glimpses of spiritual mystery through the eyes of its main character Larry Darrell that probably accounts for its continuing popularity. This commentary covers the bare bones of the story and the characters.

Larry and Isabel

Larry Darrell is a young American who has been away in the war in France flying planes. He is engaged to Isabel Bradley, who is charming, attractive, and from a good Chicago family. The only thing standing in the way of their marriage is Larry's strange reluctance to get a job. Though he has a small private income that allows him not to work, Isabel and her mother think it only right that a man should have an office to go to every day, and that he should want to get ahead in the fastest-growing economy in the world.

Their friend Gray Maturin is the plodding but pleasant son of a millionaire. Gray's father offers Larry a position in his company, effectively setting him up for life, but still Larry demurs. His outlook is put down to a need for adjustment after the war, and when he decides to go and live in Paris, Isabel and her mother consider this as sowing wild oats before he settles down. They agree that Larry will go away for a year or two, but the engagement will remain in place.

When Larry gets to Paris, the debonair Elliot Templeton, Isabel's uncle, is willing to launch him into society, but Larry has not even brought with him a dinner suit and has taken a room in a dingy hotel.

A year passes, and another, and finally Isabel visits him. Despite their differences they are still in love, and Isabel believes that when it comes to it Larry will buckle down in order not to lose her. She wants and expects a good life with nice things and children. He tries to convince her that his life is incredibly rich, and that she should join him on his travels and intellectual and spiritual seeking. But it becomes obvious that they have totally different agendas and they agree to break off the engagement.

Isabel marries Gray Maturin one year later. She does not love him as she does Larry, but she wants to be married.

Larry's journey

Maugham recounts these events to show that Larry was a comparatively normal young man who at some point decides that there is more to life than being comfortable. He knows that there is no security in life, and can no longer be the happy-go-lucky young guy that he was before. In the war he had known friends who were live wires one day and dead the next, therefore he values every minute of existence. He does not yet know what he is looking for, but is aware of some dimension of life that is greater than himself. When Maugham makes his entry in the book, in a meeting with Larry, he learns that Larry has been reading Spinoza and Descartes, but it is his interest in Ruysbroek, a Flemish mystic, that alerts Maugham to Larry's deeper interest. Maugham sees that Larry's spiritual search is ultimately more important to him than love.

In the years that follow, Larry spends time in a French monastery, reads his way through the mystical literature, and takes on arduous jobs "to clear his head." These include stints as a laborer in a French coalmine and on a German farm, and as a deckhand on a steamship plying its way to the Far East. The ship stops in Bombay for three days, and on the last day Larry suddenly decides that India has something to teach him. He stays for two years.

Maugham sees each of the main characters every few years, and keeps track of their movements. He learns that Larry spent time in an ashram devoted to the enlightened guru Sri Ganesha, and had a life-changing mystical experience up a mountain. Isabel and Gray, who prospered greatly in the 1920s, lose everything in the Great Depression. While trying to get back on their feet, they borrow Elliot Templeton's apartment in Paris. Due to his change in fortune Gray now suffers bad headaches. One day the couple are visited by Larry, back from the subcontinent, who seems to have gained healing powers; he quietly rids Gray of his malady through a kind of hypnosis.

When Maugham himself moves to the south of France, he has Elliot Templeton as his neighbor. Despite his ill health, Templeton drags himself out to parties and functions, noting, "If you're not seen everywhere you're forgotten." His chief aim in life has been to be recognized in European society, but in his last days he is already being forgotten. Maugham takes care in describing Templeton, if only to provide a counterfoil to Larry, who prefers anonymity and has zero interest in status and money. Not surprisingly, Templeton dies a lonely and pathetic figure, while the reader's last impression of Larry is of a person of rare serenity and self-possession.

Despite his experiences, Larry has meanwhile come to the conclusion that it is not for him to live cloistered away in an ashram or monastery, but to love the world and live in it.

A greater love

One of Maugham's themes is that people seek in life what means the most to them, and often the love of another person is not the highest thing. Partly by way of consolation for the love she lost, he suggests to Isabel that passion can wreck people's lives or simply get in the way of a productive existence. He ventures the suggestion that Larry was never really in love with her; ultimately the pleasure that being with Isabel would have given him would not match what he gained from his search for the Absolute.

In this respect, *The Razor's Edge* is an unsentimental book. It cleanly exposes each character's motivation, showing that we all define our purpose in life and live according to that end. It is better not to choose as our objective a particular thing or person, but rather to adopt a generic value that will shape our actions. While Gray sought a well-paid position and Isabel a nice life, Larry found his happiness through a sense of the reality of God. His example shows that we do not generally fall into spiritual grace by accident; we must decide that enlightenment is the goal of our life and not be distracted by a lesser path.

As Maugham admits, his book has no happy ending in a romantic sense. He is simply left with the feeling that in Larry he has witnessed an unusually successful life. Larry is free-willed and autonomous, while the other characters have been enslaved by their own neuroses or social convention. They have fates according to their habits of thought and insecurities, but Larry is truly in charge of his destiny. Maugham's last contact with him comes when he is sent a book that Larry has written. It consists of essays on a handful of historical figures—Sulla, Rubens, Goethe—each of whom, it occurs to Maugham, led unusually successful lives.

Final comments

The Razor's Edge is one of the better introductions to the spiritual path because nothing is forced on the reader. Maugham was something of a skeptic, and he could not explain what had changed Larry's life. The air of mystery that surrounded his friend was perhaps a whiff of some larger divine mystery—but he rightly leaves it up to readers to draw their own conclusions.

Although he was very much a man of the world, not overtly religious, and as a writer was able to dissect a personality with ease, Maugham clearly saw something new and special in Larry Darrell. All the characters in the book see life as essentially about survival or recognition, but Larry is comfortable enough in his own skin to seek answers to the larger questions. Maugham had met Larry when he was only 20, but even at this age he seemed free of the normal vanities, wants, and cares of this world. He found some kind of spiritual secret that allowed him not to be worried about getting ahead, but simply to be ecstatic about being alive. Larry might be seen as an embodiment of the "perfect man" celebrated in the Taoist classic *The Book of Chuang Tzu*; that is, a person who has found the calm center after penetrating the rings of fear and desire that ensnare most of us.

While not especially insightful into eastern religion or the process of spiritual awakening, the strength of *The Razor's Edge* is that it demonstrates the different paths that people take in life and whether or not those paths ultimately bring them satisfaction. It shows that how we live is really a spiritual matter, because by our actions and decisions we express our deepest views of the purpose of existence.

William Somerset Maugham

Born in 1874, Maugham grew up in the English town of Whitstable and then in Paris until he was 10. He was schooled in England and attended university in Germany. He studied for a while to become a doctor in London, but became a full-time writer after the success of his first novel, Liza of Lambeth *(1897).*

Maugham married and had other female relationships, but later in life was openly homosexual. In 1927 he settled in the south of France and lived at Villa Mauresque on Cap Ferrat and was very well connected socially. He worked as a spy during the Second World War.

His 70-plus books include Of Human Bondage *(1915), generally considered his greatest work,* The Moon and Sixpence *(1919),* Cakes and Ale *(1930), and the autobiographical* The Summing Up. *He was also famous as a playwright and for his collections of short stories. Maugham died in 1965, aged 91.*

The Way of the Peaceful Warrior

"Soc, I've been battling illusions my whole life, preoccupied with every petty personal problem. I've dedicated my life to self-improvement without grasping the one problem that sent me seeking in the first place. While trying to make everything in the world work out for me, I kept getting sucked back into my own mind, always preoccupied with me, me, me."

In a nutshell

Lose your self-importance and adopt a strategy of unreasonable happiness.

In a similar vein

Carlos Castaneda *Journey to Ixtlan* (p. 48)
Robert M. Pirsig *Zen and the Art of Motorcycle Maintenance* (p. 204)
James Redfield *The Celestine Prophecy* (p. 210)
Shunryu Suzuki *Zen Mind, Beginner's Mind* (p. 240)
Chögyam Trungpa *Cutting through Spiritual Materialism* (p. 270)

CHAPTER 29

Dan Millman

*T*he Way of the Peaceful Warrior: A Book that Changes Lives opens with its main character, Dan, beginning his first year of college at Berkeley in California. Life has been pretty good for him, both as an academic success and as a gymnastics and trampoline champion.

But he feels there is something missing and begins having nightmares. Unable to get back to sleep one night, he wanders the streets and finds an open Texaco gas station. Running it is an older man with a twinkle in his eye, and the two get talking.

Dan asks the man his name, and is told: "My name doesn't matter; neither does yours. What is important is what lies beyond names and beyond questions." These obscure remarks prompt Dan to give the man the name Socrates. This mysterious garage sage becomes his mentor.

"Dan" is the author, Dan Millman, who wrote up his real-life experiences as a novel, embroidered with extra thoughts, scenes, and stories for dramatic impact. Now 25 years old, *The Way of the Peaceful Warrior* has the appearance of a lightweight novel for teenagers, but by the end of it you realize that it contains many spiritual truths. This, combined with the simple enjoyment of a story that includes romance and high adventure, has made it a perennial bestseller.

Noticing the bars

Socrates takes Dan through a series of mental and physical trials that use up all his energy. Their purpose is to reveal to him his illusions, the things that he chases for ego's sake. Cutting himself free from the illusions, Socrates tells him, will require more courage and strength than any movie hero. Disillusionment, he notes, is the best thing that can happen to someone, because it reveals what does not have real meaning. We go to movies, have sex, even play sport to escape from

181

the anxieties of our normal thinking minds, but in this pursuit, Socrates says, we avoid facing the source of our suffering. He notes the predicament of most people: they suffer when they don't get what they want; they also suffer when they do get it. He leaves Dan with only one conclusion: "Your *mind* is your predicament." Dan realizes why he loves gymnastics—because when he is going through his routine, he is just doing, not thinking. It is a holiday from his mind.

Dan has always prided himself on his willingness to experience new things and change. But Socrates sees that these changes are all superficial, a protection from a real willingness to change his thoughts. We are in a prison of our own making, he says, but the bars are invisible. To get out of the prison, you must first realize that you are in it. Dan begins to feel the enormous bulk of his thoughts and also the depth of his negativity. They leave little room for anything else.

Sleepwalking through life

Socrates describes himself as a humorous fool before the mystery of the universe. In contrast, Dan is a "serious jackass" who thinks he knows a few things but in reality is sleepwalking through life. His mentor starts him on a program of awakening.

Dan is told that he is like most people in that he has been taught to get his information from outside himself, and the result is that his mind is like the gas tank of a car, "overflowing with preconceptions, full of useless knowledge." To know anything, he first needs to empty his tank. Dan learns that he does have some understanding of things, but understanding is a product of the intellect—it enables us to know something without having experience of it. Realization, on the other hand, is when we grasp something by both the head and the heart, the experience of truth at first hand.

Socrates teaches that the best way to clear the cluttered mind is through meditation. Meditation is the sword of the peaceful warrior, he says, which "cuts the mind to ribbons, slashing through thoughts to reveal their lack of substance." He tells the story of Alexander the Great in the desert with his armies, who came to two massive ropes tied together—the Gordian Knot—which no one had ever been able to untie. Alexander simply slashed the rope into two with his sword, and moved on.

Warrior action

We must attack the knots of our mind in the same way, not by thinking laboriously via logic but by coming at the problem from a totally different plane. Seated meditation is only the beginning of the warrior's practice. The real warrior must have the same clarity of meditation—but while acting. The warrior, Socrates explains, "meditates an action." In normal action, you are very aware of yourself doing the action. There is an "I" doing it. But when you meditate your actions, they are powerful and free because they do not have ambition or fear (the I) weighing them down.

Dan is told that his feelings and actions are predictable; he is effectively a machine that will react a certain way if stimulated. Socrates tells him: "You still believe that you are your thoughts and defend them as if they were treasures." He orders Dan about the garage, giving him a hard time to see whether he takes it personally. Dan's hurt reactions only reveal that his thoughts about himself as a sole entity are very strong; his defenses and pride at any provocation—which he should be laughing off—provide him with the lesson of how much he believes that he *is* his thinking mind. He can't control his own reactions. His teacher, on the other hand, always acts in creative spontaneity. Later in the book, Millman sums up the distinction between a normal person and a warrior, when Socrates says: "The warrior acts... and the fool only reacts."

Unreasonable happiness

Dan has a complicated emotional life and many burdens; Socrates is amused because from his enlightened perspective, Dan's issues have been created by himself. There is a critical point in the book when Dan realizes that it is not situations that cause his anger or melancholy but his reactions to them.

We perceive things as good luck or bad luck, or as a loss or a gain, but the character of Socrates represents the eastern idea that we should be the same in failure or success. We think of failure as being "bad reality" and success as "good reality," but it is all reality. This does not mean that we forget about trying to improve things or create better habits—we exist for these purposes—it means rather that we need to forge a new friendship with reality.

Happiness resulting from the satisfaction of cravings, Socrates notes, is the happiness of a fool. A warrior is "happy without reason." Dan comes to the sad realization that his life has been about achieving happiness through victory, but even as a winner he experiences the same unhappiness as most people. He sees that his life has been about ambition, looking forward, not enjoying life but seeing what he can get out of it. However, through Socrates he discovers that the only way to have peace of mind and really to love life is to have a philosophy of "unreasonable happiness."

There is a well-known remark that life comes down to a few important moments, and that is true—and those moments are the ones we have now. Dan begins to appreciate the new freedom that this realization brings. His *eureka* moment comes when he shouts: "There are no ordinary moments!" In an instant he grasps the meaning of that famous line from the Bible that we must become like a little child to enter the kingdom of heaven. A child lives fully in the present, delighted at the wonder of simple things. It is through this route—not through heavy ambition—that we take up permanent residence of the kingdom of happiness. Dan discovers that his ambition has actually held him back from happiness, and that greater personal power can be his if, paradoxically, he takes himself less seriously.

Final comments

Personal development is usually understood to be self-improvement, but this project can quite easily end up as mere gratification of the ego. To someone who is not self-important, like the book's Socrates, one who *is*—like Dan—seems insane. Such people go about making the world a playground for their greatness, while all the time missing great moments. Real personal development is more about unlearning a particular image we have of ourselves, and our mental habits and frameworks. The idea that we are not simply the sum of our thoughts and emotions and past, but can be new in every moment, is a strange one to most of us. Instead, we get by on old beliefs and reactions, never realizing the tension and stress this causes us.

We think of a warrior as some violent egomaniac, but the peaceful warrior kills only misperception, and in doing so destroys a self that was miserable and weak.

If you have read Castaneda's *Journey to Ixtlan*, Millman's book may seem like a rehash. However, Millman also incorporates ideas from Zen Buddhism and Sufism, and his masterful synthesis of serious concepts into a truly enjoyable story really works. Like the writings of Wayne Dyer and James Redfield, it has enlightened legions of people who ordinarily would not have picked up a "spiritual" book.

In an Afterword to mark the twentieth anniversary of *The Way of the Peaceful Warrior*, Millman responded to the question every reader wants to know: Was Socrates real? He answers that individuals are only "symbols and signposts." Our identities are less important than the question of whether we are able to show compassion—which, as anyone who has felt it knows, points to something greater than ourselves.

Dan Millman

Millman grew up in Los Angeles and has a degree from the University of California at Berkeley. He is a former trampoline champion, and has held coaching and teaching positions at Stanford University and Oberlin. He lives in Northern California.

Millman's other books include Sacred Journey of the Peaceful Warrior *(the 1990 companion to* The Way of the Peaceful Warrior*),* The Laws of the Spirit, No Ordinary Moments, *and* The Life You Were Born to Live, *a guide to finding your life purpose.*

The first published edition of The Way of the Peaceful Warrior *went out of print, but the second edition became a hit through word of mouth. It is now published in over 20 languages.*

Journey of Souls

"People associate death as losing our life force, when actually the opposite is true. We forfeit our body in death, but our eternal life energy unites with the force of a divine oversoul. Death is not darkness, but light."

"I am not a religious person, but I found the place where we go after death to be one of order and direction, and I have come to appreciate that there is a grand design to life and afterlife."

In a nutshell

Physical death is merely an event in the movement of a soul from one domain to another.

In a similar vein

Ghazzali *The Alchemy of Happiness* (p. 90)
Emanuel Swedenborg *Heaven and Hell* (p. 246)
Neale Donald Walsch *Conversations with God* (p. 276)

CHAPTER 30

Michael Newton

As a counselor and hypnotherapist, part of Michael Newton's work was to enable clients to access memories of earlier life experiences that had contributed to their current psychological conditions. That was all well and good, but some clients began talking under trance not just about incidents in life, but about other *lives.*

Newton did have an interest in reincarnation, but considered delving into this area to be non-clinical, and turned down requests to perform what is known as "past life regression." He remained skeptical until he was working with a man who felt stabbing pains in his side. Under hypnosis, the man talked about a former incarnation as a soldier in France, where he had been killed by a bayonet. Through similar cases, Newton began to accept that some current-life problems could be linked to previous-life experiences.

Amazing as it was to uncover the past lives of his clients, Newton became more interested in what they were saying about the space *between* lives. Through careful questioning, he built up data that supported the long-held religious belief that the mind or spirit does not die along with the body, but that it goes through certain definite stages before being re-incarnated in physical form. Some of Newton's clients were religious, others were not, but he was struck by the consistency in how they described their between-life experiences.

Now over 10 years old, *Journey of Souls: Case Studies of Life between Lives* has not been revealed as a fraud, although the contentions expressed in it remain at the fringes of psychology. Newton's conclusions seem credible because he retains the voice of an objective professional, and he carries the wariness of a former atheist. Knowing that he was dealing with fairly way-out stuff, his introduction is careful to outline the science behind hypnosis, explaining why it is a credible source of truth.

Surprise at not dying
Journey of Souls includes 29 transcripts of hypnosis sessions, and they make for compelling reading. For instance, a man in trance state

recounted the actual moment of death in his last life, in the 1918 influenza epidemic. The transcript conveys his disbelief and awe when he floats above his body at the moment after death, and realizes that he is not actually dead as a thinking entity: "This is so incredible... the nurses are pulling a sheet over my head... people I know are crying. I'm supposed to be dead, but I'm still alive!"

Newton's second subject is a man who had experienced throat discomfort for many years. In hypnosis it emerges that his last earthly life was as a woman named Sally, killed by Native Americans during an attack on her wagon in 1866. Sally had died from an arrow tearing through her neck, and the event had clearly reverberated beyond a single lifetime.

Generally, souls may be jolted by their bodily death but are not devastated, because they no longer experience any of the emotional or physical pain of their life as a person. However, particularly if they die young, souls may not be ready to leave the scene of their death for several days, wanting to reach out and comfort loved ones. Eventually, they are pulled toward the spirit world and its brilliant light, experiencing feelings of great euphoria and peace.

Newton's subjects, on leaving their bodies behind, feel that they have come back "home." The trip to Earth required a loss of consciousness of their real state of being; that is, as a spirit. This concurs with Plato's idea that when we are born, we are made to forget where we are from, purposely isolated so that we can fully experience life.

Journey to self-judgment

People who have had near-death experiences often report moving through a tunnel toward a very bright light, before being pulled back to human consciousness. These experiences are well documented, but in *Journey of Souls* we are taken beyond that point to what actually happens to the soul once it has fully entered the spirit world.

After coming out of the tunnel, souls are often met by a personal spiritual guide (or "guardian angel") to help them through the experience. Others are met by long-lost friends or relatives, and the transcripts record the ecstasy and amazement of subjects who thought they would never see their loved ones again. Then comes the process, led by the guide, of analyzing the life just led, to see whether it measured up to the soul's expectations before the life began. This culminates in the subject's meeting with a "council of elders," a panel of superior beings that, rather than handing down judgments, leaves subjects to draw their own conclusions about their life on Earth. (Since the afterlife is a telepathic world, souls are able to hide nothing from other souls.) Souls are then absorbed back into the specific communities to which they belong.

Newton learned the following: "These tightly-knit clusters are often composed of like-minded souls with common objectives which they continually work out with each other. Usually they choose lives together as relatives and close friends during their incarnations on earth." Thus the people we consider important to us in life have most likely been close to us in other lives, hence the feeling we sometimes get of having known a person forever even when we meet for the first time. Newton includes diagrams of the groupings and how they interact.

How much can a soul determine the actions of its host body? Newton's surprising conclusion, taken from what his subjects have told him, is that the body and brain often override what the soul wishes. The strength of human emotion can easily overwhelm the quiet urgings of the soul, or conscience. There are no evil souls, Newton's subjects tell him, it is the human ego and the circumstances in which we find ourselves that often take control and push a life on a spiral toward destruction.

Neither is there a Hell in which people suffer interminably. Instead, some souls who have done bad things in life are separated from the main spirit world for a time of solitary reflection. Spirit guides may work with them, going over the life they have just led to see what went wrong, and to evaluate how their next life may, in a karmic way, correct the previous one. For instance, one soul who had abused a girl in his last life chose for his next incarnation to be a woman in an abusive environment.

Divining our purpose

What is the point of having a progression of lives? Souls, it seems, are on learning curves that take many centuries to unfold in Earth time, and they are only able to refine themselves through physical experience of natural worlds. A soul tells Newton: "Being in many physical bodies and different settings expands the nature of our real self." The goal of life on Earth is therefore personal development, though on a greater, more finely worked-out scale than we had imagined. For millennia humans have wondered about the meaning of life, but Newton is told quite matter-of-factly that the purpose of life is "self-actualization of the soul identity."

If the meaning of life is the development of the soul, why as humans are we born without memories of previous lives? Newton's subjects explains that it is simply because knowledge of them may interfere with the goals we create for ourselves in this life. However, our spirit guides do try to give us flashes of intuition so that we are helped to make the right choices. Via meditation, prayer, or reflection we are better able to recognize these directions and live in accord with what our soul really wants.

Why life is difficult

Newton asks his in-trance subjects another question over which humans have agonized for time immemorial: Why does God allow suffering? He is informed that suffering is part of the equation of the world because in a perfect state we would learn nothing. The desire to escape suffering leads us to think, create, and strive, thereby fulfilling our potential. Even our guides, which are frequently helping us out in small ways as our guardian angels, will allow seemingly negative things to happen because they can see the larger picture in terms of what good the event will do for us in the long term. That is real love. The greatest of the Buddhist truths is that "life is suffering." But in *Journey of Souls* this takes on a new meaning—suffering was not created for its own sake, but only to spur us on to new heights through dissatisfaction with the status quo. Life was literally not *designed* to go through with ease. Challenges, if we meet them well, are what makes the soul grow.

Human life is one of the hardest tasks a soul can give itself, and the effort is appreciated in the spirit world. Newton mentions a soul who volunteered for a very difficult life assignment—as a Jewish woman who died at the age of 18 in Dachau concentration camp. Her courage and comforting of fellow prisoners meant that her life, paradoxically, was a success. Our spirit guides represent the voice inside us calling for greater risks to be taken, and to choose what often seems like the path of most resistance.

While the soul belongs to God and the body to human nature, there is a gap of free will between the two. Those who consistently choose in life what Emanuel Swedenborg called "the good and the true" clearly progress as souls, while others who live only to satisfy the body and indulge destructive emotions must return to the physical world to make better choices.

Final comments

Readers whose instant reaction to this book is that it is "made up" will be surprised just how much of the world described by Newton's clients is also found in Swedenborg's *Heaven and Hell* (see p. 246), a richly detailed description of the afterlife by one of the eighteenth century's great psychics and mystics.

Books such as these should never be blindly accepted as truth, however with *Journey of Souls* it is fair to ask: If we accept the results of hypnotherapy as they relate to earlier experiences in life, why not lives previously lived? *Journey of Souls* can certainly break open your whole understanding of life and death, planting the idea that our existence on Earth is merely one form of reality, and that what we wistfully call the world of spirits is better understood as the larger reality enclosing the created physical worlds.

The contention that Earth is only one of many places in the universe where souls incarnate is one of the book's many surprises. Indeed, it tends to become more intriguing as it moves along, and if this commentary piques your interest at all you should get the book for the details. If you can keep an open mind, it will be one of the more startling titles you will read in the modern spiritual canon.

Michael Newton

Newton grew up in Los Angeles. He has a doctorate in counseling psychology and is a certified master hypnotist, and for many years combined college teaching with his private practice in Los Angeles.

Journey of Souls has been translated into ten languages. The sequel, Destiny of Souls, *includes 70 more case histories.*

Newton lives in the Sierra Nevada Mountains in northern California.

The Miracle of Mindfulness

"Don't drink your tea like someone who gulps down a cup of coffee during a workbreak. Drink your tea slowly and reverently, as if it is the axis on which the whole earth revolves—slowly, evenly, without rushing towards the future. Live the actual moment. Only this actual moment is life."

"People usually consider walking on water or in thin air a miracle. But I think the real miracle is not to walk on water or in thin air, but to walk on earth. Every day we are engaged in a miracle which we don't even recognize: a blue sky, white clouds, green leaves, the black, curious eyes of a child—our own two eyes. All is a miracle."

In a nutshell

You become a different person when you are fully aware of your thoughts and actions in each moment.

In a similar vein
Pema Chödrön *The Places that Scare You* (p. 60)
Ram Dass *Be Here Now* (p. 72)
Mohandas Gandhi *An Autobiography* (p. 84)
Shunryu Suzuki *Zen Mind, Beginner's Mind* (p. 240)
Eckhart Tolle *The Power of Now* (p. 264)

CHAPTER 31

Thich Nhat Hanh

Thich Nhat Hanh, a Vietnamese monk, conducted a speaking tour of America in 1968 while the United States was bombing Vietnamese villages. In these talks he described village life in his country, and was able to show that the "enemy" was just like everyone else. It was partly through his influence that Martin Luther King decided to oppose the Vietnam War, and King nominated Thich Nhat Hanh (pronounced Tick-Naught-Han) for the Nobel Peace Prize.

The Miracle of Mindfulness: An Introduction to the Practice of Meditation is basically a long letter written while Nhat Hanh was living in exile in France. A few years before he had founded a Buddhist school in South Vietnam, and was now writing to Brother Qang, a senior staff member. The school had refused to be aligned with either side in the war, opposing all fighting. Nhat Hanh's communication aimed to help its staff stay the course and maintain their practices of right breathing and non-violence, even if they felt justified in doing otherwise. Yet *The Miracle of Mindfulness* has little to do with the big issues of war and peace, instead looking into the daily habits of thought and action that create our personal world.

Peace through patience

The book begins with an interesting conversation. Nhat Hanh is with a friend who has a young family, and asks him how difficult family life is. Not giving a direct answer, the man notes that he used to divide his day into time spent with his son or daughter, time spent with his wife, and time for household tasks or work. Whatever was left over was "his time." But then he tried to think of the moments he spent with others as his time too, instead of wishing that he was doing something else. The surprising result, he discovered, was: "I now have unlimited time for myself!"

193

Nhat Hanh knew exactly what he meant. Many years before, when he was a Buddhist novice in Vietnam, he had the job of washing mountains of dishes in his monastery using only ashes and coconut husks. The only way he found to get through the task was to be very aware that he was washing dishes, not thinking about anything else. This willingness actually made the job enjoyable, because he was fully alive in the moment.

Nhat Hanh admits that most people are so busy they don't have time to be mindful—there are major problems to resolve and work to be done. But he also asks, what is the value of this activity if it is done with impatience or anger? Mindfulness allows us to reclaim the peace that comes through doing things one small step at a time. When we don't do this, energy is dispersed, we become forgetful, and life seems a struggle. But to be mindful is to have new energy and life in every moment.

Ways to be mindful

The irony of mindfulness is that it is so easy to forget to be mindful. Our thoughts quickly wander. The book includes many ways and strategies to retain mindfulness, even amid great pressure and emotion, some of which are outlined below.

Breathing

"To master our breath is to be in control of our bodies and our minds," Nhat Hanh says. Many people think it is impossible to meditate or be mindful when you are upset or worried, but by "returning to your breath" these things are put in perspective. When your head is full of thoughts, return to your body and engage in conscious breathing, which reconciles the body and mind to each other. Watch your breathing until it becomes deeper, be aware of all your thoughts, and gradually they will subside until you have peace. Someone who knows how to breathe properly can remain calm in any situation, and also has the key to constant revitalization of their body.

Self-watching

You should not worry when you cannot seem to quiet your mind and stop your thoughts and feelings flowing. Instead, observe the thoughts that occur, and if you have sad thoughts, for instance, say to yourself:

"A feeling of sadness has just arisen in me." Nhat Hanh says that you should be like a palace guard who does not let any thought pass without making sure that you know who or what it is.

One way to keep mindful is to silently describe to yourself what you are doing as you do it, for example, "I am walking along this path toward the village." Then you can appreciate the wonder of taking each step. Mindfulness is not merely when you are meditating, it should be 24 hours a day, 7 days a week. Whatever you are doing, that task should be the most important thing for you. You should not be trying to get it over with. If you are in a conversation or a meeting, be fully aware that this is what you are doing and give your attention to the person in front of you. Don't be thinking about some abstraction or what you will do afterwards.

The half-smile
An interesting way to retain mindfulness is to adopt a half-smile when you wake up, then keep it through the day. Half smile in your free moments, when you are irritated, when you listen to music. The half-smile enables you not to be lost in your emotions, but instead to be reminded of the moment.

A day of mindfulness
Nhat Hanh encourages readers to devote a whole day in the week to the practice of mindfulness. Take plenty of time to clean the house or have a bath, not rushing anything. Do everything slowly and deliberately, without your usual reluctance.

One day of mindfulness has a great effect on the rest of the week. If you don't observe it, Nhat Hanh says, you will lose yourself in busyness and worry and become totally ineffective.

Mindful meditations
As a young monk, Nhat Hanh was told to meditate on the image of a corpse. He didn't want to do it, thinking that this sort of meditation should be only for older monks. But later, after he had seen the dead bodies of 14- and 15-year-old soldiers, he realized that you need to prepare for death, however young you are: "Now I see that if one doesn't know how to die, one can hardly know how to live—because death is a part of life." In this meditation, there is a point when you get over the revulsion and instead you start to feel the preciousness of life.

Another path toward mindfulness is to meditate on the inter-dependence of all things. Nhat Hanh refutes the idea that humans are "some private entity traveling unaffected through time and space"; that is, separate from other people. This is the thinking of the false self, who cannot or is not willing to see that another person is just you in a different form. Fear, pain, doubt, anger, and anxiety all derive from a separate sense of self.

Developing compassion for the person you despise the most is another of Nhat Hanh's challenging exercises. It is a way of seeing that a person is not so separate, but in fact may be expressing ideas that would be your own in another context. Nhat Hanh's surprising teaching is that you are flooded with compassion only after you have liberated your mind, not the other way around. Compassion enables you to see things to which others are blind.

Only ever now

Nhat Hanh recounts a story that Tolstoy had told about a king who tries to find the answer to three questions: What is the best time to do each thing? Who are the most important people to work with? What is the most important thing to do at all times?

The questions might be those of any person leading a busy life and striving to achieve things, but the answers revealed by the story are not exactly what everyone would like to hear: the most important time is now; the most important person is always the one you are with; the most important pursuit is making the person standing at your side happy.

You should not think about some larger service for humanity, but only how you can help now, where you are, Nhat Hanh says. If you cannot serve those around you and make them happy, you are not going to make the world at large a better place.

Final comments

As translator Mobi Ho notes in her Preface, *The Miracle of Mindfulness* was not intended for a large general audience, but the simplicity of its message and intimate style have endeared it to people around the world. Though ostensibly a guide to meditation practice, there is something deeper in the book that can make reading it a peaceful, renewing experience. That something is the idea that we can bring a dimension of quality to all our moments, even if we are not in a good mood or are experiencing pain. Better than a temporary happiness is being mindful of all our thoughts and actions, which allows us to be truly in control of our experience of life.

There is a commonly held view that Buddhism is a pessimistic religion, but Nhat Hanh says that its real value does not lie in focusing on suffering but on encountering reality. The purpose of meditation is to lift the veil on misperception, and when this happens there can only be serenity and happiness as a result. We cannot come out of a deep meditation and be unhappy, because we are truly aware of the wondrous present. It is only when we become unmindful, when we think of the past or the future, that misery finds a way in.

What is the connection between mindfulness and peace? Simply, that mindfulness leads us to understand the roots of our suffering, which in turn leads to compassion for ourselves and others. This lessens the likelihood of anger, which causes conflict.

Thich Nhat Hanh

Now in his 70s, Thich Nhat Hanh became a Buddhist monk when he was 16. He began the "engaged Buddhism" movement based on meditation practice and peaceful action for change, which included his School of Youth for Social Service and relief efforts to help war refugees.

Nhat Hanh has been living in exile from Vietnam since he was 40. His base is the Plum Village community in southwestern France, but he speaks around the world and holds mindfulness retreats for, among others, police officers, politicians, artists, psychotherapists, and Israelis and Palestinians.

Nhat Hanh has written over 75 books, including A Guide to Walking Meditation, Being Peace, The Sun My Heart, Peace Is Every Step, Living Buddha, Living Christ, *and* The Blooming of a Lotus.

Anam Cara

"*Fashioned from the earth, we are souls in clay form. We need to remain in rhythm with our inner clay voice and longing. Yet this voice is no longer audible in the modern world. We are not even aware of our loss, consequently, the pain of our spiritual exile is more intense in being largely unintelligible.*"

"*Your body knows you very intimately; it is aware of your whole spirit and soul life. Far sooner than your mind, your body knows how privileged it is to be here.*"

In a nutshell

Approach everything in life in a spirit of friendship.

In a similar vein
J. Krishnamurti *Think on These Things* (p. 148)
Starhawk *The Spiral Dance* (p. 234)
Shunryu Suzuki *Zen Mind, Beginner's Mind* (p. 240)
Chögyam Trungpa *Cutting through Spiritual Materialism* (p. 270)
Thomas Moore *Care of the Soul* (50SHC)

CHAPTER 32

John O'Donohue

We easily forget the beauty and mystery of the world we are in: rain falling outside the window; the greenness of a leaf; a laugh with a friend; hearing much-loved music. For people who lead quiet lives such things are rightly appreciated, but for most of us these moments fall into the shadows of the various battles we are fighting: to succeed, to be recognized, to be spiritually advanced.

John O'Donohue's meditation on living the soulful life, *Anam Cara: Spiritual Wisdom from the Celtic World*, has been popular around the globe, possibly because it goes against everything we might get taught at a motivational seminar. Instead, it teaches us to get off the merry-go-round of success and actually live. Though it is never really clear what Celtic wisdom actually consists of, the reader takes it to involve whimsy, spontaneity, attunement with nature, and appreciating the mystery of our souls. We unknowingly kill off our own potential for joy, O'Donohue says, by trying to "hammer our lives into predetermined shape" with plans or programs. Instead of paying attention to our senses and to the seasonal rhythm of our lives, we end up with a somewhat mechanical existence.

The Celtic mind

The Celtic imagination, O'Donohue notes, loves the circle and the spiral and abhors the straight line. Celtic culture is about the circular movement of life, in rhythm with the seasons. This ancient awareness is at odds with our modern, linear idea of constant progress.

The Celtic mind is not systematic or dualistic. In Celtic wisdom there are no great distinctions between spirit and matter, or time and eternity. We live in physical and material realms at once, and we are therefore both an earthly being and a spiritual one, a "soul in clay form."

Anam is the Gaelic word for soul. *Cara* means friend. In the Ireland of old, such "friends of the soul" were often teachers or spiritual guides with whom you could share your innermost self. In someone's

199

understanding you could find a home. O'Donohue's book is about friendship, but not just that of other people. *Anam Cara* asks us to truly become friends with ourselves, with nature, even with the idea of our own death. When you approach everything in life in a spirit of friendship, he says, much of it loses its terror.

Celtic wisdom is also about seeing the eternal in everyday life. Poetry, art, friendship, and love are some of the ways that eternity is expressed within the fixed space and time that we call our world. Eternity is all around us, trying to break through to show us that it is real, while the world we inhabit has created the illusion that it alone is real. With our segmented focus on matter, we are poorer for this lack of imagination.

Sense of mystery

O'Donohue notes the paradox that if we immerse ourselves in our senses, rediscovering the simple things, through this very physical route we might regain a deep spiritual appreciation of life. Touch, smell, and taste, in particular, provide wisdom that have nothing to do with words or thoughts. We need to think a bit less and feel a bit more, and to trust what we feel. Because we are a soul in clay form, our route to the spiritual is through recognition of our earthliness. Celtic poetry, for instance, is a great celebration of the experience of seeing mountains, feeling the wind on your body, and hearing the breaking of waves.

"If we become addicted to the external," O'Donohue says, "our interiority will haunt us." In a wonderful metaphor, he suggests that the way we see ourselves and others is often by the harsh light of the fluorescent, but the light of the soul is like that found in a Rembrandt painting, softly illuminating and revealing mystery the more you look at it. We should be in awe of the mystery that is each person. O'Donohue argues that technology and the media have not united the world, but in fact made things less intimate, and that our obsession with relationships is a sign that we don't have good ones. That non-committal word "hello" that we offer in greeting does not exist in Gaelic. Instead, when you meet someone you recognize their divine spark by saying *Dia dhuit*—God be with you.

O'Donohue asks why it is so nice to have someone visit you in your home. It is because an entity comes into the room with a lifetime of memory and experience, and that being sits right in front of you. When they leave, "their body stands up, walks out and carries this hidden world away." A mystery has come and gone.

Letting the soul speak

It is not doing stressful things that creates stress, O'Donohue points out, but allowing hardly any time for silence so that our minds can recharge. If we live an extroverted life with no time to ourselves, we always pay a price. The voice inside us that brings wisdom rarely shouts.

We have replaced religion with psychology, but psychology often lacks the depth to find out what is really going on. The soul is reserved and will reveal its wisdom and provide direction only if we are quiet enough to let it speak. While in danger of stating the obvious, O'Donohue comments, "Your soul has more refined antennae than your mind or ego." Yet we rarely try to stop the mind's incessant chatter and allow what is true to emerge. He recalls Pascal's famous remark that most of our problems come from not being able to sit alone in a room and be still.

Living a full life

Anam Cara discusses the need to integrate what we consider to be our negative side: we should not try to discard our "bad" traits so quickly, since they may tell us a great deal about ourselves. The other meaning of the command to love your enemies is to love that side of ourselves that we have been taught not to like.

However, many people go too far the opposite way. There is a difference between accepting our unsocial traits, and consciously deciding to be negative. We have become a culture of overanalysis, of too much thinking when we should be living. The worst type of analysis is mixed with ideas of guilt and punishment, for example when someone believes that God rewards them for long suffering and "carrying a cross." In fact, O'Donohue says, this is more an example of wasting the right to freedom and possibility inherent in their nature. Negativity is like a blister on your life that you need not have, trapping you for years in mindsets of your own making.

O'Donohue's Catholic background taught him about sin, but he complains that we are not told of the greatest sin: the unlived life. The soul inherently loves risk, because taking risks is the way to real growth. It is the ego that likes things to be just so, looking for permanency. It is possible to achieve perfection in life, O'Donohue says, but it is a perfection based on having lived life to the full, to be able to say, as Edith Piaf did, "*Je ne regrette rien*" (I regret nothing).

O'Donohue is reminiscent of eastern meditation teachers when he suggests: "There is no spiritual program." We should not look to foist some new practice onto our daily regimen, or believe in stages of spiritual growth, but go deeper into the existence we have now. "If there were a spiritual journey," he notes, "it would be only a quarter-inch long, though many miles deep." The full spiritual life is not about how many monasteries you have visited or how much meditation you have done, but to what degree you have been willing to let go of fear and give something of yourself.

Final comments

If your life feels like a collection of compartmentalized experiences and you long for a sense of community or love, there is something in this book that may feel like home.

While the motivational literature teaches us to assume maximum control over our life and many spiritual books urge drastic changes, this book says the opposite—loosen up and see what is special in ordinariness. It may represent a softer view of existence, but it is one that offers a truer understanding of life.

The concept of *Anam Cara* is simply that we be friends with ourselves, and through that increase our warmth and sensitivity. O'Donohue notes that one of the hallmarks of modern life is indifference. If we seek power, as most of us do, then we have to be indifferent to those we try to control, but in doing so we lose our deeper power of compassion and healing.

The Celtic way of seeing may form the philosophical background of *Anam Cara*, but its real subject is bringing the soul back into contemporary life. If this is important to you, read also Thomas Moore's *Care of the Soul*.

John O'Donohue

O'Donohue grew up in County Clare, Ireland. He is known as a poet and a Catholic scholar, and has a doctorate in philosophical theology from the University of Tubingen in Germany.

O'Donohue's other books include a scholarly work on Hegel, Person als Vermittlung *(in German),* Stone as the Tabernacle of Memory, Fire: At Home at the Hearth of Spirit, Air: The Breath of God, *and* Water: The Tears of the Earth.

Zen and the Art of Motorcycle Maintenance

"What I would like to do is use the time that is coming now to talk about some things that have come to mind. We're in such a hurry most of the time we never get much chance to talk. The result is a kind of endless day-to-day shallowness, a monotony that leaves a person wondering years later where all the time went and sorry that it's all gone. Now that we do have some time, and know it, I would like to use the time to talk in some depth about things that seem important."

In a nutshell

A purely rational approach to life leads to madness. Peace requires us to look for the unseen quality or truth behind appearances.

In a similar vein

Fritjof Capra *The Tao of Physics* (p. 42)
Chuang Tzu *The Book of Chuang Tzu* (p. 66)
Ram Dass *Be Here Now* (p. 72)
Aldous Huxley *The Doors of Perception* (p. 124)
J. Krishnamurti *Think on These Things* (p. 148)
Shunryu Suzuki *Zen Mind, Beginner's Mind* (p. 240)

CHAPTER 33

Robert M. Pirsig

Z*en and the Art of Motorcycle Maintenance: An Inquiry into Values* is the story of a middle-aged man and his son, Chris, who go on a motorcycling trip, accompanied by an adult couple. They journey from Minnesota to California, taking the back roads and camping or sleeping overnight in motels. The man describes what it is like to hear the wind moving across the plains, to see birds rise up from marshes next to the road, to ride through a ferocious storm, and to breathe the fresh air of a mountain above the tree line. He tells also about the people they meet, the towns they stop in, and the quarrels and conversations of the journey.

There is nothing particularly remarkable about the narrator (who is never given a name but is assumed to be Robert Pirsig), a writer of technical manuals living a normal suburban existence. However, with the miles come snatches of memory of having traveled the same roads before, fragments that alert the reader to a deeper story.

Along with the record of the trip itself come the narrator's philosophical reflections, which aim to slow the reader down to a pace at which important things can be discussed. Fittingly, he has taken *Walden* with him to read, Henry David Thoreau's poetic record of a time spent away from the busyness of regular life.

Zen and the Art of Motorcycle Maintenance is a book to read while on a trip of your own, or when you find yourself at a crossroads in life. Easy to get through, although not always easy to understand, it is inspirational in a no-frills way.

What is the meaning of the title? Zen is a form of Buddhism that does not look toward great enlightenments or ecstasies, instead suggesting that the soul grows through actively engaging with life as it is. In this case it is the narrator's maintenance of his motorbike that expresses his understanding of how to approach life.

Quality

Much of the book focuses on a rather surprising topic: quality. We think of quality as a measure of a product or a person, and we feel the right to make judgments about it because it is clear when something is of quality or not. The narrator recounts taking his motorcycle to a garage and reluctantly handing it over to a crew of young men playing loud music. Instead of fixing the machine, they butchered it, and he learned a lesson: it is the attitude toward a technological problem, not simply rational knowledge of how a thing works, that makes all the difference. Merely going by the manual was a clumsy, low-quality approach. Thereafter, he did the work himself.

Quality cannot be defined in a rational way; it can only be noticed when it happens. Yet quality is everything: the difference between someone who cares and someone who does not; between a machine that can enrich your life and one that explodes into a heap of useless material. Yet instruction manuals, the narrator observes, totally leave out of the picture the person who is putting something together. If you are angry or unmotivated, you will not succeed in tuning the machine or finding the problem, but if you make the effort to put yourself into the head of the designer, you come to see that a machine is really just the physical expression of a set of ideas.

Paradoxically, it is only when you go beyond the classical idea that we can separate our mind from the world that "objects" begin to come alive. Quality is appreciated not as a thing, but as the force that drives the universe. The narrator notes, "Obviously some things are better than others... but what's the 'betterness'?" His epiphany comes when reading the ancient *Tao Te Ching*, when he realizes that what we call quality, or "betterness," is the same as the eastern concept of Tao, the universal power or essence that can never be identified as such, but the presence of which makes something good.

As a college professor, the narrator had become obsessed with Aristotle and the damage that the purely rational way of thinking caused to people's appreciation of the world. Aristotelean logic had provided the foundation of our civilization, but it had pushed aside the one element, quality, that made it tick. In our world, quality had become merely an idle attribute, when in fact, the narrator notes, it was "the *parent*, the source of all subjects and objects."

Though never explicitly stated in the book, quality is clearly also love. We have created a world that puts the highest store by objects and definitions, yet what actually makes the world go round—quality or love—is now considered an optional extra. In his earlier career as a college professor, this realization literally drove the narrator mad. A world without quality is a world in which he is no longer able to live.

Getting back the gumption

Years before, he had traveled with some black Americans, from whom he had learned the idea of "squareness." Too much intellectuality and too little soul made a person square. Such a person could not recognize quality, and nothing was real for them unless it was put into boring categories and defined. The narrator learns that quality is simply "reality" before it is thought about or categorized. Quality is just knowing. Even talking about "quality" is not quality! The person who can see quality has what Suzuki called a "beginner mind": a blank slate of a mind that is fully open to seeing things as they truly are in the moment, without putting layers of meaning on.

While the book includes many road-trip scenes of despair, tiredness, or boredom, it is uplifting in other ways. As the party ride west towards California, they leave behind a slower America where people wave and have time to chat, and start to see ego-driven people traveling along with grim expressions. This America, of big freeways and television and celebrities, makes people feel that the important things are happening somewhere else.

The narrator discusses the idea of "gumption," an old Scottish word meaning a certain zest for life that many in the modern world have lost. As he explains it:

"The gumption-filling process occurs when one is quiet long enough to see and hear and feel the real universe, not just one's own stale opinions about it."

When someone comes back from a road trip or fishing trip, or any experience that has forced them to live in the present or revel in the senses, we notice that they have got their gumption back. They have forgotten how they were *meant* to live and just lived.

The Greeks had a word, *areté*, meaning excellence or virtue. As the narrator discovers, it was not virtue of a moralistic kind, more a duty toward ourselves—a powerful, instinctive thing far removed from dry ethics or prim moralistic virtue. It had nothing to do with reason, but was an attitude, "an understanding of what it is to be a part of the world, and not an enemy of it." That is, it welcomed an immediacy about living life that says "yes" to everything that comes our way. But because we put logic and reason and objective truth first, this outlook becomes the opposite to how we live today.

Final comments

Years after his obsessive quest for the origins of quality, the narrator has become "just another middle-class, middle-aged person getting along." He is now able to get some perspective on what happened to him. Taken to hospital after his breakdown and zapped with electrodes, he came out a different person, with only fragments of memory of the philosopher he once was. But as the book progresses, and as he explains the ideas that drove him to mental illness, the reader is led to the understanding that perhaps it was society—its *mythos* or collective way of thinking—that was mad, not him.

Zen and the Art of Motorcycle Maintenance tells us that we won't get to the truth about life by pursuing answers through the rational mind only. The narrator hungered for a rational explanation for everything, but in the end found that both science and philosophy are just *maps* of the truth. However, in the love of another person, in the experience of nature, or in a feeling of closeness to God, we can access truths that cannot be broken down. The book makes you think about the technological culture we live in and where we can find room in it for quality and things of the spirit. It shows how a life drained of gumption is not really a life.

Considered a classic virtually from the day of publication, *Zen and the Art of Motorcycle Maintenance* is a complex, multilevel work that may require some meditation before we can really appreciate it. Pirsig has noted that his book was a "culture-bearer," expressing a latent feeling that many people had in the 1960s and 1970s that an exclusively rational way of seeing the world was too small a container. It had been adopted to ensure survival, but as the world had got richer, many people did not want to merely survive. The book took on a larger conception of success that was not only about getting a good job, but about being able to see differently. The sense of fragmentation and alienation had come from the classical belief that people are fundamentally separate from the world around them, but such a concept was emotionally and spiritually hollow, and in the end made us less human.

The book does not say that reason is bad, only that it needs to expand to accommodate the irrational. If society could accept abstract art, hippies, and beat novels, then maybe it could save itself from the dullness of its mental structures, which were after all an inheritance over 2,000 years old. Paradoxically, acceptance of the unreasonable provided the lifeblood for a culture based on reason.

Robert M. Pirsig

Born in 1928 in Minnesota, as a teenager Robert Maynard Pirsig registered an extremely high IQ (170). He enrolled to study biochemistry at the University of Minnesota, but after getting expelled traveled around the United States. After three years in the army and a stint in Korea he returned to the same university to read philosophy, and later studied Asian philosophy at India's Benares Hindu University. On his return to the US, Pirsig got a job as a journalist, married, had two children, and at various times also worked as a science writer, copywriter, and technical writer.

When writing Zen and the Art of Motorcycle Maintenance, *Pirsig sent out 122 letters to publishers. A few showed interest but only one made an offer and Pirsig received a standard $3,000 advance. His editor at William Morrow did not expect it to make much money but felt it should be published anyway. The work received rave reviews and has sold millions of copies. The title was inspired by Eugen Herrigel's* Zen in the Art of Archery (1953).

Pirsig's other main work is Lila: An Inquiry into Morals.

The Celestine Prophecy

"I could almost see the momentum of the Modern Age slowing as we approached the end of the millennium. A four-hundred-year-old obsession had been completed. We had created the means of material security, and now we seemed ready—poised, in fact—to find out why we had done it."

In a nutshell

Meaningful coincidences are a sign of the spiritual evolution of the human race.

In a similar vein

R. M. Bucke *Cosmic Consciousness* (p. 36)
Carl Gustav Jung *Memories, Dreams, Reflections* (p. 136)
Dan Millman *The Way of the Peaceful Warrior* (p. 180)
Ken Wilber *A Theory of Everything* (p. 294)
Gary Zukav *The Seat of the Soul* (p. 306)

CHAPTER 34

James Redfield

*T*he *Celestine Prophecy: An Adventure* was the biggest-selling book in the world for three years in the late 1990s. The two most common reactions to it are "This is trash" and "It changed my life." The first group of readers focus on the style of the writing; the second hone in on Redfield's messages, codified in the nine insights woven into the story. While this might not be highbrow literature, on the other hand critical praise or condemnation is irrelevant for a large portion of the reading public—we want to know if our friends liked a book—and it was word of mouth that made *The Celestine Prophecy* a hyperseller.

Redfield has admitted that he is more of a social commentator than a novelist, and the book reads as if it is a set of ideas with the convention of a novel foisted onto it. He could easily have written *The Celestine Prophecy* as non-fiction, forming a chapter out of each of the insights, but would more than a few thousand people have read it? The grand theme—an emerging humanity-wide consciousness—required a fictional narrative to make it really come alive, in this case an adventure story that carries the reader into the Peruvian Andes, where an ancient manuscript surfaces in jungle ruins. The manuscript states that the end of the twentieth century will be a time of spiritual awakening.

The insights

The originality of *The Celestine Prophecy* lies in its combination of the soul-searching character of the New Age with a Hollywood screenplay sequence of close scrapes and sexual attraction. But what is it about the ideas that makes the novel so alluring?

Some creative works stand out because they were the first to express in a popular way what was latent in the culture, and this book really tapped into something. The idea of synchronicity, first postulated by Carl Jung (see *Memories, Dreams, Reflections*, p. 136), is no longer new, but Redfield revived interest in it by saying that coincidences were happening more often, to a greater number of people, and that they were somehow linked to our evolution as a species. His book focused on a growing belief that some or all coincidences are not instances of mere chance but carry meaning.

The first of the book's nine insights claims that it is awareness of synchronicity more than anything else that will lead us to a cultural transformation, because once we admit it is real, our whole view of how the universe works must change—it becomes a meaningful universe.

It is no surprise that in the later *The Celestine Vision*, Redfield refers to Thomas Kuhn, whose book *The Structure of Scientific Revolutions* showed how small anomalies can eventually turn upside down a whole theory or way of seeing the world. *The Celestine Vision* is Redfield's non-fictional account of his influences and philosophy. In it he suggests that only in direct experience do we find truth, yet we hang on to models of how the world works that do not fit our experience. This view has little respect for both the western tradition of objective scientific proof or Christianity's demand for blind faith. It is genuinely democratic, because we are asked only to believe in what we have actually experienced, whether or not science or religion has validated it. In *The Celestine Prophecy* Redfield sets up the Peruvian church and army as the bad guys who seek to control dissemination of the insights, but in the age of freedom of information we know they cannot win. Spiritual knowledge is a matter for the individual and cannot be "instructed."

The second insight that Redfield describes is the "longer now," an enlargement of the circle of our thinking beyond our life, our job, our country, to appreciate humanity across the ages. We see the evolution of humankind almost as the story of a single person. A character in the book explains that in the last 1,000 years we have moved from a world centered on God to one based on our own achievements and discoveries. The philosophical security we felt in the Middle Ages was replaced by a drive for secular material security, but now this is being questioned. The attachment to "scarcity consciousness" is being eclipsed by the realization that we must now pursue what has most meaning for us. The past few hundred years have set the stage for a new era of "mystery appreciation"—whatever we find amazing, and nothing less, will determine how we spend our time.

The third insight says that the universe is pure energy. Our way of seeing the world is based on the apparent solidity of matter, but our science is yet to detect the subtle energies that flow through and around things, including the living. Astounding experiments in particle physics show that the forms in which particles manifest depends on whether they are being observed. Other experiments show that among two sets of plants in the same conditions, those that are given "loving attention" grow more rapidly. Redfield's question is: To what extent does the universe as a whole—since it is made up of the same particles—respond to our expectations?

The fourth insight extends the concept of "everything is energy" to human relationships. Because we don't know exactly how to restore the energy flowing around the universe to ourselves, we seek to steal it from other people. The fifth insight is the antidote to the fourth: we know that at any time we can access the "higher source" and regain any lost energy. Instead of the crime of using other people to get energy, we go into ourselves and access it through meditation, silence, or being with nature.

The sixth insight is about the "control dramas" that we all develop in order to direct energy to ourselves, taking on the roles, for example, of "Intimidator," "Poor Me," or "Aloof." Control dramas do not let us progress as human beings, but seeing them objectively gives us the power to kill them off.

You will have to get the book to find out the last three insights, and subsequent Redfield novels reveal yet more.

Final comments

The Celestine Prophecy was successful because it renewed interest in spirituality while being tough on traditional religion. In asserting the idea of direct intuition of spiritual knowledge it was a genuine Gnostic work.

Redfield tapped into the feeling that "the truth is out there," and by merging the ancient spiritual quest with a racy adventure set in the here and now (the first chapter begins in a parking lot), he masterfully satisfied a market thirst for danger and sacredness.

It is easy to be cynical about *The Celestine Prophecy*, but the fact is that it has had a transformative effect on many people, and its insights relate directly to the concerns of our time: the preoccupation with relationships and their fragile balance; environmental awareness, particularly the healing power of nature and the energy radiating from old forests; and the desire to see the human experiment in its entirety.

Perhaps Redfield's main theme is that the resolution and avoidance of conflict in human relationships is *the* most important issue in the universal scheme of things. Conflict and ill will create friction against the natural flow of energy in the universe, whereas to love unconditionally is to move with this energy and take on its grace and power. In this state we actually exist at a higher mental and physical vibration.

In this respect, though initially attractive as a spiritual self-development book, what makes *The Celestine Prophecy* so compelling is its broader theme of the non-physical evolution of the human species.

James Redfield

Born in 1950, Redfield grew up in a Methodist family near Birmingham, Alabama. He attended Auburn University, where he studied eastern philosophies, including Taoism and Zen Buddhism, as part of a sociology major. He later received a Master's degree in counseling and spent more than 15 years as a therapist to abused adolescents.

Quitting his job in 1989 to write full time, Redfield took almost two and a half years to write The Celestine Prophecy. *The first edition was self-published, but word of mouth spread quickly and Warner Books bought the rights. The book spent 145 weeks on the* New York Times *bestseller list.*

Redfield's other books include the sequel, The Tenth Insight: The Afterlife Dimension, The Celestine Vision, The Celestine Prophecy: An Experiential Guide *(with Carol Adrienne), and* The Secret of Shambhala: In Search of the Eleventh Insight, *another adventure, set in Tibet.*

Redfield lives in Alabama and Florida.

The Four Agreements

"Your whole mind is a fog which the Toltecs called a mitote
*(pronounced MIH-TOE'-TAY). Your mind is a dream where a thousand
people talk at the same time, and nobody understands each other. This
is the condition of the human mind—a big* mitote, *and with that big*
mitote *you cannot see what you really are."*

In a nutshell

By consciously adopting agreements with ourselves on how to act
with integrity, we begin to take control of our lives.

In a similar vein

Carlos Castaneda *Journey to Ixtlan* (p. 48)
Dan Millman *The Way of the Peaceful Warrior* (p. 180)
John O'Donohue *Anam Cara* (p. 198)

CHAPTER 35

Miguel Ruiz

n the early 1970s, in his final year of medical school, Miguel Ruiz had a terrible car accident that changed the course of his life. Despite the severity of the accident Ruiz was miraculously unhurt, and he had a spiritual experience that he could not explain. In the aftermath he turned to his family's ancient Toltec wisdom.

Ruiz had been raised in rural Mexico by a mother who was a *curandera* (healer) and a grandfather who was a *nagual* (shaman), but he had left behind their traditional ways. He now set about becoming a *nagual* himself, committed to guiding people to greater mental freedom.

The Four Agreements: A Practical Guide to Personal Freedom leapt to public attention after the actor Ellen DeGeneres mentioned its transforming effect on her life on Oprah Winfrey's television show. The idea of adopting four rules for living sounds simple, but in this commentary we try to explain Ruiz's interpretation of Toltec wisdom as well as taking a brief look at the agreements themselves.

Awaking from the dream

Essential to Toltec wisdom is the idea that the world, "reality," is a collective dream. The word used for this fog of perception is *mitote*, which is similar to the Hindu word for illusion, *maya*. This dream is the same as the dreams of the night, except that its rules and customs of understanding and behaving enable it to seem more real. We are born into a ready-made dream that includes language, culture, religion, and family, and we agree to go along with it because it is too difficult to resist. Ruiz describes this process as the "domestication of humans."

In order to get by, we make invisible agreements with others—spouse, children, society, God—but the most important agreements we make are with ourselves. Some of them benefit us, but many others make us suffer. We hang onto them because we believe we would be something less without them. According to Toltec wisdom, most people's problems stem from not being able to forgive themselves for the fact that they are not perfect, yet it is other people's rules that they are trying to measure up to, not their own.

The good news, Ruiz notes, is that by becoming conscious of our agreements we can begin to control our lives. We can declare a "war of independence" in which we decide how we will view the world. In shamanic traditions, he observes, individuals are called warriors not for their skill with weapons but because they fight the parasite in their own minds.

Impeccability of word

The first of the agreements we must keep with ourselves is to be impeccable with our word. Ruiz does not mean simply keeping commitments, but realizing that what we say (both speaking to the world and to ourselves) determines the person we are and the world we live in. What we say is creative; that is, we can use our words to create anger or jealousy, or use them to heal. Our words are seeds that go out into the world and come back to us as full-grown reality. No other animal can speak as we do, and no other has the same ability to create a wonderful reality or a terrible one.

We keep each other in a state of fear and doubt by our misuse of words. Ruiz argues that gossiping is a bad use of words, and he compares it to a computer virus with harmful intent. By adopting the first agreement, we become more resistant to the "word spells" that others may cast on us, but more importantly we are cleansed of emotional poison in our own minds.

Nothing personal

Why do we take offense? Ruiz draws the connection between a person's being offended at even small things, and that person's belief that they are the center of everything. The problem with taking things personally is that you feel the need to lash back and defend yourself, to prove the other person wrong. This, of course, only creates more conflict.

Yet few things said to us or about us, Ruiz observes, reflect the truth of who we are. The criticism says more about the other person's state of mind and conditioning than it does about us. Thus the second agreement, "don't take things personally," includes even criticism that is directed very clearly toward us.

We don't want to become the prey of what Ruiz calls "black magicians," people who can damage us with their words:

"You eat all their emotional garbage, and now it becomes your garbage. But if you do not take it personally, you are immune in the middle of hell."

Assume nothing

The *mitote* of the human mind causes us to see things incorrectly, to make assumptions that lead only to further mistruth. Because we are quick to assume, Ruiz says, we don't have the ability to see things as they are. Human beings fear not knowing, so we make up answers for all our questions to make us feel safe—whether they are wrong or right. Hence the third agreement, "don't make assumptions."

Assumptions create lots of problems in relationships because we assume that if a person loves us, they should know what we are thinking. On a larger level, problems are created because we assume that other people see the world as we do. Instead of making assumptions, Ruiz says, ask questions. Without the clarity that comes from questioning, your relationships will not work, and your relations with the world will be poor. The "dream of hell" that many people exist in, he suggests, stems from their practice of making one wrong assumption after another, never questioning.

The best is all you can be

The fourth agreement, "always do your best," sounds a little elementary, so why did Ruiz make it so central to living the good life? One of our main problems is that we continually judge ourselves harshly according to some external measure. But if we always do our best, it is difficult to judge ourselves and create guilt and regret. Doing our best sets us free.

In always doing our best, we are happy simply because we are taking action, making an effort. We revel in the action itself, without thinking about the reward. If we are fully engaged in what we are doing in this moment, we are fully alive; there is no time for missing anyone or anything.

The fourth agreement is a key to the first three, Ruiz says, because while we will not always be able to be impeccable with our word, or not take things personally or make assumptions, we are always free to do our best.

The four agreements represent a way of getting our real selves back, and remaining steadfast about who we are and what we believe in. The world is set up to make it likely that we will break the agreements, Ruiz says, but we have to persevere. Getting free of our mind, our *mitote* based on false agreements, is like climbing a mountain. It is hardest in the beginning, but when the four agreements become a habit it is easier to keep them.

Final comments

In Carlos Castaneda's *Journey to Ixtlan*, the author is told by the old *nagual* don Juan to have a strategy for his life. If he did not, he would end up a mere reflection of society, with his original self all but buried. The premise of *The Four Agreements* is similar, except that the strategy becomes a story that we tell ourselves to justify the paths we take. Ruiz's question is: Is that story really ours or someone else's? There is a real person that hides under our layers of conformity, and the strange thing is that many of us want to keep it wrapped up. Ruiz's plea is: Whatever strategy you come up with for your life, or whatever story you tell yourself, you have to make sure that it is a conscious creation.

The Four Agreements may seem like a very basic interpretation of shamanistic wisdom, but the book's inspirational message about a reemergence of the self from the bubble of conditioning is powerful. While not a great piece of writing, the work has been a gift to many people who are asserting their true identity for the first time, and need to remain steadfast.

Don Miguel Ruiz

Ruiz began teaching in the United States in 1987 with his mother, Sarita. As his renown grew he increased his teaching and speaking work, but since a heart attack in 2002 he has limited his appearances. His son, Don Jose Louis, has now also been initiated as a nagual.

Ruiz's other books include The Mastery of Love, The Four Agreements Companion Book, Prayers, *and* The Voice of Knowledge. The Four Agreements *has sold over two million copies.*

A Course in Miracles

"Nothing real can be threatened.
Nothing unreal exists.
Herein lies the peace of God."

"You have every reason to feel afraid as you perceive yourself. This is why you cannot escape from fear until you realize that you did not and could not create yourself."

"Prayer is the medium of miracles. It is a means of communicating of the created with the Creator. Through prayer love is received, and through miracles love is expressed."

In a nutshell

Miracles lift the veil of misperception, revealing truth and love.

In a similar vein
The Bible (50SHC)
Marianne Williamson *A Return to Love* (50SHC)

CHAPTER 36

Helen Schucman & William Thetford

A landmark modern spiritual text, *A Course in Miracles* has unusual origins. In 1965, Dr. Helen Schucman was a research psychologist at Columbia-Presbyterian Medical Center in New York. Her workplace was no different to millions of others in that politics and status seeking among staff had created a strained atmosphere. One day, the head of her department, Dr. William Thetford, announced he was tired of what was going on and that there must be another, better way. Schucman agreed to help him find it, and soon after began having strange dreams, then hearing a voice that seemed to want her to write down what it was saying. The first sentence she recorded in her shorthand notebook was "This is a course in miracles." Thetford typed up the notes, beginning a process that would last seven years and result in the 1,200-page *A Course in Miracles* that we know today. In *Course* circles, Schucman and Thetford are considered the vehicles for the book's appearance, rather than its authors.

Is the book a delusion? You might think so, except that the text itself has a diamond-like clarity, and apart from the fact that Schucman, who died in 1981, was a professed atheist who never capitalized on the *Course* phenomenon.

With its distinctive blue binding and gold lettering, including a workbook for students and manual for teachers, the book has sold over a million copies and spawned self-study groups around the world. Marianne Williamson's *A Return to Love* popularized its message and is a masterful introduction to *Course* ideas, and Gary R. Renard's *The Disappearance of the Universe* has further illuminated its teachings.

A course in true awareness

"This is a course in miracles. It is a required course. Only the time you take it is voluntary. Free will does not mean that you can establish the curriculum."

This droll opening statement presents *A Course in Miracles* as a book revealing "house rules" for being a human in this universe, principles that operate unerringly whether we take heed of them or not.

But why a course in *miracles*? A miracle can be expressed in many forms, physical and mental, but its essential feature is a sudden freedom from misperception. In the book's words, a miracle is simply "removing the blocks to the awareness of love's presence." When this moment takes place—called the "holy instant"—we feel the peace of God because we see things as they really are, not though the self's normal clouds of arrogance and ignorance. This event is a miracle because it is permanent; we may forget that it happened, but as soon as we remind ourselves of it the same effect is felt.

The book's distinction between reality and unreality (or knowledge and perception) is important. Reality/knowledge is what God is and what comes of God: "It can be unrecognized, but it cannot be changed." It is also beyond time. In contrast, unreality/perception is the world that we normally perceive, involving interpretation rather than facts. What we perceive seems true, but it is only true through our lens. What is given by God, on the other hand, is not perceived but *known*. It is unmistakable, and therefore dependable.

Holy relationships

The *Course*'s popularity probably owes much to its insights into relationships. One of its memorable distinctions is that between "special" relationships and "holy" relationships. Special relationships are built on the ego's desires, and many people will only ever have relationships on this basis. Such relationships, the *Course* says, are a way of excluding God from our life. Their holy alternative, in contrast, happens when we let God in on it: "The holy relationship is the old, special relationship transformed." On this issue the book can make uncomfortable reading, as we may realize just how much our relationships have been forged from selfishness rather than a desire for truthful, loving partnerships.

When we ask God, or more specifically the "Holy Spirit," to enter our relationship, changes happen quickly: "At once His goal replaces yours." In an unholy relationship, it is our goal for the relationship that makes it meaningful. In a normal relationship, if we don't get what we want we usually try to end it, because the emphasis is on what *we* want (i.e., the ego). The problem with this is that we will always feel slightly uneasy about our relationships, because they have no solid foundation. We think we know what is best for us, but in truth the ego does not really have a goal for our relationships except using them for its own benefit.

God, on the other hand, does have a definite goal for the relationship, so it is a matter of having faith in that goal being revealed. The experience of the Holy Spirit being present initially gives us faith, but that faith turns to conviction. We are given the chance to save our relationship from our own selves. "Whom God has joined as one," the *Course* says, "the ego cannot put asunder."

One of the themes of *A Course in Miracles* is the need to forgive, not because it is a nice thing to do, but because it allows us to cast off misperception and see truth again:

"Forgiveness is the means by which we will remember. Through forgiveness the thinking of the world is reversed."

To forgive is to see through to the essential innocence of a person, the truth behind the façade. When we are able to do this, instead of constantly feeling the need to judge or attack, we will have a healed relationship.

Miracle answers

A recurring idea in the *Course* is that "only love is real." Logically, this means that everything else—the whole world—is an illusion. The purpose of prayer and meditation is to have our misperceptions about this reality healed. When a misperception is seen for what it is, it is never our ego that has allowed us to see the light, but only the appreciation of true reality from outside the ego. It is impossible to get a right answer amid conflict, the *Course* says, because the answer will be shaped by that conflict. We try to solve our problems by thought alone, but this only results in both questions and answers that relate to the ego.

An honest question, on the other hand, "asks for something that you do not know." A real answer is one that is right today and right tomorrow, which comes in a "holy instant"; that is, a momentary flash of awareness that is delivered as a gift from God. When truth is experienced, it seems like a miracle, because it did not come from us as we currently know ourselves to be, but from the self that has always been one with God. Our separation from God is illusory.

To receive this sort of guidance, we have to forget about thinking and just be still: "In quietness are all things answered, and is every problem quietly resolved."

Who is in control?

When we are confused about who or what we are, it means that we are torn between what our ego may desire and what is naturally ours. The ego loves busyness and creating and sustaining problems, which should be an indicator that these problems may not be as real as we think they are, but are created by a part of us that wants to maintain itself.

This belief that we are a solitary entity floating along in the world is "the depth of madness," the *Course* says, because in reality we are one with the God that created us, and have always been so. The word "atonement" (at-one-ment) means the remembrance of this fact, and when we admit it, no room is left for doubt and insecurity. As the *Course* asserts:

> "All things work together for good. There are no exceptions except in the ego's judgment."

The book further points out why many people do not even like thinking about God or spiritual matters: because any recognition of God points "to the nonexistence of the ego itself," and most people identify with their ego. Since the ego believes in itself as a self-created entity, it cannot accept the wholeness of God. What is meant by the concept of the second coming of Christ? Not the physical arrival of a Christ-person on Earth, the *Course* says, but rather the end of the ego's dominion. The Holy Spirit is God's messenger to bring this about, sent to cure the tortured misconceptions that the ego makes us believe are real.

Final comments

There are countless examples of "channeled" writings, but *A Course in Miracles* remains the gold standard. It has been described as a bible for the new millennium, and the comparison is not ridiculous. Like the

Bible, it seems to contain an answer for just about every issue, and it is so big that you are unlikely to read it cover to cover. It employs biblical language and references, but instead of parables uses plain logic and rigorous distinctions to change the reader's mind. The writing is often beautiful.

Some readers will be put off by the Christian terminology, but this is simply the form used to express universal truths that can be found in all religions. Despite the Christian references, fundamentalists do not like the *Course*, claiming it to be an amalgam of blasphemous New Age ideas. Mainstream religions are quick to denounce such books because they lay claim to being the wisdom of God channeled through a human author, but is this not the way nearly all religions began? That is, as a particularly well-attuned individual receiving the divine word, which followers later turned into a system of organized practice.

Whether its source is divine or not, if you have an open mind it would be difficult not to take away something inspirational from reading *A Course in Miracles*. If you have ever felt a miracle happen to you in terms of a sudden awareness or greater understanding, you will see where it is coming from. All religions teach that separation is an illusion, and that a reawakened awareness of our unity with God makes all things possible. The *Course* simply confirms the "normality" of miracles when we are aligned with a higher power, and gives us the wonderful idea that life is simply a course in understanding the spiritual laws that can make us happy.

The Way of the Sufi

"*Asked why a certain Sufi sheikh did not appear to the outward eye to follow a religiously devout life, Nizamuddin Awliya said: 'Kings bury their treasures in one of two places. The first, and obvious one, is in the strong-room, which can be burgled, emptied or usurped. The other, and more enduring one, is in the earth, in a ruin where nobody would think of looking for it.*"

In a nutshell

Spirituality is not about emotional security, it is about finding truth.

In a similar vein

Ghazzali *The Alchemy of Happiness* (p. 90)
G. I. Gurdjieff *Meetings with Remarkable Men* (p. 102)
Shunryu Suzuki *Zen Mind, Beginner's Mind* (p. 240)

CHAPTER 37

Idries Shah

What do William Shakespeare, Roger Bacon, Geoffrey Chaucer and Dante Alighieri have in common? Is there anything connecting Hindu philosophy, Kabbalah knowledge, the teachings of Rosicrucianism and Freemasonry, and Japanese Zen stories? In *The Way of the Sufi*, Idries Shah suggested that these were all influenced by a body of teaching now given the name Sufism. Usually understood as the more mystical and personal dimension of Islam, Shah made a case that Sufi wisdom goes back well beyond the era of Muhammad, possibly to the time of Hermes in ancient Egypt.

Shah's many books expanded awareness of Sufi philosophy and writings in the West, and *The Way of the Sufi* is perhaps his best-known work. An enjoyable introduction to the subject, it includes brief portraits of well-known Islamic figures that he believed to be Sufi masters, including Ghazzali of Persia, Omar Khayyam of *Rubaiyat* fame, Attar of Nishapur (author of *Conference of the Birds*), Ibn El-Arabi of Spain, Saadi of Shiraz (author of *The Rose Garden*), Hakim Sanai, and Jalaludin Rumi (author of the famous *Masnavi*, or "Couplets of Inner Meaning"). The four main Sufi orders, the Chishti, Qadiri, Suhrawardi, and Naqshbandi, are also described.

The work's real power, however, is as an anthology of hundreds of Sufi or dervish tales, riddles, and sayings that could take a lifetime to fully appreciate and understand. As it would be impossible to go into these in this commentary, instead we will look at the broader Sufi ethic of mental and spiritual freedom.

The deconditioned mind

There are several possible origins of the word "Sufi," from Arabic, Greek, and Hebrew, but Shah asserts that its etymology is not tied to a particular language but created simply for the *sound* of the letters S U F and their effect on the brain. This gives a hint of the Sufi masters' deep knowledge of how the brain works, and indeed it is their insights into psychology and the human condition that we find most valuable today. Sufi writings going back to the twelfth and thirteenth centuries speak of certain psychological states and procedures that were only "discovered" in the twentieth century by the likes of Freud and Jung.

Shah notes that eight centuries prior to Pavlov, Ghazzali highlighted the question of conditioning or indoctrination—the enemy of genuine spirituality. Most people were not independent because they accepted beliefs given to them without much question; in religion they did not seek real enlightenment, but security. On this subject Shah also quotes the seventh-century Sufi teacher Abdul-Azziz, who said: "Offer a donkey a salad, and he will ask you what kind of thistle it is." If we only know thistles, we will never think that anything else could be good. Applied to a person, our minds always favor the existing thistles of knowledge, never knowing what other marvelous wisdom exists.

The way of the Sufi is not to get bogged down in believing that one religion or philosophy is the truth, but to develop an openness that frees us to be able to reconcile opposing parties and ideas (Sufis, Shah notes, have often been advisers to kings and worked behind the lines to bridge differences between peoples and religions). However, most people feel comfortable with religion because it keeps them within the walls of their own thinking and habits, never tasting the freedom that exists beyond.

Levels of knowing

Shah notes that it is possible to study Sufism as a cultural or religious movement and still come away with nothing meaningful from the effort. He quotes the Sufi master Saadi of Shiraz:

> *"The learned man who only talks will never*
> *Penetrate to the inner heart of man."*

Sufi wisdom can't be gained from mere scholarship, which is why its form of teaching has always been through stories, legends, riddles, and jokes. Like the Japanese *koan*, it aims to shock or surprise the mind into a sudden realization of wisdom.

The great mystic and poet Rumi said that his poems were so much rubbish compared with the actual self-development of the individual. Academic appreciation of art, literature, and religion is all very well, but these can only be aids to the greater task of attaining Sufihood.

Ibn El-Arabi told followers that there were three forms of knowledge: intellectual, or the collection of facts; knowledge of states, or having a "spiritual feeling"; and knowledge of the true reality that underlies everything. About this third form he wrote:

> *"Of this there is no academic proof in the world;*
> *For it is hidden, hidden, and hidden."*

Sheikh Abu Nasr Sarraj distinguished three kinds of culture: worldly culture, or conventional opinions and knowledge; religious culture—discipline and ethical behavior; and Sufi culture—self-development that takes you to the door of truth. Shah also includes a short and simple quotation from Ibn El-Jalali that sums up the beyond-religion, beyond-academic nature of this wisdom: "Sufism is truth without form."

An idea threading through *The Way of the Sufi* is that people pretend to seek God, but really just want their disappointments massaged and their problems solved. Saadi of Shiraz was something of a genius, Shah noted, and because he was a genius, the people wanted to make him a hero. Yet Saadi was more concerned with getting these same people to work on themselves. He said:

> *"Seekers there are in plenty, but they are almost all seekers of personal*
> *advantage. I can find so very few Seekers after Truth."*

The way of Sufism

Today there are many Sufi organizations existing within Islam, but Sufi teachings have always played down the importance of formal structures, including organized religion, instead placing the development of the *individual* before all else. It is this emphasis on truth before form, on the personal above the institutional, that has allowed Sufi ideas to crop up repeatedly through history.

Sufism acknowledges that people have different capacities to understand esoteric and mystical learning, and its writings commonly have several layers so that different readers will learn at the level appropriate to them. Jalaludin Rumi knew that people loved poetry, so his beautiful poems were like the honey that attracted the bee, but he embedded in them deeper ideas. He noted: "You get out of it what is in it for you."

Genuine Sufis do not seek to transcend the culture in which they live, Shah notes, but work *through* the language, customs, prejudices, even religion of a place in order to have maximum effect. This camouflaged method of instruction ensures the enduring influence of the Sufi.

Final comments

Many Sufi stories try to show that the only real wealth a person can have is their knowledge and wisdom; everything else is ephemeral. The Sufi student does not wish to become wedded to dogma, but seeks to have their eyes opened to truth in whatever form it arises. The paradox of Sufism is that although it is usually described as mystical, its purpose is to increase the store of rational truth in the world.

Sufism tries to show us that what we think is important may be just a façade, that seen from another level of thinking the fundamentals of our life can easily be swept away. To some, this makes Sufi ideas dangerous and unorthodox. Yet the Sufi ideal is the "completed" person who has seen to the heart of truth, and from this vantage point is able to see the vanities and blinkered vision of the majority. Even a dabbler in Sufi writings, although they can seem obscure and difficult to grasp, will discover a treasury of human wisdom going back many centuries. They open up a higher form of awareness that lessens the chances of our sleepwalking through life.

Idries Shah

Idries Abutahir Shah was a controversial figure whose life straddled East and West.

Raised in his father's Sunni Muslim faith and claiming a family lineage stretching back to Muhammed, Shah was born in 1924 in Simla, India, to a Scottish woman his father had met while studying in Edinburgh. The family moved to England when Shah was still young, and he attended high school in Oxford. Shah did not actually come into contact with Sufi dervishes until the age of 30, after which he wrote the books Oriental Magic *and* Destination Mecca.

A polymath, he was active in a range of social and cultural issues, and founded the Institute for Cultural Research. He lectured in many countries. Popular in society circles for his wit and wisdom, Shah attracted literary figures such as Doris Lessing and Robert Graves. In his sixties he made an undercover trip to Afghanistan during the Russian occupation and created a relief organization to help the Afghan people.

Shah produced over 35 books, many of which were bestsellers. *They include* The Sufis, The Commanding Self, Wisdom of the Idiots, Thinkers of the East, *and* Learning How to Learn. *He died in 1996.*

1979

The Spiral Dance

"The Old Religion, as we call it, is not based on dogma or a set of beliefs, nor on scriptures or a sacred book revealed by a great man. Witchcraft takes its teachings from nature, and reads inspiration in the movements of the sun, moon, and stars, the flight of the birds, the slow growth of trees, and the cycles of the seasons."

"Modern Witches are thought to be members of a kooky cult, primarily concerned with cursing enemies by jabbing wax images with pins, and lacking the depth, the dignity, and seriousness of purpose of a true religion. But Witchcraft is a religion, perhaps the oldest religion extant in the West."

In a nutshell

Belief in the sacred feminine and the spirit in nature is the oldest religion.

In a similar vein

Black Elk *Black Elk Speaks* (p. 26)
Carlos Castaneda *Journey to Ixtlan* (p. 42)
John O'Donohue *Anam Cara* (p. 198)
Clarissa Pinkola Estés *Women Who Run with the Wolves* (50SHC)

CHAPTER 38

Starhawk

Though the book was written in her mid-twenties, the seed for *The Spiral Dance: A Rebirth of the Ancient Religion of the Great Goddess* was planted in Miriam Simos (now known as Starhawk) when she was only 17. In the summer between finishing school and starting college, she hitchhiked up and down the Californian coast, camping and sleeping on beaches, and for the first time felt an almost erotic connection to nature. In her first year in college she took a class in anthropology, and as a side project began giving a seminar in witchcraft.

Though raised as a Jew, Simos was deeply attracted to goddess spirituality and its celebration of nature and the female body, and began to immerse herself in the Wiccan and pagan traditions. At a time when virtually every religious figure—priest, minister, guru, or rabbi—was male, it was an epiphany for her to discover that for the majority of history people had lived with an essentially female cosmology, preceding the emergence of the patriarchal or male-centered religions of Judaism, Islam, Buddhism, Hinduism, and Christianity.

Her mother had hoped that witchcraft was just a phase she would grow out of, but Simos's years of reading and practice eventually resulted in this bestselling introduction, which made her an influential figure in a re-emerging religion. Taking a new name that combined a dream about a hawk and the star card from the tarot, Starhawk began her mission to re-empower women through drawing attention to the sacred feminine in western culture, and to have Witchcraft recognized as a legitimate religion.

The Old Religion

According to Starhawk, Witchcraft began some 35,000 years ago in northern Europe. As the ice caps ventured further south, clans needed an edge to survive, and some among them—shamans—had certain powers of attunement to animals. By getting into the mind of a particular animal, its moves could be anticipated and hunted down. In Anglo-Saxon, the word *wicce* from which the religion took its name simply means to bend or shape, and such people had special powers to change their consciousness at will so that the world around them could be shaped according to the clan's needs. Their symbol for the endless cycle of birth, death, and rebirth was a double spiral, with the universe as a whole understood as a "spiral dance." Each clan or group had its group or "coven" of wise ones who were well versed in esoteric knowledge.

The religion of these peoples, whose names included the Picts and the Faeries, revolved around the sacred feminine. The Goddess, rather than a father God, was the giver of life. Though in time they were driven out of their lowland homes and replaced by patriarchal warrior cultures, such as the Celts, the myths and rituals of the "Old Religion" did not die out with the advent of Christianity, but changed form. The Christian myth of mother and child is remarkably similar, Starhawk notes, to the ancient myth of the mother Goddess and divine child who is sacrificed and born again, and many medieval cathedrals were built to honor Mary, whose figure absorbed traditional reverence for the Goddess. Another vestige were the Troubadours of the twelfth and thirteenth centuries, who disguised love for the Goddess in poems and songs ostensibly aimed at individual women.

Driven underground

In the fourteenth century, the Church began in earnest to associate witchcraft with evil, and in 1484 Pope Innocent VIII initiated the Inquisition that aimed to snuff out any remaining practices of the Old Religion. The male horned God of Wiccan tradition, an expression of wild but non-violent masculinity, became simply the devil, and the infamous *Malleus Malificarum* or "Hammer of the Witches," written by two Dominican priests, was the final nail in the coffin of Witchcraft's right to be recognized as a legitimate set of beliefs and practices. Given the basic misogyny of medieval Christianity, a religion revolving around the Goddess was a tremendous threat to the Church, and women went from being the revered sex of childbirth to the symbol of sinful sexuality. Witch trials were a chance, Starhawk notes, for villagers to get rid of uppity or unattractive women, and to entrench male dominance in work and politics. How many died? At least a few hundred thousand, possibly as many as several million.

Starhawk suggests a deeper reason the Old Religion was so demonized: in addition to being female-centric, the basic political outlook and structure of witchcraft was anti-institutional, non-dogmatic, decentralized, and focused on personal truths, none of which could be reconciled with the patriarchal Church.

She observes the irony that come the nineteenth century, Witchcraft's persecution was replaced by simple disbelief. In a rational scientific age, it became just another superstition. After centuries of character assassination, it was always going to be difficult to shake off the general association with the diabolical, but the reinstatement of Witchcraft as a proper religion had begun. The words "witch" and "coven" still carry frightening and ungodly connotations for most people, but Starhawk says that "to reclaim the word Witch is to reclaim our right, as women, to be powerful." The Craft should no longer have to hide or change itself simply to please public opinion.

The coven

As churches have congregations, so Witchcraft has covens. Originally, coveners were the group of elders who guided the larger clan or tribe. Today they are the "heart of the Craft," Starhawk notes, both support group and training college.

Usually consisting of 13 people (normally women but many include men), when it meets the coven joins hands, forming a circle. Members go "sky-clad" (naked) to symbolize unclothed truth. Through invocation, chant, or rituals, a "raith" or spirit is generated that creates an energy field greater than the sum of the individuals. Megalithic stone circles worked on the same principle—if energy is contained, its power increases. One important ritual is the repeated "calling of the name" of each person, which serves to affirm strong identity. Another is the chant "You are a Goddess" directed at every member.

Given that modern life often produces a sense of fragmentation and often a crisis of identity, such rituals are understandably powerful. Starhawk notes the purpose of most rituals to be bringing forth a "power-from-within," as opposed to the external power-over-others that underlies patriarchal society. Covens have the popular image of being circles of evil, but it turns out that they mainly exist for personal development. Coven leaders emerge only through peer recognition of their practice of certain qualities such as self-control, courage, honesty, and keeping commitments.

Having herself been in a number of covens, Starhawk admits that, like families, they have their squabbles. Some exist for particular purposes such as healing rituals, while others are more general. Some focus exclusively on the Goddess, while others include worship of the male horned God in their ceremonies. All aim to return members to the mystery of our human roots and a reconnection with the power of nature.

With such power comes responsibility, and Starhawk goes to some length to dispel the myth that witches spend their time casting hexes and spells on people they don't like. Covens do teach the ways of magic, but more as a means of attracting things we need and as a form of empowerment. Any power or technology can be used for bad ends, but negative uses are considered a dishonoring of the Craft. Magic powers, Starhawk says, are like the Ring of Sauron in *Lord of the Rings*—if used in the wrong way, the ring will destroy the owner.

The goddess religion

Starhawk repeatedly makes the point that Witchcraft is not an intellectual or theological religion—there is no sacred book or set of rules by which to live—but instead it requires a reveling in life and in the senses. Against common perception, Witchcraft is not a solemn affair, but takes it as given that pleasure and joy are routes to the divine. Sex is acknowledged as the basis of the life force that drives the universe, and is therefore sacred.

Unlike some religions, Starhawk notes, Witchcraft does not require self-abnegation, poverty, chastity, or obedience. The idea of purposefully "going without" is alien to its way of thinking, because it recognizes the universe as physically abundant, not to be transcended but to be enjoyed.

Another feature of Craft spirituality is its conception of the godhead. While the Christian "God the father" sits high above the world, there is nothing separate about the Wicca Goddess. She does not rule over a kingdom but is expressed in everything we can see, hear, feel, and smell; she is seen in the roundness of a stone, the color of a leaf, the glow of the moon, and the warmth of the sun, making Witchcraft the religion of both poetic nature and the science of ecology.

The history of religion, Starhawk observes, is mostly a history of one "great man" after another revealing great truths to a grateful public. Wicca gives women back a spiritual system that does not depend on obedience or revealed truths, but celebrates inner wildness and wisdom. The Goddess reawakens such an intensity of female power that it can never again be pushed into traditional roles.

Final comments

If you have no knowledge of the Craft tradition, this book can be a revelation. In her preface to the twentieth anniversary edition, Starhawk reflects on the evolution of Witchcraft, and notes that her original summary of its history did not properly take into account the strong Witchcraft traditions of non-European cultures. Her implication is that the sheer commonness of Goddess worship makes it not simply the Old Religion but the *world* religion, an ancient heritage that later faiths have attempted to paper over, borrow from, or destroy. Critics will say that a pagan or nature religion can never raise people to the spiritual heights of Christianity or Islam because of the lack of theological sophistication. It is true that Wicca has no Thomas Aquinas or Ghazzali, but it makes up for that in the intensity of ritual experience. Nor do the mainstream religions come close to matching the Craft in terms of an ecological sensibility or the focus on female empowerment.

Though the Craft is a broad spiritual tradition, The Spiral Dance is a masterful overview of its core elements and is well supported by notes and an extensive bibliography. Yet for most people the work is a practical handbook, containing copious invocations, rituals, and exercises—many quite alluring.

Starhawk

Born Miriam Samos in 1950, after school Starhawk enrolled at UCLA, taking courses in psychology, art, and anthropology. While at graduate film school she wrote a prize-winning novel that was never published but provided a foundation in writing skills. After some time living in New York, Starhawk returned to San Francisco and deepened her involvement in its burgeoning Witchcraft scene.

In 1979 she found a publisher for The Spiral Dance *after presenting a paper at the American Academy of Religion convention. She also organized the first public Spiral Dance Ritual, which became an annual event in San Francisco, and with others formed a collective called Reclaiming, which has since evolved into a global non-violent action group involved in political, environmental, and other protests.*

Her other books include Dreaming the Dark *and* Truth or Dare.

1970

Zen Mind, Beginner's Mind

"*If your mind is empty, it is always ready for anything; it is open to everything. In the beginner's mind there are many possibilities; in the expert's mind there are few.*"

"*In the beginner's mind there is no thought, 'I have attained something.' All self-centered thoughts limit our vast mind. When we have no thought of achievement, no thought of self, we are true beginners. Then we can really learn something.*"

In a nutshell

A peaceful and intelligent mind can be attained through simply sitting and breathing.

In a similar vein
Pema Chödrön *The Places that Scare You* (p. 60)
J. Krishnamurti *Think on These Things* (p. 148)
Dan Millman *The Way of the Peaceful Warrior* (p. 180)
Robert M. Pirsig *Zen and the Art of Motorcycle Maintenance* (p. 204)
Eckhart Tolle *The Power of Now* (p. 264)
Chögyam Trungpa *Cutting through Spiritual Materialism* (p. 270)

CHAPTER 39

Shunryu Suzuki

Zen has become a familiar word to us, but what is it? When Buddhism spread to Japan, it gained its own distinctive flavor and practices, and became known as Zen Buddhism. One of these practices, *zazen*, is a meditation posture that involves little more than sitting and breathing.

Daisetz T. Suzuki was the first to bring Zen philosophy to the West, but Zen master Shunryu Suzuki consolidated its influence by establishing the Zen Center in San Francisco in the 1960s. *Zen Mind, Beginner's Mind: Informal Talks on Zen Meditation and Practice* was his one and only book, but has been treasured for its beautiful expression and life-changing insights.

What is meant by his term "beginner's mind"? The purpose of Zen practice, Suzuki explains, is to have a simple, pure mind, open to possibilities. Our normal mind congratulates itself for achieving certain things, but such self-centered thoughts prevent us from really learning and seeing. The beginner's mind goes beyond "me" to the realization that it is just an expression of the larger universal Mind, and this naturally produces compassion. It ceases to think in a dualistic way, in terms of polarities such as good and bad, or agreeable and disagreeable, and consequently can focus on the fullness of the moment, as it is.

If you feel that your life is chaotic and lacks any real peace, this book may have a profound impact.

Ordered mind, ordered life

Zazen practice is not done to "achieve" a certain state of mind. When we try this, our mind only wanders. The book gives simple instructions on the relaxed sitting position that is the core of *zazen* practice. The posture provides stability and puts us into a state of mind that provides freedom from the tyranny of constant thought.

Breathing is at the heart of the practice. The mind follows the pattern of breathing, its inhaling and exhaling, and in doing so begins to lose its focus on the "I," the small self that normally generates our thoughts. In its place, our universal nature, the "Buddha nature," comes into focus. We go from the small mind, as Suzuki described it, to "big mind."

Why is breathing so important? Concentrating on our breathing reminds us that we are totally dependent on the world around us, on the very air we breathe. It also reminds us that if we are breathing, then we are alive and therefore independent. If you realize the fact of this dependence/independence, it can free you. This is not some intellectual idea, but a very real, physical thing.

Through *zazen* practice we understand that the world is fundamentally out of balance, that it is always changing and often chaotic. This gives the world and our life within it the flavor of suffering. But the invisible background to the world, the realm that generates it, is perfect, and it is this awareness of perfect harmony that we can experience in *zazen*. Naturally, this experience puts the world with all its created things into perspective. It allows us to think, "Well, that is only the nature of the world."

However, this does not mean that we can never take positive action. On the contrary, the action we take following *zazen*, when we have just been in attunement with perfection, will necessarily be right action. Normally, our actions are not generated from the peace of this moment; they are distorted by desire or ambition, and therefore create more disorder. Therefore, the more time we spend in meditation, the more ordered our world becomes. If we have a calm mind, in touch with what is real and stable, our life has a way of sorting itself out. This is the intelligent, natural way of being.

Zen practice

It may seem obvious, but the best way to soften the extremes of the mind, Suzuki says, is to sit, be still, and breathe. See your thoughts as waves that, with constant breathing, gradually get smaller, until the water of your mind grows calm. Leave your mind to itself, and this will always happen. The mind of "I" will become big mind, or the field of pure being.

Sitting and breathing will take us away from the ego's idea that we are someone special. We think that the part of ourselves that wants special things is who we are, but our true nature, which comes out in Zen practice, is more powerful than this. It is attuned to the larger Mind, so when we are in touch with it we go beyond the I, which paradoxically makes us more compassionate and more joyful. When everything is based on the I, we struggle all the time.

Suzuki cautions us not to have a thought of gaining something through *zazen* practice, just to do it for the sake of it. Using an analogy, he says: "To cook is not just to prepare food for someone or for yourself; it is to express your sincerity." Meditation is the highest form of self-expression.

Yet *zazen* practice requires discipline. Repetition, constancy, sameness are the way of Zen. Not looking for excitement or great joys, which imply a loss of our true nature, but just seeing the "is-ness" and beauty of each moment. Suzuki looked to the humble frog to demonstrate Zen practice. Frogs sit, without thinking that they are anything special, yet their sitting does not take anything away from their identity. They are clearly still frogs. Suzuki talked of the purity of practice. He did not mean wanting to make ourselves pure, turning something bad into good, but just to see things as they are—their "quality."

What is enlightenment?

We tend to think of enlightenment as some great flash of understanding, achieved by decades of spiritual work, and indeed there is a Zen term, *satori*, for the sudden realization of Buddhahood. But most of the time, Suzuki says, enlightenment is quite ordinary—it is actually just the understanding of a simple fact. First comes realization of the fact, then practice to remind ourselves of it, which in turn is expressed in thought and action.

What is the fact? That everything comes out of nothing, that there is a formless, colorless "nothingness" that constantly generates the color and forms of our world. Because all emerges from nothing, "nothing" must be something. It is an indefinable quality.

Sanity requires that we believe in this creative field of potentiality as the basic reality of life, behind all the forms that it creates. In daily practice, we must be able to go through the "gate of emptiness," clearing our mind of the illusions that we habitually take to be real. Everyone thinks that the forms—the world as we know it—are "reality," but they are only a representation of what creates it. Everyone acts as if they have something, Suzuki says, because they possess a bit of the representation, but when we come to think of these forms as permanent and "ours" it causes problems.

Suzuki points out that 99 per cent of our thinking is about ourselves and our troubles. He does not discount the pain we experience in our minds. But someone who recognizes that life is in essence about change and problems, and yet still recognizes that before all that there is a perfect something at the heart of it all, will see that anxious worrying about how life is going can solve little. Only by re-experiencing the source of it all can life as it is be fully accepted and put into perspective.

The person who can freely acknowledge that life is full of difficulties can be free, because they are acknowledging the nature of life—that it cannot be much else. Yet in doing this, we lose the idea that we are the center of life, and the pain of self-centeredness. We are a "temporal embodiment of the truth," Suzuki says, a brief expression of the essential truth contained in nothingness, and if we can appreciate this our problems lose their bite. As he puts it more eloquently:

"Because you think you have body or mind, you have lonely feelings, but when you realize that everything is just a flashing into the vast universe, you become very strong, and your existence becomes very meaningful."

Suzuki warns us not to expect great demonstrations of the worth of his practice. Remember, all you are doing is sitting and breathing—nothing special. However, he gives this hint: "Just continue your calm, ordinary practice and your character will be built up." You may not experience any great spiritual awakening, but the practice will have an effect on your life. It gets you to understand things as they are, and that the rest is "just delusion." This in itself is enlightenment, and can usher in a quiet revolution in how you live.

Final comments

Zen Mind, Beginner's Mind shatters the belief that we can achieve salvation or happiness through looking elsewhere, beyond who we are and where we are now. We want to escape because of suffering, but Suzuki says that finding pleasure in the transient nature of life—which we often label suffering—is the only way to live in the world successfully. This outlook of coping with and even enjoying the experience of suffering as part of life is a radical thought, but is it not closer to reality than a belief that we can only be happy when we have a perfect existence? Equanimity is perhaps the greatest spiritual gift, not in a fatalistic sense, but in affirming the beauty of life in all its imperfections.

Some of Suzuki's thoughts may be difficult to grasp, but *Zen Mind, Beginner's Mind* is not an intellectual exercise to read. If you are inspired by it, you may also want to read Lao Tzu's ancient *Tao Te Ching*. The colorless, flavorless, nothingness of the Tao, or universal energy, is what Suzuki also tries to draw our mind to—the "is-ness" that seems like nothing, looks like nothing, but is the constant generator of the world. Knowing it and attuning to it provides an ever-ready store of peace.

We usually seek to gain knowledge by gathering information, Suzuki says, but in Buddhism the reverse is true. Its purpose is clear the mind of "stuff," to be empty-minded. This is not dumbness, but how we access the universe's endless and perfect intelligence.

Shunryu Suzuki

Born in 1905 in Japan, Suzuki was only 12 when he was taken on as a disciple of Gyokujun So-on-roshi, a Zen master who had been his father's disciple. He studied at a Buddhist university, Komazawa, then at the Eiheiji and Sojiji training monasteries. On his master's death, Suzuki had to take over the running of his temple and its associated responsibilities.

He traveled to the United States in 1959 as a visitor but became a permanent resident, based in San Francisco. He established three Zen centers, including the first Zen training monastery in America.

Zen Mind, Beginner's Mind was conceived by Marian Derby, a Suzuki disciple, and is based on talks given by him at Los Altos. Trudy Dixon and Richard Baker (who was anointed Suzuki's successor) edited the work and brought it to publication.

Suzuki died at the San Francisco Zen Center in 1971.

Heaven and Hell

"Angels are baffled at hearing that there actually are people who ascribe everything to nature and nothing to the Divine, people who believe that their bodies, where so many heavenly marvels are assembled, are just put together out of natural elements—who believe nature to be the source even of man's rationality.

Yet if only they could raise their minds a bit, they would see that things like this are from the Divine, not from nature, that nature was created simply to enclose the spiritual, supporting it as its correspondent on the lowest rung of the sequence. Angels compare people like this to owls, who see in the dark but not in the light."

In a nutshell

The heavenly world is as real as the mundane one.

In a similar vein
Black Elk *Black Elk Speaks* (p. 30)
Michael Newton *Journey of Souls* (p. 186)

CHAPTER 40

Emanuel Swedenborg

For more than half his life, Emanuel Swedenborg was known for his work in science and engineering, and he wrote copiously on metallurgy, mathematics, physiology, anatomy, and navigation. But in his mid-fifties, this "Aristotle of the north" (he was Swedish) had a profound religious awakening that transformed him from scientist to visionary. After this point his life was devoted to what he had witnessed during his meditative visionary states, and to revealing fresh interpretations of the Bible.

What makes Swedenborg interesting is that even with this spiritual knowledge he did not abandon his skill as a scientific observer, but simply transferred it the non-physical world. His matter-of-fact tone seems to cut through the superstition and mystery that Christianity had built up around its teachings, and as a result his name was generally regarded with distrust and alarm in eighteenth-century Christendom. When you pick up his *De Coelo et eius Mirabilibus et de Inferno* (*Heaven and Hell*), it is a surprise to find none of the theological surmising you might expect from a book of this time. Instead, you get a detached and quite convincing description, reminiscent of a travel guide, of the celestial kingdoms. *Heaven and Hell* is surprisingly easy to read for this reason (particularly George F. Dale's excellent translation from the original Latin), and should be acquired by anyone with an interest in theories of the afterlife.

The structure of heaven

Part of Swedenborg's purpose was to explode the myth that heaven is some amorphous mass of billowing clouds and spirits. His psychic journeys revealed that the afterlife was a realm of great order, with different regions, levels, and communities. As a man of science, he was interested in accurate descriptions. He makes the following points:

❖ Heaven has two kingdoms: the celestial kingdom and the spiritual kingdom. Angels in the celestial kingdom (where God lives) are of a higher type, accepting the truth of God instinctively and therefore enjoying celestial love. They are very closely bonded to the Lord.

247

Angels in the spiritual kingdom are more concerned with love for their neighbor. Their love for God has come through thought and memory, making them one step removed from God.

❖ There are actually three heavens: an inmost, an intermediate, and an outer heaven. A person's mind and spirit is arranged in the same way, therefore we are all representations of the structure of heaven. On death we are greeted by angels of the outer or intermediate heaven, depending on the degree to which we accept the good and the true. For those in the most inward heaven, there has never been any gap between direct appreciation of truth and acting on this truth.

❖ The light in heaven varies according to different communities. The more inward you get to the center of heaven, the purer the light. The further away you get, the more crude things are, yet it is still bathed in the light of heaven, which is nothing like Earth's.

❖ Heaven works as a unit, with every element coming together to make up the whole, yet with each element being a representation of the whole. As Swedenborg put it: "Each community is a heaven in a smaller form, and each angel a heaven in the smallest form." The principle of "many makes One" is the principle of God.

❖ There is a clear separation between the heavens. Someone who finds themselves in one cannot not really enter another. If you try to go to a purer level and you are not of that level, you will only experience pain on moving into it.

❖ Since it is a realm of pure love, spirits cannot hide anything from each other: "In heaven, there is no way to have a face different from one's affections." At a material level, heaven is a commonwealth in which everything is shared.

❖ Heaven has many dwellings and buildings, like on Earth, hence Jesus's statement "in my Father's house are many mansions" (John 14:2).

The life of angels

Much of Swedenborg's knowledge of heaven was gained from actually conversing with angels, who note that people on Earth live in "blind ignorance" about the spirit world. They are amazed that many, particularly smart people and intellectuals who base their beliefs only on sensory data, do not believe they exist. Yet it is the simple people, who base their beliefs on inner feelings of truth, who are right. Swedenborg confirms that angels are as real as people on Earth. Some points:

- ❖ Angels have an ego, just as humans do, and their love of self can for a time turn them away from the love of God. Angels experience changes in condition, or state—pleasant, disagreeable, etc.—depending on their exposure to heavenly love and light. When angels are in an ego state they get depressed: "for them, heaven is being kept away from their 'ego.'"
- ❖ Angels have power, but their strength depends on the extent to which they admit that it comes from God and not themselves.
- ❖ In heaven, the clothes of angels correspond with their intelligence: the more intelligent, the more radiant. People in hell are dressed in rags.
- ❖ Angels live in communities, and they are drawn toward each other by their likeness.
- ❖ Angels live in beautiful houses and have gardens. This explains why on Earth gardens have always been symbolic of the peace and beauty of heaven.
- ❖ Angels have little understanding of space and time because these dimensions don't exist as they do on Earth. For humans, everything happens according to time, in sequences, but in heaven what matters is condition: "Angels understand eternity to mean an infinite state, not an infinite time." Our thoughts are limited because they involve time and space, but celestial beings are unlimited mentally and spiritually because they transcend time and space.

The good and the true

Those people who have found themselves in heaven are those who are attracted to things that are good and true for their own sake. People who love themselves more than they love the good and the true find themselves in hell. This is the meaning of Matthew 6:33: "Seek the kingdom of God first, and its righteousness, and everything will be added to you."

Every person on Earth, Swedenborg discovered, has within them an entryway into their body into which God flows. Only humans possess this. It is up to us to accept the love, intelligence, and wisdom that flow into this higher part of the self. We think that our intentions are our own, but God helps to implant intention so that it can shape thinking and action. Again, we can either go with these good intentions or reject them.

On several occasions in *Heaven and Hell* we find this emphasis on intention, for Swedenborg was told that what we intend, more than anything else, defines who we are. This "ruling love," as he called it, is all-important because it is what determines the quality of our life and the community in which we live in the spirit world.

He makes a crucial distinction: There are those who seek the good and the true, and then there are those who seek for themselves under the guise of the good and the true. The former will genuinely act for the good of the whole without worrying about the results.

Rich in heaven

People think that the life of an ascetic or hermit is the path to God, but Swedenborg was told that such people are often too mournful and do not really care about others. In contrast, there are many people in business who live a very worldly life, carrying on their trade and eating and drinking well. These people have no problem entering heaven if they live in good conscience, acknowledging God first and doing well by their fellow men. Swedenborg's conclusion is interesting: "People can be formed for heaven only in the world." The spiritual person may wish to escape the hurly-burly of life to be alone with God, but actually the reason we have earthly lives is to throw ourselves into the maelstrom and do what good we can within it.

The Bible says: "It is easier for a camel to go through the eye of a needle than for a rich man to enter the kingdom of God." Ever a genius at biblical interpretation, Swedenborg comments that the camel represents knowledge and information, and the needle's eye refers to spiritual truths. Hubris and self-love, symbolized by the rich man, will never please God, whereas a person of simple faith and trust will make an easy transition to the spirit world.

Final comments

Is *Heaven and Hell* simply the product of a lively imagination? To assume yes would give Swedenborg little credit, remembering that he was a scientist of the first order and showed no signs of mental deterioration before or after having his visions. Restricted by our normal five senses, it may be hard to accept that a grown man held conversations with angels and with the souls of Cicero and Luther (as he also claimed), yet his book should be seen within the context of an ancient tradition of a person with special powers, or "second sight," being able to report back their journeying beyond space and time. Greater recognition of

Swedenborg's powers came after an incident in which he was dining with friends in Gothenburg and stated in horror that a great fire had broken out in Stockholm (300 miles away). A couple of days later a messenger duly brought news of the fire, exactly as Swedenborg had described it.

Heaven and Hell contains many statements that challenged official Church dogma, yet Swedenborg's scientific background, combined with his conscience, compelled him to state exactly what he had seen. What he discovered was that the simple faithful people—who had all along believed in heaven and tried to improve their lives in relation to that belief—were right, while the intellectual Christians, who had "grown out of" such notions, were wrong.

Emanuel Swedenborg

Swedenborg was born in 1688 in Stockholm, the son of a clergyman and theology professor. He attended Uppsala University and after graduating traveled for several years in England, Holland, France, and Germany, educating himself across a range of sciences. In 1716 the King of Sweden appointed him an Assessor in the Royal College of Mines. Three years later he took up a seat in the House of Nobles in the Swedish legislature, beginning a half-century of state service that included advising on many engineering projects. Between 1729 and 1734 he published his three volume Philosophical and Mineralogical Works.

Swedenborg's transcendent experiences came in 1743 and 1745, in Holland and England. Arcana Coelestia *was his first major theological work, published in 1758.*

Between 1769 and 1771 he endured a trial for heresy at Gothenburg involving church accusations against his theology. His last major theological work, the two-volume True Christian Religion, *was published in Holland in 1771–72.*

Swedenborg died in 1772 in London, aged 84, and around his writings followers founded the New Jerusalem Church in 1787. William Blake, Ralph Waldo Emerson, Fyodor Dostoevsky, Helen Keller, John Wesley, and Carl Jung were among those who have been inspired by Swedenborg.

Interior Castle

"Would it not be a sign of great ignorance, my daughters, if a person were asked who he was, and could not say, and had not idea who his father or his mother was, or from what country he came? Though that is great stupidity, our own is incomparably greater if we make no attempt to discover what we are, and only know that we are living in these bodies, and have a vague idea, because we have heard it and because our Faith tells it so, that we possess souls."

"As I see it, we shall never succeed in knowing ourselves unless we seek to know God: let us think of His greatness and then come back to our own baseness; by looking at His purity we shall see our foulness; by meditating upon His humility, we shall see how far we are from being humble."

In a nutshell

Inner spiritual progress can motivate great earthly achievements.

In a similar vein
St. Augustine *Confessions* (p. 20)
G. K. Chesterton *St Francis of Assisi* (p. 54)
Margery Kempe *The Book of Margery Kempe* (p. 142)
Mother Teresa *A Simple Path* (p. 258)
Gary Zukav *The Seat of the Soul* (p. 306)

CHAPTER 41

Teresa of Avila

As a teenager in sixteenth-century Catholic Spain, Teresa de Cepeda y Ahumada enjoyed dressing up and reading novels of knightly chivalry and romance. Vivacious, with alabaster skin and shiny black hair, she enjoyed her own flirtations and little romances, but was sure to keep them secret to preserve family honor.

As she moved toward adulthood, her choices were limited to marriage or becoming a nun. The Carmelite Order's Convent of the Incarnation, just outside Avila, was one where the sisters could have their own rooms, receive visitors, and read. These freedoms appealed to Teresa, and against the wishes of her father, who expected her to marry, she joined up as a novice. Although she had felt no vocation or special closeness to God, she found convent life to her liking.

With her intellect and way with people, Teresa might have risen to the head of her convent, but otherwise lived an unremarkable life. However, she began to have raptures and visions, mystical experiences that turned her into a something of a holy celebrity. Spain was in the grip of the Inquisition, and Teresa's claim that her raptures allowed her to converse directly with God bypassed the authority of the Church. Many believed that these conversations were not with the Lord but with Satan. She had to be careful. Teresa turned to confessors, learned religious men who had the authority to correctly diagnose her states as real or imaginary. Their probing luckily led to a consensus that her experiences were a genuine gift from God.

Teresa worked to reform the Carmelite order (toward stricter observance) and founded 17 new convents and two monasteries. These activities are chronicled in her popular and influential *Life*. It is nevertheless *Interior Castle* that is considered to be her masterpiece.

A description of the stages of her soul's growth, the book was originally intended for the eyes of the Carmelite sisters only, in order that they may feel less alone in their spiritual trials. Teresa's inspiration was her imagining of the soul "as if it were a castle made of a single diamond or of very clear crystal, in which there are many rooms, just as in Heaven there are many mansions."

253

In Spanish the book is known as *Las Moradas* ("The Mansions"). We will now briefly visit these dwelling places.

First mansions

This initial level of the life of the soul is likened to a courtyard surrounding the castle, in which prowl the "venomous creatures" of sin. Here humility is slowly learned through the effects of sinful action. Souls are challenged to find the discipline required to act from beyond base impulses. Though God desires the best for the soul, its ability to recognize and love God is not great, and therefore self-knowledge also will be limited.

Teresa speaks of those who are continually busying themselves with their affairs, never realizing the treasure that lies within. Some do have the honest desire to enter the door of the castle through prayer and meditation, but their prayer is too infrequent and weak. They cannot concentrate on much beside their preoccupations and attachments.

Most people would fit this picture, yet Teresa says that, even if it does not do much for you, just the attempt to get in on the first floor of the castle is a great step.

Second mansions

We now appreciate the need for regular prayer to stave off our old ways and so feel a comforting nearness to God. God makes a great effort to beckon us closer, even though we are very much still involved in the "pastimes and businesses and pleasures and hagglings" of this world. The devil continues to try to make us believe that material things and relationships are of an eternal nature and all-important. Teresa says of this crucial point: "What confusion the devils bring about in the poor soul, and how distressed it is, not knowing if it ought to proceed farther or return to the room where it was before!" Here we must keep foremost in mind that all earthly things come to an end, while God's love is eternal, and we come to realize that life outside the castle of the soul never gives us full security or the peace that we desire.

In the second mansions, the soul starts to get more in charge of itself, and seeks out the things of God to keep it on the spiritual path. Through prayer it becomes more able to resist temptations. Yet in this first flush of real love for the divine realm, we tend to look for spiritual favors. Instead, we should be willing to suffer more, offering our suffering to God.

Third mansions

By this point we may be perceived by others as being good or religious, yet these rarefied heights are a dangerous place for the seeker of God. Whatever faith and godliness we have achieved so far, in the third mansions of the soul they are at risk of evaporating through hubris and forgetting to fear God. Teresa counsels us to remain humble, for "the more we have received of Him, the more deeply do we remain in His debt." We may experience periods of aridity when we do not feel the rush of love or faith, but we must plow through them and not be restless.

At this level of the interior castle we stand on a threshold: full surrender to the divine—or going back to relying on our own reason.

Fourth mansions

This is the first mystical level of the castle, when we are depending less on ourselves and relying on God, falling into his embrace with trust. Instead of always thinking about God, we begin to receive the gift of natural understanding. Teresa tells the reader "not to think much but to love much."

These mansions are of such beauty that we are not able to describe them to those who have yet to see. We start to get natural blessings or consolations without even praying for them. This is the long-awaited takeoff point in our awakening, when striving gives way to grace.

Fifth mansions

Within these walls unity with God is achieved. We can pray all we like, but spiritual union is a mystery. When it happens it is unmistakable. Teresa here uses her famous analogy of the silkworm. The soul is like the silkworm that feeds on the sustenance of God, and when we are in a state of full trust we are cocooned in divine love. Only from this parcel of piety can we emerge as a butterfly, imbued with a lightness never before possessed. Teresa writes: "It sets no store by the things it did when it was a worm—that is, by its gradual weaving of the cocoon. It has wings now: how can it be content to crawl along slowly when it is able to fly?"

Sixth mansions

The soul is now engaged to the spouse (God), but God seeks to test it a little more before marriage. The soul is awarded even greater favors, but also greater trials. This is the time when we are most vulnerable to a "dark night of the soul."

A soul in this mansion is enraptured by the face of God and a feeling of great humility occurs. Given what we have seen and felt, to return to the Earth seems like an affliction. We would dismiss the world entirely, except that we can do works for God while still here.

Seventh mansions

Finally, betrothal to God, with perfect peace and tranquility. As the soul dies to itself, a person becomes a perfect expression of God on earth: a saint. Though events and trials still happen, they occur as if around the person, not really affecting them.

The medium of advancement

For Teresa, the soul's journey was divided into two stages: in the first to third mansions striving on one's own to get closer to God, and thereafter progress that comes from God's grace.

Yet only through prayer and meditation, she warns, can we begin to progress. Prayer is not for getting things, but for drawing closer to God and his will. It is the act of admitting that we don't know everything, that there is a higher power who will help if he is let in on a problem. The chance of experiencing grace or divine favors increases the more we engage in thoughts about God in prayer. Pray, Teresa urged, even when you don't think it is effective. The divine timescale is different from the human.

Going to church, saying prayers, reading holy works, forgiving people—all seem old-fashioned now, yet such things take us out of the incessant chatter of our minds, elevating us to greater and more lasting things. Simple worship and contemplation keeps us on the straight and narrow, providing a clear path through the thickets of our mind.

Final comments

Throughout *Interior Castle* Teresa states her ignorance before "learned men" and describes herself as a "bird with a broken wing," hopeless at writing and offering nothing new. Yet this picture of a demure sister who knew little was largely false, because when she wrote it Teresa was a powerful figure who did not suffer fools gladly. Single-minded, even brash, she was a good negotiator and had learned something of finance and law. She enjoyed conversations about books, cultivated society figures, and liked having a good meal and a laugh. "There is a time for penance," she is reputed to have said, "and a time for partridge."

The non-religious mind finds it hard to comprehend how someone can channel their love toward something invisible, but in Teresa's case it only served to awaken her individuality and powers. If she had married, it is unlikely much would have come of her life, but as a "bride of Christ" she beat a path that not even her teenage books of chivalric romance could match in excitement or purpose. Indeed, there is a famous Bernini sculpture of Teresa in one of her prayerful ecstasies, in which she appears as if having an orgasm. It is this sort of passion that motivated the great earthly achievements of the saints.

St. Teresa of Avila

Teresa was born in 1515. Her grandfather was a Jew who had converted to Catholicism, and her father retained a life-long fear of being exposed as not genuine Christian nobility. Teresa joined the Carmelite order in 1533, taking her vows two years later. In 1562 she left the convent where she had lived for almost 30 years to found, in a small house in Avila, the Convent of St Joseph. In 1567 the general of the Carmelite order requested that she extend her convent reforms.

Teresa died in 1582 at the convent of Alba, but her body was exhumed a few months later. The total lack of decomposition indicated that she was a saint, and her body parts were given away to various convents as holy relics. It was said that her unearthed body emitted the "odor of sanctity." She was canonized in 1622, and in 1970 was the first woman to achieve the Vatican's distinction of Doctor of the Church.

Interior Castle was written in only three months and edited by her friend Padre Gracian, provincial of the Discalced (barefoot) Carmelites. The original unedited version is generally read today, and the classic English translation (used here) is by Edgar Allison Peers.

A Simple Path

"The poverty in the West is a different kind of poverty—it is not only a poverty of loneliness but also of spirituality."

*"The fruit of silence is prayer
The fruit of prayer is faith
The fruit of faith is love
The fruit of love is service
The fruit of service is peace."*
Mother Teresa

In a nutshell

In addition to physical help, give spiritual solace to those in need.

In a similar vein
G. K. Chesterton *St Francis of Assisi* (p. 54)
Mohatmas Gandhi *An Autobiography* (p. 84)
Teresa of Avila *Interior Castle* (p. 252)

CHAPTER 42

Mother Teresa

One of the few well-known facts of Mother Teresa's life was the timing of her death, which came in the same week as Princess Diana's in 1997. They were two of the most significant women of our time, loved in different ways, but many thought it characteristic of Mother Teresa's humility that her passing would be overshadowed by someone even more famous than her. But what do we really know about her and what is her legacy?

Despite many biographies, she did not write a complete book of her own. *A Simple Path* comes close. Compiled by the religious writer Lucinda Vardey, it is written from Mother Teresa's point of view and based on conversations with her and with other sisters and brothers of her Missionaries of Charity order, plus volunteers who have worked in its homes around the world.

Though an uncritical portrait, you cannot come away from reading it with anything but admiration for Mother Teresa's work. It will be a bit too Christian for some, with prayers included in the text and many mentions of the power of Jesus, but this book is perhaps the clearest expression of what she stood for, and its description of sad lives given some dignity will bring a tear to many a reader's eye.

The bare bones of Mother Teresa's story are these: Born Agnes Gonxha Bojaxhiu in Skopjet, Albania in 1910, the youngest of three children, she had a middle-class upbringing; her father was a building contractor and importer. When he died prematurely her mother formed a business selling cloth and doing embroidery, creating a strong model of female resilience.

At 18, Agnes went to Ireland to become a nun with the Loreto Sisters, who she knew did missionary work in India. Transferred to Calcutta, and taking the name of Teresa after St. Thérèse of Lisieux, she taught in a Loreto school for many years before becoming headmistress. A period of illness gave her for time for reflection, and in 1946 she received her "second calling": to help "the poorest of the poor" in the slums of Calcutta. Though the Sisters required her to continue teaching, in 1950 she was able to establish her own order, the Missionaries of Charity, with its familiar blue and white habit.

The order grew swiftly. By 1960 there were 25 homes across India, and in 1966 the Missionaries of Charity Brothers was founded. Through the 1970s and 1980s Mother Teresa founded many branches outside India, including hospices, homes for drug addicts, alcoholics, and prostitutes, and centers in US and European cities to care for people suffering from AIDS. Also established were homes for abused or abandoned children, people with leprosy, tuberculosis sufferers, and those with mental illnesses. The order's work also includes family planning clinics and Bible study groups.

Though the most common image people have is of the famous nun walking the streets of Calcutta, the order now has a presence in 100 countries, with over 500 missions from Tokyo to Bogotá to Los Angeles. While vocations in the Catholic church have been steadily declining in the last 50 years, the Missionaries of Charity has had huge growth, even since Mother Teresa's death.

Mother Teresa's motivation

In *A Simple Path*, Mother Teresa recounts a visit to a soup kitchen for the homeless in London. She reached out to a man who had been living in a cardboard box, and he said, "It's been a long time since I felt the warmth of a human hand."

Mother Teresa would often note that many people who came to the order's missions were not necessarily hungry; they wanted to be recognized, to have a sense of peace, to relax. The job of the Missionaries of Charity, she says, is not to figure out the hows and whys of homelessness, but to allow a person to experience some dignity, particularly if they are dying. In her words: "There are many in the world dying for a piece of bread but there are many more dying for a little love."

The Sisters take a vow of poverty in order to be able to rely fully on the providence of God. They can own only two sets of clothes, a bucket, sandals, a metal plate for meals, and basic bedding. Without suffering themselves, Mother Teresa explains, their work would just be social work. The primary motivation of the order is always religious; their work is dedicated to Jesus. She is fond of the phrase "love until it hurts," because the Sisters appreciate the paradoxical joy of suffering if it is directed toward a purpose. By saving others they save themselves, an idea backed up by the order's volunteers.

Voluntary life-change

The section of *A Simple Path* dealing with the experiences of volunteers is the most powerful. Clearly, you can't be a volunteer for any length of time without it changing your life in some way, and many come to see that in normal secular life they are unhappy without really realizing it.

Penny, a beauty therapist, found herself virtually by accident at the Nirmal Hriday home in Calcutta, and ended up staying for six months. Her work involved washing destitute people, and although what she saw and did was traumatic, the experience became the catalyst for a desired career change into psychotherapy. Part of the idea of the homes, Mother Teresa says, is simply to let people come in contact with the poor, so that "it's not just these 'millions' of people, but somebody you've actually touched."

A Simple Path does make you think about the value of pursuing wealth and secular things. Peter, another volunteer, says: "I've come to realize that the fewer possessions you have the happier you are. When you see the simple way the sisters live it can totally change your life… I believe the simplest way is the easiest way to God." Another volunteer realized that his office job back home was not the real world; working with the Missionaries of Charity seemed more real. Seeing life and death every day put trivial matters into perspective.

Life in rich countries can make people feel isolated and vulnerable, but this sort of selfless work provides focus and a level of emotional integration that normal secular life may not. One of the principles guiding the order is "The fruit of service is peace."

Prayer as fuel

In 1976, Mother Teresa opened a contemplative branch of her order in New York, known as Sisters of the Word. The vocation of these women is simply to pray most of the day in silence. If you become silent, Mother Teresa points out, God can speak to you: "Prayer feeds the soul—as blood is to the body."

The book has several stories about the right people turning up at the right time to help the order, as the result of prayer. With their crushing demands to serve the destitute and sick, for many of the nuns and brothers prayer provides a chance to recharge with spiritual motivation. As Mother Teresa herself remarks, "Without prayer I could not work for even half an hour. I get my strength from God through prayer."

In the book, praying and forgiving emerge as the answer to every kind of difficulty. By getting our own emotions out of the way we are able to let God use us in the best way possible, and this begins with prayer.

Mother Teresa as leader

When a number of sisters were interviewed about their impressions of Mother Teresa after her 19 years spent at the Loreto school before starting the Missionaries of Charity, collectively they noted nothing really remarkable about her except for fragile health. Yet this was the same person, Lucinda Vardey comments, who became "the quintessential, energetic entrepreneur, who has perceived a need and done something about it, built an organization against all odds, formulated its constitution, and sent out branches all over the world."

What made her such a visionary? The portrait we are given in *A Simple Path* is of a person combining the strongest will with complete surrender to God. She had a powerful mixture of practicality and holiness that allowed her to build an organization comparable to a large company in complexity, at the same time inspiring anyone who met her with her simple zeal for goodness and hope. Yet Mother Teresa must have had a level of ambition and shrewdness to make her dream come alive, and she did not shy from courting kings and presidents when she felt it in the order's or the Church's interests to do so.

Final comments

Though Teresa took her religious name from the simple and childlike St. Thérèse of Lisieux, in her own life she was more similar to Teresa of Avila, the pious but forthright founder of 17 Spanish convents who could converse easily with powerful men (see *Interior Castle*, p. 252). Like the Avilan, who was 40 by the time she founded her first convent, Mother Teresa was also a comparatively late starter. Most people don't know that she spent almost 20 years as a teacher and then head of a school before embarking on her famous work in the Calcutta slums, and was 40 by the time the Missionaries of Charity was fully under way. Yet from this point she became one of the twentieth century's leading "entrepreneurs for God," spreading her organization onto every continent. Its growth resembled a successful business franchise whose unchanging principles allowed it to grow fast without losing its strong identity and purpose.

The greater world only started taking note of Mother Teresa after Malcolm Muggeridge's 1969 documentary, *Something Beautiful for God*. Since then most appraisals of her have been hagiographic, but in recent years critics have suggested that we need to take a look behind the myth of Mother Teresa. Author Christopher Hitchens has been the most strident, his charges including the following:

❖ Teresa was a wily operator who always sided with the most conservative political forces in every country where her order had a presence. She praised the Albanian dictator Enver Hoxha, for example, and was a friend of the Duvalier family in Haiti.
❖ She was a Catholic fundamentalist who opposed the Vatican Council reforms of the 1960s, and tried to intervene in an Irish referendum on abortion. The Church accepted her only because she attracted new believers.
❖ Despite hefty financial donations, care facilities under her management remained primitive, supporting the accusation that the aim of her order was not to save lives but to give people a "good Catholic death."

Though these charges may well be true, on balance the good that Mother Teresa did outweighs any negatives. There are hundreds of thousands of lepers, abused children, addicts, and others whose lot has improved because of the Sisters. Any large organization has its downside and its agendas to push, and the Missionaries of Charity are no different. If they did not exist to spread the word of Jesus, then there would be little to distinguish them from the Red Cross.

Standards of physical care are obviously a major issue, yet as Mother Teresa says throughout her book, what people hunger for most is for someone to look them in the eye and extend a warm hand. While hospitals fix people's bodies, the Missionaries of Charity are a reminder that a life gone wrong is as important as any other life, and that a person is above all a soul.

The Power of Now

"Don't look for any other state than the one you are in now; otherwise, you will set up inner conflict and unconscious resistance. Forgive yourself for not being at peace. The moment you completely accept your non-peace, your non-peace becomes transmuted into peace. Anything you accept fully will get you there, will take you into peace. This is the miracle of surrender."

"To offer no resistance to life is to be in a state of grace, ease, and lightness. This state is then no longer dependent upon things being in a certain way, good or bad. It seems paradoxical, yet when your inner dependency on form is gone, the general conditions of your life, the outer forms, tend to improve greatly."

In a nutshell

Transform your life by the simple realization that the only time you ever have is this moment.

In a similar vein
St. Augustine *Confessions* (p. 20)
Ram Dass *Be Here Now* (p. 72)
Thich Nhat Hanh *The Miracle of Mindfulness* (p. 192)
Shunryu Suzuki *Zen Mind, Beginner's Mind* (p. 240)
Neale Donald Walsch *Conversations with God* (p. 276)

CHAPTER 43

Eckhart Tolle

Amodern masterpiece of spiritual writing, *The Power of Now: A Guide to Spiritual Enlightenment* was first published in Canada. Released in the United States, it became a sleeper hit and made Eckhart Tolle into a sought-after teacher.

While the majority of spiritual and New Age writings contain ethereal concepts for "achieving transcendence," *The Power of Now* is intensely focused on the problems we have today and the person we are at this moment. It is perhaps the most practical of any self-help, success, or spiritual classic because it denies our usual tendency to imagine some bright future without ever really coming to grips with the present.

The book is also a masterful synthesis of ideas from Buddhism, Christianity, Taoism, and other traditions, satisfying our twenty-first-century desire to think outside the boxes of conventional religion, and recognizing that ultimately all religions say the same thing.

Tolle's immersion in spiritual texts came only after he had glimpsed their truth in a flash of enlightenment at the age of 29. His recounting of this scene in the first few pages, reminiscent of some of the great spiritual autobiographies, leads us into the work, which takes the form of questions and answers. His sudden transformation from self-loathing to lasting inner peace and joy may be difficult to believe at first, but it is worth reading on.

You are not your mind

Our civilization is built on the achievements of the mind, Tolle writes, and many of them are remarkable. We are naturally apt to confuse the mind, in its constantly thinking state, as being *us*. However, there is a "Being-ness" behind the mind that is the real "I"; by getting in tune with it, we can control our thoughts and put our emotions into perspective.

Until we have control of our mind, it controls us. The mind has continual conversations with itself that are difficult to turn off. It has lots of opinions, but they are all based on what has happened in the past.

This makes it difficult to experience things afresh in the present. Today is never as good as the great times to come or the ones that were.

You have probably come to believe that this constantly thinking voice is "you," but in fact it is only part of who you are. We are addicted to thinking, Tolle says, because by getting us to think all the time the ego gives us a sense of identity. Yet continual thinking prevents us from simply enjoying the moment.

How do we free ourselves of compulsive thinking? We begin by putting the mind into perspective by watching what it says and thinks, being a witness to the rolling seas of thought and emotion that we experience every day. You will of course continue to use your thinking mind to solve problems and survive, but by getting some objectivity from it and embracing the real you behind it, Tolle says, you are taking the single most important step toward enlightenment. When you can be still and shut off your thinking mind, if only for a moment, you do not go into a dreamy or comatose state. The opposite happens: You get a burst of appreciation for the present and for everything around you, and suddenly feel more together.

A new life of now-ness

Given the way our minds usually work, to access the state of "now" may seem very difficult. However, just the acknowledgment that it does exist will help us to increase the amount of time we are fully "awake." We can admit to ourselves that, for example, in the last hour we were totally swept up by an emotion or thoughts of worry or regret. We can admit that we couldn't turn off. Every time we recognize that we were not living in the present, the chances that we may do so in the future increase.

Tolle suggests that we get more into the "now" through the routines of everyday life: washing our hands, sitting in our car, walking up steps, breathing—being aware of all of these movements. If they are mechanical and automatic, we are not fully experiencing the present.

Tolle's basic law is that the more we resist our current situation, the more painful it is. Obviously, if we are thinking "This can't be happening," the fact that it is makes it unbearable. Waiting and looking forward to the day when we will be happy or prosperous, for instance, only makes resistance to the present situation stronger. The thought that we could be somewhere else, be with someone else, doing something else can turn our life into a living hell. Is there a way out? The author provides a paradoxical solution: we have to forgive the situation and accept its right to be; even if we hate the situation, accept our hatred as part of it, but don't keep saying to ourselves, "This is not happening, this can't be."

Tolle also talks about the basic existential dislike that people have of the present. He describes the normal state of the thinking mind as "an almost continuous low level of unease, discontent, boredom or nervousness—a kind of background static." We are always trying to get away from the rawness of the present moment, whether it be through dulling it or making it more exciting through drink or drugs, or having grand dreams of the future or nostalgia for the past. Feelings of regret or longing are created when we fail to appreciate the present, which is the only time we ever have. Yet through our surrender to what is, we will find ways to deal with what is happening. We can begin to see that our life, our essential being, is not the same as our life situation.

The present moment, Tolle dares us to consider, is actually problem-free. Problems need to exist in time, so the more we live in the present the less life we give them. He asks us to withhold judgment about situations, so that instead of an event being good or bad it just *is*. Hold the fear and loathing for a second, and we will find that a solution emerges.

When we act from a sense of deep being, instead of restlessly striving to become something, we are free from fear. Paradoxically, this relaxed state makes it easier to succeed in the situations of our life. We take things as they come and adapt quickly to what is, rather than being crushed when things don't turn out as we planned.

Relationships of presence

In a chapter on enlightened relationships, Tolle observes that "most 'love relationships' become love/hate relationships before long." It is considered normal that we switch suddenly from love and affection to savage hostility and back again; as the saying goes, can't live with a person, can't live without them. We believe that if we could just get rid of the negative states all would be well, but Tolle says that this can never happen. Both polarities of love and hate depend on each other, and are merely "different aspects of the same dysfunction."

When we are in love, the other person makes us feel whole, but the downside is a growing addictiveness to this individual and the horror of any possibility of losing them. The ego has a need for wholeness, yet romantic relationships are not the right place to look for this because they give us a sense of self that is dependent on something or someone outside of us. We all carry a body of pain inside us that appears to be healed when we are in love, but the pain is still there and emerges again when the honeymoon is over.

The purpose of real, long-term relationships, Tolle says, is not to make us happy or fulfilled; they are to bring out the pain within us so that it can be transmuted. They are to make us more conscious, and if we can accept this we can move to another level, and the relationship will flower naturally, free of our unreal expectations.

If your current relationship seems like an "insane drama," instead of trying to escape from it, go into it more deeply and accept the fact. Tolle's assertion is that close relationships have never been more difficult than they are now, yet they also offer possibly the greatest opportunities for spiritual advancement.

Final comments

Rather than presenting some grand scheme for success, *The Power of Now* asks us to be more present in the minutiae of everyday life, to see if we can make every moment mean something. What is regret but that we were not more fully present in a situation, or to be more "there" in a relationship that we have now lost?

Some forms of mental illness involve an inability to shut off internal conversations. In contrast, someone in the fullest mental health will have the ability to quiet their mind, and from this stillness access the true state of being that offers up perfect solutions to our problems.

Though it has the style of personal revelation common to many spiritual classics, *The Power of Now* seems new, even revolutionary, and it is one of the most practical books for changing your life in a sustainable way.

Be sure to read this book, if you do acquire it, more than once. The writing style is beautifully clear, so on first reading you may think that you have "got the message," but the work is only fully realized when its teachings are put into practice.

Eckhart Tolle

Born in Germany, Tolle is a graduate of the University of London and Cambridge University, where he was a research scholar and supervisor.

For the last decade he has been a spiritual teacher working with groups and individuals in Europe and North America, and is based in Vancouver, British Columbia.

The Power of Now *has been translated into 17 languages. Tolle's other books include* Practicing the Power of Now *and* Stillness Speaks.

1973

Cutting through Spiritual Materialism

"Ego is constantly attempting to acquire and apply the teachings of spirituality for its own benefit."

"To the conventional way of thinking, compassion simply means being kind and warm... But true compassion is ruthless, from ego's point of view, because it does not consider ego's drive to maintain itself. It is 'crazy wisdom'. It is totally wise, but is crazy as well, because it does not relate to ego's literal and simple-minded attempts to secure its own comfort."

In a nutshell

Sometimes the desire to be spiritual is really a hankering after psychological security.

In a similar vein

Pema Chödrön *The Places that Scare You* (p. 60)
G. I. Gurdjieff *Meetings with Remarkable Men* (p. 102)
Shunryu Suzuki *Zen Mind, Beginner's Mind* (p. 240)

Chögyam Trungpa

Cutting through Spiritual Materialism is based on talks given by the Buddhist master and scholar Chögyam Trungpa in 1970 and 1971. He was setting up a meditation center in Colorado, and noticed that the students were bringing with them unreal expectations regarding the spiritual path. They seemed to be earnest in their desire for truth, but their real motivation was to feel good about themselves.

For those who have spent years pursuing various spiritual practices, the book can be shocking. It ruthlessly demonstrates how the ego is behind our attempts to be spiritually advanced individuals, when it should be clear that just having such a desire is the mark of ego.

The first part of the book studies the traps we get ourselves into believing that we are on our way to enlightenment; in the second Trungpa describes the real spiritual path through concepts such as the four noble truths, *shunyata*, and Bhoddisatva. This commentary focuses on the first part.

Lords of materialism

What is "spiritual materialism"? Surely the two words do not belong together?

In Tibetan Buddhism there are Three Lords of Materialism: the mental Lords of Form, of Speech, and of Mind. The Lord of Form, Trungpa said, is a representation of our attempts to create a "manageable, safe, predictable, pleasurable world." In response to the unpredictability of life, "It is the ego's ambition to secure and entertain itself, trying to avoid all irritation."

The Lord of Speech refers to our attempts to categorize and turn everything into concepts, so that we don't have to experience reality directly. Everything is screened through our established forms of perception. As with the Lord of Form, the purpose of this type of materialism is to try to solidify the world around us and our place within it.

The Lord of Mind represents our effort not to lose awareness of our separate self. Though it may not seem so, any kind of yoga or prayer or meditation can be used not to lose our sense of self into something larger, but to maintain self-consciousness. A person who wants to isolate themselves from the world and live in a cave in the mountains, so avoiding all of life's irritations to get close to God, is a classic example of the Lord of Mind at work.

Trungpa notes that the ego's sense of solidity stops it from absorbing anything new, and therefore it will only really want to imitate spiritual practice, not be changed by it. After all, why would the ego sincerely want to get involved with something that might see its elimination? It naturally only seeks that which will confirm its own identity, and if becoming "religious" serves this, it will be taken on as another layer of ego consciousness. This is spiritual materialism.

Real spirituality, in contrast, involves peeling back the layers and wittling away the ego's management over our behavior and awareness.

The solid illusion

Trungpa's distinctions have us re-examining what we have taken to be our spirituality. Are we merely trying to buttress our sense of identity as a good, spiritual person, or are we prepared to cut ourselves open and see what is really there? There may be a hard core of self that, in truth, we will protect at all costs.

After this shock of admission, you may wisely conclude that you are not really up to the spiritual path and what it involves, that you don't want to lose yourself in some greater universal Mind. And anyway, you may decide that there is no way that your ego, having infiltrated every aspect of your thoughts, even your seemingly noble desire for the spiritual life, is ever going to give up its grip over your existence. You are a hopeless vassal of the mental Lords.

Yet at this point, Trungpa says, you could be open to genuine insight, for only when you see that you are not much more than a bundle of self-protectiveness do you have a small chance to be otherwise. The more we think, the more convinced we become that we are our thoughts. With so much worry and anxiety going on, nothing can seem more real that our thinking selves. The ego wants us to believe that there is nothing beyond our thoughts, and in so doing our ego mind becomes a rock-hard, inescapable reality.

The purpose of meditation, in contrast, is to allow all our categories and fixations to evaporate, to let the illusion of solidity be viewed as such. When we see that there is no need to struggle to prove that we exist, we have the beginnings of sanity and enlightenment.

Beginning the real work

The ego prefers heroic acts of spiritual seeking, Trungpa notes, such as doing a week-long retreat or becoming a vegetarian. Such experiences may give us a high because we are leaving behind our bad old unenlightened self, but we always come down from them and are left with ourselves again. We can "throw away the suit to enter the ashram," as Trungpa puts it, but such grandiose change will only entrench our sense of identity, of the "I" that is going to change our life.

Only when we see that our ego controls even our attempts to *lose* the ego are we able to stop the act of striving toward some great enlightenment experience and just let things be. We can stop our spiritual shopping and decide to work with the person we are, not the exulted self that we think these experiences will make us.

We are on the real spiritual path when we can laugh at our pretenses, whereas the zealous convert or person who has joined a cult tends to lose all sense of humor. Everything becomes black and white, they have "found the way." Their relief comes from having the world made simple: they no longer have to accept reality as it is, but can live according to some belief that lifts them above it all. They will not admit that they were looking for security, but this is what they have gained. But as Trungpa observes, this is all the work of the ego, wanting to make things more solid and more definite, and to render itself even more invulnerable.

Real spirituality is more ordinary, even tedious. We have to surrender our hopes and get acquainted with disappointment. Disappointment is a sign of intelligence, Trungpa says, because "it does not confirm the existence of our ego and its dreams." Instead, it lets us know that there is something beyond ego's control, an awareness of self that is not self-deceiving. We need to say to ourselves: "I am willing to open my eyes to the circumstances of life as they are. I am not willing to view them as spiritual or mystical."

This is the paradox of *Cutting through Spiritual Materialism*, echoed in Suzuki's *Zen Mind, Beginner's Mind* (see p. 240)—that the spiritual path, once you are on it, is nothing special. It is merely looking at life as it is, without so many mental structures—beliefs, theories, salvation fantasies—built up over it.

The savior myth

Trungpa comments that no one would listen to him if they just bumped into him in the street or in a restaurant, but when they learn he is from Tibet and is the eleventh reincarnation of the Trungpa Tulku, they are suddenly all over him. He discusses the familiar pattern of someone who has found a spiritual adviser, excited with their wonderful teacher who will open the door to universal mysteries. But having been through the heroic stage, it is a shock to find out that on the real spiritual path, no one is going to do anything for you; and you have to do it through the boring present.

Another of Trungpa's secrets is that we should not be "looking for the good" or "focusing on the light." Real spirituality means accepting everything, good and bad, darkness and light, as part of the whole. Trying to be good, and trying not to be bad, is a duality. In meditation we do not think in dualistic terms—this is a naïve way of being. We want to experience what is.

Final comments

With his prolific, high-quality writing and achievements as a founder of meditation centers and educational institutions in America and around the world, Trungpa was one of the major figures in twentieth-century Buddhism.

However, he was not a typical Tibetan monk. Trungpa had renounced his vows and married, was a heavy drinker and smoker (his early death was caused by cirrhosis of the liver), and he had sex with his female students. Yet he apparently did not see these facts as contradictory to his work as a spiritual educator, but rather put them down to "crazy wisdom" or natural spontaneity.

Whatever your view of Trungpa as a person, *Cutting through Spiritual Materialism* is a landmark work not simply in eastern philosophy but in spiritual thought generally. Unlike figures such as Shunryu Suzuki and Paramahansa Yogananda, who brought eastern religion to the West but very much retained their Orientalness, Trungpa's lifestyle as a modern (very free-thinking) American perhaps gave him greater insight into the secular mind, a mind that could see spirituality as something separate to itself that might be acquired.

Trungpa warned that the spiritual seeker could end up as just a collector of interesting cultural experiences, not someone who truly gives something of themselves. Instead, we have to approach spiritual matters with "a hard kind of intelligence," remaining wary of over-pious or charismatic gurus. This no-nonsense approach is attractive to anyone wanting real answers, not mere inspiration, and in a world that offers thousands of enticing spiritual paths and experiences this book is like a lighthouse that can stop you crashing into the spiritual rocks.

Chögyam Trungpa Rinpoche

Born in 1939 in eastern Tibet, Trungpa was the 11th tulku or reincarnation of a line of Tibetan teachers of the Kagyü lineage, a school of Buddhism focusing on meditation. He was made abbot of the Surmang monasteries while still in his late teens, but in 1959 had to flee to India when China invaded Tibet, making a perilous journey by horse and foot. For the next few years he worked in a school for young Lamas in Dalhousie, under the appointment of the Dalai Lama.

In 1963, Trungpa went to Oxford University under a fellowship to study comparative religion, philosophy, and fine arts. In 1967 he founded the first Tibetan Buddhist practice center in the West, Samye Ling in Scotland, but not long after had a serious car accident that resulted in partial paralysis on his left side. He rescinded his vows, married, and moved to the United States, establishing a meditation center in Vermont. Through the 1970s he opened many more centers, wrote prolifically, and established the Naropa Institute, a Buddhist liberal arts college in Colorado. His teaching and meditation organization, Shambala Training, operates in many countries.

Trungpa died in 1987. His use of the term "egolessness" is included in the Oxford English Dictionary.

Conversations
with God

"You are in a partnership with God. We share an eternal covenant. My promise to you is to always give you what you ask. Your promise is to ask; to understand the process of the asking and the answering."

In a nutshell

God's thoughts may be more accessible than you think.

In a similar vein
St. Augustine *Confessions* (p. 20)
Helen Schucman & William Thetford *A Course in Miracles* (p. 222)
Teresa of Avila *Interior Castle* (p. 252)
Eckhart Tolle *The Power of Now* (p. 264)

CHAPTER 45

Neale Donald Walsch

N eale Donald Walsch was in the habit of writing down his thoughts in the form of letters, and during a very difficult period of his life he drafted a particularly angry letter to God. He demanded to know: Why was his life always a struggle? Why did his relationships always fail? Why did he never have enough money?

Then something remarkable happened: he felt his pen move almost with a will of its own, and answers started to flow. He began to have, he says, a "conversation with God," one question following another until there was enough material to fill a book. The book even in manuscript form had a powerful effect on people, and when published became a bestseller.

It is easy to be skeptical about the *Conversations with God* series (this commentary relates to Book One). Are these actually God's thoughts channeled through a man, or a brilliant synthesis of all Walsch has learned in his spiritual searching? Even if you believe the latter, it will be difficult to deny the profound and radical nature of some of the answers offered. For example, Walsch wonders why God has not before provided definite guidance for life as a human being. God rejoinders that he has, but most people are not willing to listen, and one reason is that we do not want to hear what to us seems wrong:

"Go ahead and act on all that you know. But notice that you've all been doing that since time began. And look at the shape the world is in."

Particularly when it moves through the deeper issues about the human soul, its connection to God, and the concept of free will, the book can inspire reflection and even awe in the reader. The question-and-answer sessions range over subjects as diverse as war, sex, reincarnation, relationships, and the body. Here we focus on the themes of life as creation, personal power, and abundance.

Waking up to our power

Most people think of life as a series of tests or a process of discovery. In *Conversations with God*, the point is made over and over that life is, in fact, about creation. God is above all a creator, and as expressions of God it is our job to spend life creating, not by living unconsciously according to other people's rules or, indeed, the expectations of conventional religion.

When Walsch asks in desperation "When will my life take off?" God replies that it will do so when he becomes crystal clear what it is that he wants to be, do, and have:

> *"For most of your life you've lived as the effect of your experiences. Now, you're invited to be the cause of them."*

Whether consciously or not, we all live according to the creation formula of thought followed by word followed by action, never realizing exactly how much idle thoughts create our world. With fuzzy or incorrect thinking, we are not ever likely to rise above mediocrity. God, of course, is less concerned with our worldly achievements than with our state of being, but it is logical that optimal states of being lead effortlessly to excellent doing, to results. The more fully we are ourselves—that is, clear about what we stand for and what we choose to create—the more authentic and lasting our success will be.

The certainty of greatness

What seems to humans like shooting too high, from the Almighty's point of view is expected. We have to assume our power to create in the manner that God does, to have a much larger conception of ourselves:

> *"you choose constantly the lesser thought, the smaller idea, the tiniest concept of yourself and your power, to say nothing of Me and Mine."*

God, it turns out, is not the fearful master demanding obedience, but has implanted in us the idea of "thinking big." Our mistake is believing that we are not great and must spend our lives improving. This is a life of struggle, when in fact God wants us to recognize that we are divinity in material form, already perfect, already wonderful. By accepting our greatness, we eliminate the struggle of life stemming from internal debate about whether we deserve this or that.

Humanity's illusion, Walsch learns, is that great outcomes are ever in doubt. God says:

"For thousands of years people have disbelieved the promises of God for the most extraordinary reason: they were too good to be true."

That is, too good for our limited conception; if we expand our appreciation of what we and God are capable of, all of the pronouncements in our religious texts begin to ring true.

Agreeing to co-create

Conversations with God throws out the idea that there is a perfect divine plan for each of us and that if we err from it we will be punished. We were given free will, which means what it says. Logically, then, the relationship between God and us is not one of master and servant, but of equals engaged in creating the world.

God informs Walsch that there are well-established laws in the universe that, if followed, will give a person exactly what they choose. We follow these laws or resist them, but we can't ignore them, for by them the universe is run. One of God's laws is that whatever a person asks for, they will receive ("ask and you shall receive, seek and you shall find"); our task, in return, is to understand how this process actually works.

In our traditional relationship with God, we pray for things and hope that our requests will be granted. Yet praying, hoping, bending down, supplicating—are these consistent with a co-creating partnership? Walsch has an "aha" moment when he discovers why he usually doesn't get what he prays for: his requests and wishes are a statement to the universe of what he lacks, and since our reality reflects back to us perfectly our state of mind, the actual conditions he finds himself in are somewhat lacking.

Praying for something therefore often has the opposite effect: it pushes it away from us. A supplicating prayer suggests a weak relationship with God, so the results will be correspondingly weak and small. The way to manifest things is to give thanks that they already exist, whether yet in material form or not. God, or the universe, rewards those who are thankful for the ease with which anything can be produced; if we recognize divine power, it is suddenly more accessible to us. When choosing to have something, God tells Walsch, the Master (the advanced human being) "knows in advance that the deed has been done."

Mechanics of abundance

Walsch is told that if he wants financial success, he has to change his root or sponsoring thought about money. If this underlying thought is that he rarely gets what he wants, that he never has enough to survive, so this situation will surely remain.

Thoughts become words and words become action. This is simply the law of cause and effect, God tells him. Start being more spontaneously generous with your money, for instance, and you will find that you live in an abundant world. The universe simply reflects our words back to us as reality, so that if you are wanting money or wanting success, you do not have either. You will just be creating a state of wanting, not of being. If you project into the universe mixed messages about how you feel about money, your attempts to get more of it will be mixed to say the least.

Therefore, God suggests, make statements to the universe and to yourself that involve not what you want but what you are grateful for already having and being—for example: "Thank you, God, for bringing success into my life."

Final comments

From a traditional Christian perspective that values sacrifice and long-suffering, the messages in the book may seem very selfish. Walsch's God commands us to think above all of our own personal development in our journey through life. Traditional religions put God up there and us down here, but this book says that we can be co-creating partners.

This may seem like a blasphemous concept, but try to have an open mind. If nothing else, you can experience Walsch's thrill at the chance to bypass prayer and commune directly with a voice that he believes to be the Creator. The series has become a new bible for many people because the language is so direct and there are many references to contemporary life. While the parable and the myth were once the best way to communicate spiritual ideas, *Conversations with God* caters to our modern liking for Q&A and Frequently Asked Questions. While this can take some of the mystery out of our holy relationship, it also breaks us free from the belief that spiritual intelligence only comes from saintly self-sacrifice or knowledge of the mystical.

Neale Donald Walsch

Walsch grew up in Milwaukee, Wisconsin, in a Roman Catholic house-hold, although his mother encouraged him to be a theological free-thinker. After school graduation he enrolled at the University of Wisconsin, but dropped out after two years to pursue a career in radio. He became a radio station director, then a newspaper reporter, and then a public information officer for public schools. After a move to the West Coast he formed his own PR and marketing firm, but could never settle down professionally. In his private life he married and divorced four times.

Things got worse before they got better. His neck was broken in a car accident, and the ensuing rehabilitation cost him his job. He found himself homeless and had to claw his way back into full-time work. In 1992, at the age of 49, Walsch began to write down Conversations with God: Book One.

Book One *spent two and half years on the* New York Times *bestseller list, and the* Conversations with God *series has been translated into 27 languages. The most recent work is* The New Revelations.

The Purpose-Driven Life

"The purpose of your life is far greater than your own personal fulfillment, your peace of mind, or even your happiness. It's far greater than your family, your career, or even your wildest dreams and ambitions. If you want to know why you were placed on this planet, you must begin with God."

In a nutshell

We were created by God for a reason. If we know God, that reason will be revealed.

In a similar vein

Ghazzali *The Alchemy of Happiness* (p. 90)
C. S. Lewis *The Screwtape Letters* (p. 154)
Emanuel Swedenborg *Heaven and Hell* (p. 246)

CHAPTER 46

Rick Warren

Rick Warren's book makes a big claim: that by the end of it, you will know the purpose of your life. Just as Jesus was transformed by his 40 days in the wilderness, and Moses by his 40 days on Mount Sinai, you are told that you can be transformed by reading *The Purpose-Driven Life* one chapter a day for 40 days.

The book has been a massive bestseller (over 10 million copies) and it is not difficult to see why. Its powerful ideas, backed by the authority of the Bible, are presented in an attractive layout and conversational style, and the air of revolution, if only of the personal type, pervades its pages. Warren's basic idea is that human beings were hard-wired by God to seek out the meaning of their life, and therefore we cannot fulfill our potential or achieve any real satisfaction until we recognize ourselves as divine progeny.

A definite reason

At the outset, Warren stresses that his book is quite different to regular self-help volumes on the subject of life purpose. These books get the reader to ask what they want from life, to set goals and clarify aims, but such a focus on "me," he argues, can never reveal our real purpose. His radical point is that worldly success and living according to purpose, even though we are quite capable of having both, are quite different things. "What people fail to realize," he says, "is that all achievements are eventually surpassed, records are broken, reputations fade, and tributes are forgotten." What you think will last forever ends up on history's scrapheap.

The only way to know that what you are doing in life is really worth it is to make sure that it is part of God's plan. The first line of the book's first chapter reads: "It's not about you." Since God created you, only God knows what purpose he has in mind for your life, and this is discovered not through the wisdom of the world, but through the word of God. Rather than "pop psychology, success-motivation, or inspirational stories," Warren says, life must be built on eternal truths.

We discover our purpose not by planning, thinking or philosophizing, but through direct revelation. And when you dare to ask why you exist, you can be sure of an answer.

Surrender

In our power-based culture, Warren notes, surrendering to anything or anyone can be taken as the sign of a loser. We want to succeed, win, overcome—not submit or yield. However, the Christian way does ask us to surrender ourselves to God, to "take our hands off the steering wheel." We think that this will ruin our lives, but Warren says that letting God take over brings freedom.

Surrendering does not require us to give up our personality; in fact it may bring it out, along with many dormant abilities. We expand into something greater and look back on our former life wondering why we wasted so much time. We admire power, but are wary about taking the path that can make us a much more powerful person that we are now. We actually believe that we know better than God, and therefore call on him only when we are in need, but we will never see our true potential unless our surrender to God's direction is total.

As Warren puts it: "Surrender is not the best way to live; it is the only way to live. Nothing else works. All other approaches lead to frustration, disappointment, and self-destruction." Surrender is reasonable, because it acknowledges the truth that we can have all the plans in the world, but if they are not the same as God's they will be fruitless. Surrender is not just a leap of faith—it is the smartest thing we can do with our life.

Relationship

What God wants more than anything, Warren says, is to be our friend. That is the purpose of all that happens to us, to bring us closer to God. He wants us to include him in all our thinking, even argue with us vehemently. God does not want "pious clichés" but a real relationship. Most people think that we have to be reverential when we talk to God, but there is little logic to this when God can see right through to all our thoughts, good and bad. The basis of a real divine relationship is honesty, often a questioning, pleading frankness that can include anger. Warren notes that God is not offended when we state our belief that things are hopeless, as long as we have the underlying thought that God still exists, that we believe anyway.

Above everything else, what we are asked for is faith, even when what we are asked to do makes no sense. Warren devotes a chapter to Noah, who obeyed God's command and started building an ark for a future big flood he was told would definitely happen, even though he lived in an area with hardly any rain and was a long way from the sea.

Warren gives this warning: "You will be tested by major changes, delayed promises, impossible problems, unanswered prayers, underserved criticism, and even senseless tragedies." A relationship with God does not mean that we escape difficulties, but it does bring an appreciation that things happen for a purpose, and that part of that purpose is to test our character, loyalty, and love. When people say in exasperation "these things are sent to try us" they are right, because in both the little and large things of life we have endless opportunities to show faith. As in marriage, without faith there is no basis for a relationship; with faith, there is no limit as to what God can accomplish through you.

Worship

There are now many books on discovering one's purpose in life, but Warren puts his finger on what is missing from nearly all of them, even the Christian ones. Our purpose, he says, is only partly to express our abilities and make a contribution in terms of career or family life. Our more fundamental reason for being is to give glory to God through worship. As a pastor of a large church Warren is naturally biased on this, but he points out that the desire to honor and delight in God was made part of human nature, so that we will never be fulfilling our true potential unless we recognize that we are created beings who serve God.

Many go to church to solve their problems or get a feeling of community, but church going is for worship, which is inherently joyful. Martin Luther famously wrote, "A dairymaid can milk cows to the glory of God." Warren recalls this to support the idea that we have endless opportunities for praise and glory, and going to church provides a wonderful focus for this to happen. We need to change from concentrating on how much pleasure we are getting out of life, to considering how much pleasure God is getting out of us.

Living for eternity

Central to Warren's idea of the purpose-driven life is the concept that
we need to live within the context of eternity. Our life on Earth is a
preparation for the afterlife in the same way that our time in the womb
was only a brief preparation for life outside. Using another metaphor,
he suggests that although we cannot understand what goes on in
heaven any more than an ant can comprehend the internet, what we
can know—what the Bible tells us—is that our earthly life greatly
affects the quality of our eternity. An awareness of eternity necessarily
changes how we see day-to-day living. Our old life of cheap
amusements and keeping up with fashions suddenly seems somewhat
shallow next to our relationship to God. As Warren puts it, "The closer
you live to God, the smaller everything else appears."

Warren notes the many references in the Bible to life on Earth being
like living in a foreign country. We may get attached to this new place,
but we should always remember where we came from and where we
will return to. Why do most us feel a constant feeling of discontent in
life? Warren says that this is God's way of getting us to realize that the
world can never really satisfy us, that our real home is eternity.

Final comments

Many readers will be turned off by the Christian fundamentalist nature
of the book. Warren's frequent suggestion that only through faith in
Jesus will we be "saved" is a little threatening. Not once does Warren
give any credence to faiths or traditions other than Christianity; religious fervor is one thing, but denying the truth of other beliefs is what
makes *The Purpose-Driven Life* seem, in places, quite narrow. Could
the rest of the world be that wrong? Many readers will also be taken
aback by the considerable attention that Warren gives to the idea of
mission, or spreading the word of Christ overseas.

Yet *The Purpose-Driven Life* is a still a brilliant contemporary spiritual work and will be read for a long time to come. Part of the reason
is that it offers an alternative to normal consumer society, and for people who have pretty well everything they need, the absence of meaning
and spiritual connection becomes a knawing hunger that must be satisfied. At one point, Warren uses the word "counter-cultural" to describe
the spiritually driven life. Non-believers look at church-going people
and think they are brainwashed, without seeing that they may them-

selves have become brainwashed by the values of popular culture. To consciously refrain from adopting prevailing attitudes and remain connected to God in everything is a powerful statement to make to the world. In contrast to the modern ethic of setting our own agenda and achieving our goals, Warren asks us to let God take over our life. In a "get what you want" culture, this is a radical message.

The other reason for this book's success is that, using hundreds of biblical quotes, its arguments are difficult to refute. Instead of trying to make the reader into a Christian clone, Warren repeatedly highlights the uniqueness of every human being (using genetic science to support his case) and why each of us has a special reason for being here. Yet *The Purpose-Driven Life* is in no way a frothy feel-good story, giving much attention to the dark aspects in each of us that can only be transformed when we make a decision to surrender. Warren notes that God "specializes in giving people a fresh start." Most of us toy with merely improving our lives, when what is available is transformation.

Rick Warren

Warren was born in San Jose, California. He is a Baptist minister whose academic qualifications include a BA from California Baptist College, a Master of Divinity degree from Southwestern Theological Seminary, and a Doctor of Ministry degree from Fuller Theological Seminary.

With his wife Kay, Warren founded Saddleback Church in Lake Forest, California in 1980, which has one of the largest congregations in the United States. His previous book, The Purpose-Driven Church, *has sold over a million copies.*

Waiting for God

"As one has to learn to read or practice a trade, so one must learn to feel in all things, first and almost solely, the obedience of the universe to God. It is really an apprenticeship. Like every apprenticeship, it requires time and effort... Whoever has finished his apprenticeship recognizes things and events, everywhere and always, as vibrations of the same divine and infinitely sweet word."

"Friendship has something universal about it. It consists of loving a human being as we should like to be able to love each soul in particular of all those who go to make up the human race."

In a nutshell

Spurn the collective mindset and create a spirituality unique to you.

In a similar vein
G. K. Chesterton *St Francis of Assisi* (p. 54)
Epictetus *Enchiridion* (p. 78)
Dag Hammarskjöld *Markings* (p. 108)
Teresa of Avila *Interior Castle* (p. 252)

CHAPTER 47

Simone Weil

How did a left-wing intellectual become one of the twentieth century's better-known mystics? This is the puzzle of Simone Weil's short life.

Born in Paris, her background was middle class, Jewish, and agnostic, and as a gifted student she sailed through school and university. From 1928 to 1931 she attended the elite École Normale Supérieure, coming second in her class in front of Simone de Beauvoir. She loved Greek Stoic philosophy, enjoyed translating Homer and Sophocles, and wrote a commentary on Pythagoras. Weil appreciated the English metaphysical poets, read the Bhagavad-Gita, learned Sanskrit, and found inspiration in Francis of Assisi and John of the Cross. Yet she saw spirituality only as an interesting part of culture, and until the last years of her life never prayed.

Through her twenties she worked in various positions as a schoolteacher, but her passion was the wellbeing of France's workers. One year she took a leave of absence to work alongside factory hands at a Renault car plant, and for several summers labored with peasants in the vineyards. She was plagued by ill health, and in 1940 moved to be with her parents in Marseilles. There she met a Catholic priest, Father Perrin, who became her friend and mentor for the last years of her life.

Waiting for God includes a number of letters that Weil wrote to Father Perrin, plus several essays. The book was never meant to be a whole work and was published after her death, but provides an excellent entrée to her thinking. Look for the edition with an insightful introduction by Leslie A. Fielder.

The outsider saint

In the chapter "Spiritual Autobiography," Weil tells of being a moody and insecure adolescent, living in the shadow of her genius brother. She did not care about her lack of outward successes, she says, but did mind the feeling that she was excluded from "the kingdom of wisdom and truth." However, she had an epiphany in which she realized that, if your heart was really set on it, you did not have to be a genius to find truth.

As a student then teacher of philosophy and agitator for social change, Weil was intent on solving the world's problems through intellectual means. But in several visits to Catholic sites and churches, including a church where St. Francis of Assisi had prayed, she experienced a kind of spiritual collapse after which she considered herself a "slave to God."

While Weil knew that she had a vocation, but simply getting baptized and becoming a nun was never really an option. All her life she had distrusted every kind of institution, so she was not about to sign up to one now, even if it was the Catholic Church. She felt that being a member of something entailed exclusion of others, and although now a believer, she didn't want to separate herself from the mass of humanity who did not believe, or to be perceived as some religious nut. Moreover, Weil loved other faiths and cultures too much to restrict herself to Christianity. Being a classicist, she could not stomach Christianity's condescension toward the Greek Stoics such as Marcus Aurelius, whose spiritual intentions, she felt, were at least Christianity's equal. And she could not forget the Inquisition, which had killed and tortured thousands in the name of dogma, and the Church's historical eagerness to support war.

In one letter to Father Perrin, Weil accused him of saying "false" when what he really meant was "unorthodox." She could not accept intellectual dishonesty or the way in which the Church through dogma had made it convenient for people not to have to think. Although she fantasized about the sense of belonging that being in the Church would give her, Weil knew that her higher calling was to seek truth outside the sphere of religion.

She mistrusted the "patriotism" that people feel when they belong to a faith and was frightened at the damage that can be done by collective feeling, noting that she was the type of person who would have been swept up by the rousing nature of Nazi war songs. Given this tendency toward spiritual swooning in the manner of Teresa of Avila, she knew that she had to be as objective about spiritual ideas and belief as she was in relation to, for instance, materialism and atheism.

Following is a brief look at three themes prominent in *Waiting for God* and Weil's thinking generally.

Love of the world

Weil wrote about three loves that are a sort of proxy for love of God ("indirect loves") but that we can experience while living on this Earth: religious ceremonies, love of our neighbor, the beauty of the world, and friendship.

Our love of increase, luxury, and beauty, she suggests, is not for the things themselves but for what lies behind them. We love objects and art for the door that they open into universal beauty. For many people, Weil says, seeing beauty is often the only way that God can find a way into their minds: "The soul's natural inclination to love beauty is the trap God most frequently uses in order to win it and open it to the breath from on high." The beautiful things of this world are a representation of the true beauty of God that underpins them all.

Similarly, love of our neighbor is not a self-conscious moral act, it is our way of recognizing the divine love behind every person. The good Samaritan stopped and helped not because it was something that made him feel good, but because neighborly love is justice; it recognizes the right order of a universe powered by love.

Mystery of affliction

Weil noted that affliction, as opposed to common-or-garden-variety suffering, is one of the mysteries of life. It is no surprise that people are enslaved or washed away in a flood or tortured, but it *is* surprising when people who have apparently done nothing bad experience a "dark night of the soul," a psychological or spiritual breakdown.

Another difference that Weil saw between suffering and affliction is that affliction is almost like physical pain: it can feel like a constricting of the breath or a terrible hunger. For a spiritual person, it brings the shocking feeling that God has abandoned you. However, if you can emerge from the darkness, your faith will be deeper and you will have experienced one of life's great mysteries.

Her idea of genuine neighborly love means being able to say to someone: "What are you going through?". There should be no condescension or pity, just a recognition of what affliction is like from one human being to another.

Naturalness of obedience

Weil made the interesting observation that it is foolish to believe that we cannot be obedient to God, since all things in the universe obey divine law in an almost mechanical sense. We have the choice to desire or not desire obedience, but we all obey in the end, since spiritual law is as unerring as the law of gravity. Criminals, she says, are like "tiles blown off a roof." Maybe they loosened themselves from the roof to be free, but gravity inevitably caused their fall back to the ground.

She remarks that the more obedient a slave is to his master, the greater the gap that widens between them. But the more a person is obedient to God, the more that person becomes an expression of God.

Final comments

Like the ancient Stoics, Weil was a universalist, loving the world too much to restrict herself to one faith or interpretation of God. This wariness of organized religion is now such a part of the modern outlook that we take it for granted, but in the time she lived Weil was courageous to stick to this position. Her torment over whether to get baptized (she never was) now seems a little strange, but the will to keep her spirituality private is what we admire about her now.

In her uncompromising view of life she often went too far, and that included the circumstances of her death. During the war she was ill, and in solidarity with her compatriots in occupied France, and against doctor's orders, she refused to consume any more than basic rations. It is clear that Weil had always had issues with food and leaped at opportunities to put principle before health. In this case it killed her, but a martyr's death was perhaps what she wanted.

Waiting for God is a dense work, but if given your full attention can be very satisfying. You know you are in the presence of an original thinker. Weil's forays into matters of Catholic theology will not be of interest to most readers, but it is when she talks about herself that we want to read more. She considered her personal history to be unimportant, but the fact of who she was made her thoughts fascinating, even to the non-Christian. Her power lay in the fact that she crossed over from godless modernity to ancient faith, but never lost her wariness when it came to the supposed power and authority of institutions.

Weil never intended to devote her life to God; rather, she was looking for truth, and it happened to come into focus through the stained-glass windows of the Church. She saw the beauty in Catholic theology and ritual, but remained an outsider in fact and in spirit.

Simone Weil

Weil was born in 1909 in Paris. Her father was a doctor and her brother was the noted mathematician André Weil. She began her career as a school philosophy teacher in 1931 at Le Puy, and for the next few years interspersed teaching with various laboring jobs to empathize with the working class.

In 1936 Weil joined the Republican side in the Spanish Civil War, but received burns in an accident with hot oil and left for Italy. In Assisi her attraction to the Catholic faith grew, assisted by a love of Gregorian chants. In 1942 she traveled to the United States with her parents, then to England where she worked in support of the French Resistance. Diagnosed with tuberculosis, she lived out her last days in an English sanatorium, and died in August 1943.

Weil's writings include Gravity and Grace, *consisting of excerpts from her diaries,* The Need for Roots, Supernatural Knowledge, Oppression and Liberty, *and* Lectures on Philosophy.

A Theory of Everything

"*The Greeks had a beautiful word, Kosmos, which means the patterned Whole of all existence, including the physical, emotional, mental, and spiritual realms... But us poor moderns have reduced the Kosmos to the cosmos, we have reduced matter and body and mind and soul and spirit to nothing but matter alone, and in this drab and dreary world of scientific materialism, we are lulled into the notion that a theory uniting the physical dimension is actually a theory of everything.*"

In a nutshell

Adopt an explanation of the universe that involves consciousness as well as matter.

In a similar vein

Richard Maurice Bucke *Cosmic Consciousness* (p. 36)
Fritjof Capra *The Tao of Physics* (p. 42)
James Redfield *The Celestine Prophecy* (p. 210)
Gary Zukav *The Seat of the Soul* (p. 306)
Abraham Maslow *Motivation and Personality* (50SHC)
Pierre Teilhard de Chardin *The Phenomenon of Man* (50SHC)

CHAPTER 48

Ken Wilber

We frequently hear about the latest advances in physics as being one step closer to a full explanation of our universe. But philosopher Ken Wilber was struck by the fact that these theories only deal with the physical world. What about the mind, soul, and spirit that actually infused life and matter with meaning? Could we not have an appreciation of the universe that took account of *consciousness*?

At this point in humanity's development, he felt, it was our task to develop a cosmology that covered not just matter but mind, soul, self, and culture—to make sense of art, physics, sociology, politics, medicine, and business as well as the movement of particles and the traverse of planets. Such a "theory of everything" was always going to be somewhat elusive, but given the fragmented and divided nature of the world, he reasoned, "a little bit of wholeness is better than none at all."

An important point on his journey was his discovery of the Greek idea of the Kosmos, which included all dimensions—physical, emotional, mental, and spiritual—in one view of the universe. The Kosmos was less a theory than an awareness that the inner and outer experiences of life were of the same importance, and this clearly had implications for how we currently see the world. The first implication was that personal development was the major factor in the unfolding of history, and the second that the scientific and spiritual worldviews could be reconciled.

Spiral of consciousness

In the 1960s, Abraham Maslow put forth the idea of "self-actualized" people who, once they had had met their basic physical and emotional needs, began to focus on psychological and spiritual fulfillment. More recently, researchers such as Clare Graves and Jenny Wade developed models that see human development as a series of unfolding waves or stages. In these models, human beings move through certain psychological "holons" that give us a certain outlook on life, and each must be fully lived before we can move onto the next one. The ethics, values, motivations, and education of a person should all be understood according to their stage in development. We cannot jump stages, as each is contained by the next one.

Wilber became interested in these models of development because they provided scientific backing for his Kosmos concept of awakening human consciousness. In *A Theory of Everything: An Integral Vision for Business, Politics, Science and Spirituality*, he devotes considerable space to a particular theory, spiral dynamics, which was applied successfully to the issues facing South Africa as it dismantled apartheid. Developed by Don Beck and Christopher Cowan, the concept looked at individuals and communities beyond the usual categories of race or gender or education, going deeper to their fundamental way of seeing the world. Each way of seeing was given a color:

❖ Beige (Archaic–Instinctual)—survival mode; satisfaction of basic wants.
❖ Purple (Magical–Animistic)—tribal; ritual; kinship; belief in spirits.
❖ Red (Power Gods)—mythical heroism; feudalism; "the world a jungle"; power always wins.
❖ Blue (Mythic Order)—rigid conformism to social hierarchies; only one right or wrong way; law and order; strong patriotism; religious fundamentalism.
❖ Orange (Scientific Achievement)—individualism; rational scientific enlightenment; focus on economic success.
❖ Green (Sensitive Self)—Ecological and emotional sensitivity; building relationships; universal humanism over dogma and tradition; political correctness; human rights.

Writing of his work in South Africa, Beck noted: "There are not black and white people; there are purple people, blue people, orange people, green people…" It was not possible to solve social and political problems by forcing solutions based on race or gender or any other old categories—most important was people's inner psychological mindset.

Wilber's own conclusion was that world problem spots are not simply the result—as is fashionably believed—of a clash of civilizations, but a clash of levels of *consciousness*.

The health of the spiral

The key point about the spiral is that none of the people in one color can really appreciate other ones. As Wilber puts it:

"Blue order is very uncomfortable with both red impulsiveness and orange individualism. Orange individualism thinks blue order is for suckers and green egalitarianism is weak and woo-woo. Green egalitarianism cannot easily abide excellence and value rankings, big pictures, hierarchies, or anything that appears authoritarian."

Green people believe that their way of thinking and being is the highest and often wish to impose it on the rest of the world. They would like the world to be pluralistic and multicultural, not bound by tradition. They do not admit hierarchies because they want to be egalitarian, but by denying the outlook of blue and orange, green people deny the whole spiral of development. They are therefore little different from religious fundamentalists who feel that their worldview is right.

However, the whole point of the spiral concept is that each stage must be fully lived before a person or culture can move on to another, and the green attitude itself must be superseded by "second-tier" thinking that is able to see with detachment the whole spiral of human development. At the second tier are two outlooks:

❖ Yellow (Integrative)—blending the best of each first-tier color's attributes to create a flexible and functional person/culture.
❖ Turquoise (Holistic)—a genuinely holistic unity of feeling and knowledge, awareness and appreciation of every facet of existence, including the material and spiritual.

At the yellow and turquoise levels, we can see the big picture of personal development and human evolution in which each color has its important place. At this level, we seek the health of the whole spiral of development instead of pushing an agenda. With second-tier thinking, we no longer have a world in which each mindset turns on the other to win.

Wilber's examples of second-tier thinking include transpersonal psychology, Teilhard de Chardin and his "noosphere," and Mandela and Gandhi (see p. 84), whose integrating philosophies went beyond individual peoples and movements to seek the health of the greater whole.

Two sides of the coin

The traditional way of seeing science and religion, Wilber says, can be likened to a multistory building that represents reality. We let science tells us about the lower floors and leave the upper floors to religion. The integral or Kosmic model, however, says that there may be both a scientific and a spiritual explanation of all phenomena. Wilber's example is a person in meditation hooked up to an EEG machine. The scientific equipment shows the changes in the brainwave patterns, while the meditator himself reports an expansion of consciousness and greater feelings of love and compassion. Both realities are true.

Science has never managed to disprove spiritual experience, and Wilber suggests that "deep spirituality is in part a broad science of the farther reaches of human potential." That is, the more advanced the spirituality, the more scientific it gets (the sophisticated categorization of human emotion and development found in Buddhism—sometimes called the "scientific religion"—is an indicator of this). Likewise, go to the edges of science and you have to deal with metaphysical questions.

Ultimately, both science and religion are expressions of truth that go toward a fully integrated understanding of the universe. To deny one or the other is like the outlook of an infant who cannot get beyond their own little mind and therefore believes that reality is only as they see it. With an integral or Kosmic outlook, both points of view are not merely tolerated but appreciated as elements of the truth.

Final comments

Wilber is a major contemporary thinker whose ideas are often complex, but *A Theory of Everything* is a good introduction to his integral philosophy because it refers to many of his other writings. Though not long, the book packs in the ideas, and this commentary is an attempt at describing only some of them.

A Theory of Everything continues the idea running through most of Wilber's writings that there are three basic levels of human consciousness, culminating in the "transpersonal," which is an awareness of the universe unclouded by the ego or the normal self. Wilber defines human development as "a successive decrease in egocentrism," meaning that our future depends on an ability to remove the blinkers and take a larger view of history. In this conception, a small number of people could be the leading edge that raises the center of gravity of the world's consciousness. However, as the color spiral suggests, this will get us nowhere unless full recognition is given to the majority who are not at such an exalted stage.

Reading Wilber is like taking a ride in a spaceship. As captain he invites you to look down on Earth and try to make sense of the course of humankind's mental and spiritual development. The trip is an exhilarating ride that will leave some dizzy and others jetlagged, but for a big-picture view there are few writers better to journey with.

Ken Wilber

Wilber was born in 1949 in Oklahoma City and attended high school in Lincoln, Nebraska. He began a medicine degree at Duke University, then tried studying biochemistry back in Nebraska, but dropped out of college altogether to devote his time to reading the literature of consciousness and to writing.

His first book, published in 1977, was the classic The Spectrum of Consciousness. *This was followed by a string of influential titles including* No Boundary, The Atman Project, *and* Up from Eden. *Other books include* The Marriage of Sense and Soul; Sex, Ecology and Spirituality; Grace and Grit: Spirituality and Healing in the Life and Death of Treya Killam Wilber *(Wilber's wife Treya was diagnosed with breast cancer shortly after their marriage in 1983, and passed away in 1989);* A Brief History of Everything; *and* Integral Psychology.

Wilber lives in Colorado.

Autobiography of a Yogi

"A 'miracle' is commonly considered to be an effect or event without law, or beyond law. But all events in our precisely adjusted universe are lawfully wrought and lawfully explicable. The so-called miraculous powers of a great master are a natural accompaniment to his exact understanding of subtle laws that operate in the inner cosmos of consciousness."

In a nutshell

The story of the man who brought yoga to the West and his revelation of spiritual secrets.

In a similar vein
Fritjof Capra *The Tao of Physics* (p. 42)
Ram Dass *Be Here Now* (p. 72)
Mohandas Gandhi *An Autobiography* (p. 84)
G. I. Gurdjieff *Meetings with Remarkable Men* (p. 102)

CHAPTER 49

Paramahansa Yogananda

W hen Paramahansa Yogananda wrote the last sentence of his autobiography, he is reported to have said, "This book will change the lives of millions. It will be my messenger when I am gone."

Indeed, on its publication in 1946 the book was widely acclaimed and became an enduring bestseller. But its origins are somewhat mysterious, having been prophesied by the nineteenth-century Indian saint, Lahiri Mahasaya. He foretold that 50 years after his death a book would be written about him that would help to spread the message of yoga around the world. It was made clear to Yogananda by his guru Swami Sri Yukteswar (himself a disciple of Lahiri Mahasaya) that the task was his to fulfill. Duly, an exact half-century after the saint's death, the book appeared, and despite its title, also incorporates the life stories of Mahasaya and Sri Yukteswar.

Autobiography of a Yogi is justifiably celebrated as one of the most entertaining and enlightening spiritual books ever written. It has that old-fashioned turn of phrase so characteristic of Indian English, and its many amusing scenes give it a warmth rarely found in spiritual writings. A marvelous picture is given of India itself, which although comparatively poor for the last two centuries, Yogananda noted, had produced "living skyscrapers of the human soul" in the form of the great swamis and yogis.

Early life

Born Mukunda Lal Ghosh in 1893 in Gorakhpur, northeastern India near the Himalayas, Yogananda was the fourth of eight children, and for most of his youth lived in Calcutta. He was only 11 when his mother died. His father held a senior position in a large railway company, and became a disciple of Lahiri Mahasaya in Benares. This saint also became Mukunda's first teacher on his *sadhana* or path to God, and heightened his sense that the spiritual life was waiting for him.

His family tried to talk Mukunda out of becoming a *sannyasi*, or renunciate, but he acquired a second guru in Sri Yukteswar, of the Swami order. Sri Yukteswar respected the ways of the West as much as the East, had female as well as male disciples, and exhibited a great knowledge of science even though he never seemed to read. Frighteningly for the young monks, Yukteswar possessed the specific yogic power of being able to attune himself to the mind of anyone he chose, not just reading their thoughts but placing thoughts into their minds. Yogananda describes him as fitting the definition found in the sacred Vedas of a person of God: "Softer than the flower, where kindness is concerned; stronger than the thunder, where principles are at stake."

Against his inclinations, Mukunda was made to do a university degree at Calcutta, on the grounds that it would make him more respected when his life took him to the West. Thus under Sri Yusteswar's guidance, his destiny began to take shape. He took the name Yogananda, which means "bliss (*ananda*) through divine union (*yoga*)."

Bringing the East to the West

Words such as "guru" and "yoga" are now part of universal English, but when Yogananda went to America in the 1930s, the world of eastern spirituality and philosophy was still very exotic. How did it actually come about that he traveled to the West?

He had founded a school in Ranchi that combined conventional learning with yoga and vedic philosophy. While meditating at the school one day, he had a vision of Americans, and took this as the long-heralded sign to go to the United States. Though his English was poor and he had little money (his father gave him a sum to get there and live on), he did go in 1920. Leaving behind everything he knew and loved, he was not to return to India for 15 years.

The voyage took two months, and when he arrived he spoke at an international religious congress in Boston. This was the first of hundreds of speeches that slowly increased the awareness of Hinduism and introduced yoga to hundreds of thousands of people. By 1925 the author had established a base at Mount Washington in Los Angeles, and became a mini-celebrity, even being called to meet President Calvin Coolidge.

Fêted when he did finally return to India, Yogananda saw his guru and his father for the last time, sorted out the affairs of his school, and enlarged the Self-Realization organization.*

Meetings with kindred spirits

The book includes Yogananda's accounts of meeting various saints around India and abroad, often in remote places. These explorations were assisted by the use of a Ford (the author describes it as the "Pride of Detroit") that a devotee had donated. Sages encountered include the Perfume Saint, who could materialize scents at will, the Tiger Swami, who had wrestled and defeated tigers, and the Levitating Saint, Bhaduri Mahasaya, who had apparently given up great family riches to become a yogi. The Levitating Saint noted that it is worldly people who are the real renunciants, having given up the bliss of communion with God for illusory things.

Yogananda also met Shankari Mai Jiew, a *yogini* (female yogi) of great age, and Nirmala Devi, the beautiful Joy-Permeated Mother, who spent much of her time in a state of *samadhi* (blissful trance). He notes that this childlike woman had solved the essential problem of life— establishing a unity with God—when the rest of us remained "befogged by a million issues."

He journeyed into the heart of Bengal to find Giri Bala, a non-eating saint who had used a certain yoga technique that had allowed her to exist without food for decades, with no ill effects and proven by close observation. Strangely, the woman enjoyed cooking for others, but when asked the purpose of her non-eating, Giri Bala replied that it was to show us that humans are essentially spirit and will gradually learn how to live from the energies of astral light, as she did. Yogananda also devotes a chapter to his visit with the German mystic Therese Neumann, who for years had existed on nothing more than a host (holy wafer) once a day, and weekly bled from her hands and side (stigmata) in empathy with the agony of Jesus's crucifixion.

Yogananda painted fascinating portraits of his meetings or friendship with scientist Jagadis Chandra Bose; Rabindranath Tagore, a great Indian poet; Luther Burbank, a pioneering plant cultivator; and Sri Ramana Maharshi, the sage of Arunachala. Fans of Mahatma Gandhi will enjoy Yogananda's description of his time at Wardha, Gandhi's ashram in central India.

Yogic powers and the law of miracles

Autobiography of a Yogi is full of tales of miraculous healings, people being raised from the dead, and strange intercessions. Yet the descriptions of these events ring true. Yogananda goes to great lengths to discuss how the seemingly impossible is of daily occurrence for yogis. He notes that Einstein's theory of relativity boiled the universe down to pure energy, or light. Matter was simply concentrated energy, and the solidity of things is to some extent illusory. Einstein showed that matter could never equal the velocity of light, which is why we class matter as solid and light as ephemeral.

What has this to do with the miraculous powers of yogis and sages? Yogananda explains that they are able to put themselves into a state in which they cease to be identified with their body, or with matter at all. From their awareness that the material world is essentially *maya*, or illusion, they can literally transform their molecular structure from matter to light energy, allowing them to be, for instance, in two places at once. A yogi sees himself as omnipresent, becoming "one with the universe," and as a result can materialize or dematerialize objects free from the principle of gravity.

A yogi's ability to "become light"—to concentrate light energy—is why divine manifestations in every religion are often described as blinding flashes. Spiritual masters see the universe as God did when it was created: as an undifferentiated mass of light. Becoming one with that light, the Hindu sage and Christian saint alike are freed from the restrictions of matter, allowing miracles to occur. In fact, such occurrences are fully in line with the laws of the universe, it is just that most humans are not able to work with them. When he visited her, Therese Neumann told Yogananda that she was energized by light and air alone. As he notes, that miracle making *is* possible for anyone "who has realized that the essence of creation is light."

While a yogi is capable of strange powers, they are not used for the entertainment of others. Yogananda felt that the adage "He is a fool that cannot conceal his wisdom" applied to his Master Sri Yukteswar. He was plainly spoken, but quietly bent the laws of the universe around himself, so attracting little attention.

Final comments

When you pick up this book you think that you are about to read an enjoyable life story of an eastern wise man; what you get is an entrée to some of the mysteries of the universe. At the beginning is the quote: "Except ye see signs and wonders, ye will not believe" (John 4:46–54). Yogananda included it because he knew that people are so set in their ways that sometimes only miracles can jolt them into pondering divine matters. Gurus usually do not like to discuss their special powers as they distract the learner from the real path, but Yogananda knew that miraculous occurrences were the honey that attracted the bees to the spiritual pot.

Yet his broader message was that self-realization through yogic control of the mind and body is a *science* (the "science of self-realization") that anyone could learn.

While the autobiography provides a fascinating introduction to the Hindu spiritual literature—the Vedas, Upanishads, Mahabarata—a great surprise of the book is that it can give us new eyes for the Bible. Yogananda was a keen biblical scholar, and the book is rich with footnotes comparing concepts and sayings from the Hindu scriptures with those found in the Old and New Testaments. He refers to Jesus as the "Galilean Master," who had similar powers over matter as that of the great yogis.

It is possible to read the whole of *Autobiography of a Yogi* without believing any of it, but see if your skepticism can withstand the last page, which contains excerpts from a letter written by the director of the Forest Lawn mortuary in Los Angeles where Yogananda's body was placed after his death in 1952. Unlike every other corpse that had come his way, Yogananda's failed to show any signs of decay even three weeks after it had come in. The actual circumstances of his death were also remarkable, but for this and a thousand other details you should read the book.

* Self-Realization Fellowship (SRF) centers in America, India, and the UK continue Yogananda's work today.

The Seat of the Soul

"It is the health of the soul that is the true purpose of the human experience."

"Every decision that you make either moves you toward your personality, or toward your soul. Each decision you make is an answer to the question, 'How do you choose to learn love?', 'How do you choose to learn authentic empowerment—through doubt and fear, or through wisdom?'"

"When you choose the energy of your soul—when you choose to create with the intentions of love, forgiveness, humbleness and clarity—you gain power."

In a nutshell

Achieve authentic power by letting your soul rather than your personality guide your life.

In a similar vein

Richard Maurice Bucke *Cosmic Consciousness* (p. 36)
Pema Chödrön *The Places that Scare You* (p. 60)
Carl Gustav Jung *Memories, Dreams, Reflections* (p. 136)
Michael Newton *Journey of Souls* (p. 186)
Ken Wilber *A Theory of Everything* (p. 294)
James Hillman *The Soul's Code* (50SHC)

CHAPTER 50

Gary Zukav

Zukav's study of figures such as the philosopher William James, psychologist Carl Jung, and scientist Albert Einstein led him to the conclusion that their great ideas concerning human life and the universe came from somewhere "beyond the personality." They were able to cut through the clouds of the ego and receive information or wisdom that was already there but needed to be tapped into.

Yet Zukav came to believe that this ability is not simply spirituality or religiosity; it is "authentic power," or the capacity to make a connection with our soul and its purpose for our life. That purpose, in turn, is intricately woven into the greater purpose of the evolving universe.

Evolution to authentic power

There is physical evolution, which we all know about, but what does it mean when we say that someone is a very evolved human being? What made Buddha or Jesus, for instance, different to other people?

What evolution means to us, Zukav says, reflects the knowledge that we have gained of our world through our five senses. However, if we were to explore the universe beyond the five senses—becoming a "multisensory being"—we would have a correspondingly larger understanding of the universe. Most of the time, if we can't observe something through the five physical senses, we doubt that it exists.

In the five-sensory world, the ability to survive is the main criterion for evolution, and therefore fear of not surviving is the defining characteristic of human relationships and psychology. The ability to control the environment, whether it be nature, other people, or economies, is the main indicator of power, and therefore power is always something external. But if you look at many of the great figures in history, those who have transformed the way we think, many of them had no external power. Zukav asks us to consider that the words and actions of a carpenter (Jesus) became more powerful that the might of the Roman Empire. He notes:

"The perception of power as external splinters the psyche, whether it is the psyche of the individual, the community, the nation or the world."

In contrast, *The Seat of the Soul: An Inspiring Vision of Humanity's Spiritual Destiny* is about authentic power, or power based on love, humility, compassion, and clarity of intention.

The personality and the soul

A soul knows what it would like to achieve before it enters a body on the Earth, but this intention is forgotten when we are born. Our personality is born with our body, but our soul lives beyond our body. Our personality has likes and dislikes, but our soul has intentions that it would like to see fulfilled. It will try to guide our life so that these are fulfilled, but the personality may have desires that override them and end up as the true shapers of our life. Because not many people understand the distinction between the soul and the personality, most people exist according to their personality. But the wise learn to let their soul shine through and allow it to express its purpose.

Only the personality can create and experience the "bad" emotions of fear, anger, greed, sorrow, regret, indifference, cynicism, and so on. Yet people who are aware of their soul are able to see beyond these states in others and in themselves. When we decide to serve the intents and purposes of our soul, we become authentically empowered. We may resist what it is asking, but our evolution depends on our listening and acting.

If we are to achieve authentic power, aligning our personality with our soul must be the main concern of our life.

Feelings and authentic power

A society focused on external power will ignore the role of feelings, but without getting to the bottom of what causes anger or sadness or joy, we won't be able to see what is true in ourselves and what are just the whims of the personality.

Our world of science and logic marginalizes feelings and subjectivity, yet those people who do not look for the deeper meaning of their lives often end up in despair or emptiness. They are, in effect, unconscious, "living out their karma" like a robot. But it is possible to live at a more conscious level, recognizing our tendencies and trying to move ourselves higher.

Comparatively few people are willing to really look at the pain they feel, but doing so makes it much more likely that we will overcome it. The easy way is to block it out, but this will mean that we never grow. Zukav suggests, "Only through emotions can you encounter the force field of your own soul." This is what is asked of us in the human experience. Get to the heart of why we feel the way you do, and we become more fully human. Project our bad feelings onto the world, and we become less so and create the potential for evil.

Emotions reflect intentions, so when we experience emotional pain we need to go deep into our intentions. We may intend to have a loving and harmonious relationship, but if we also have an unconscious intention to end it, the stronger intention will win. After the end of the relationship we might feel that things did not work out as intended, but in fact they turned out exactly as intended.

Intuition's reason

We have not been taught to trust our intuition. We tend to experience life only through our five senses, and therefore disregard hunches and unexplainable insights. To someone ruled only by their five senses, intuitions are not really considered "knowledge" and so are disregarded, treated as curiosities. The multisensory person, however, understands hunches and promptings to be their link to a wiser, larger mind that speaks the truth.

For intuitions to be received, we have to clear our mind of mental toxins in the form of unexpressed emotions. Observing our own thoughts also leaves us with a quiet mind. Zukav suggests another thing that makes it easier to cultivate intuition: having a sense of faith that what we are experiencing in life has a reason to it, and trusting that it is all for a good end. This makes us less judgmental, more open to truth.

Intuition is like a walkie-talkie, Zukav says, between the personality and the soul. Most people are unwilling to fully trust their intuition because sometimes it points us in a way not to our liking, a path of greater resistance. But if we are unwilling to take the advice of our soul, we will never be able to flower into our true potential. Our personality will choose what suits its purposes, but those purposes are usually less noble than the soul's.

The splintered personality and the healed soul

Most of us have sides: the selfish side, the loving side, the angry side, the wise side. Each of these aspects has its own intentions, and of course often they will conflict with the others. This self-sabotage is the lot of the splintered personality, with seemingly unlimited pain and anguish.

What can we do about it? First, admit that we often tear ourselves apart. Then appreciate that part of our soul's aim in incarnating on Earth was to experience different states of being and improve or heal any aspects of itself that need to be healed. Instead of living in the murky depths of our self, expose these aspects to air, examine them to see how they can serve us. Consider that if we had no issues in life we may not be drawn to the interests or activities that will provide our sense of purpose.

Zukav is very interesting on the subject of temptation. He describes temptation as "a thought form that is designed to draw possible negativity from the human energy system without harming others." The soul understands temptation, because it exposes the parts of us that still need healing, the longings and urges that need to be put in balance. Paradoxically, temptation carries with it the seeds of greater responsibility, because it makes us choose, and if we choose rightly then we are able to become the person we truly wish to be. It is only by accepting our many sides that we will gain the chance of incorporating them back into the one sense of self, and rededicating ourselves to our life purpose.

It is often said of great saints and yogis that they are like a mirror to people's souls. In their presence we can see our own splintered nature. Yet such people also give us the hope that we can become a fully conscious and integrated person. As Zukav puts it:

"When a personality is in full balance, you cannot see where it ends and the soul begins. That is a whole human being."

Final comments

The modern world seems chaotic because it is mostly a reflection of the personality in all its anger, lust, and insecurities. The original meaning of the word psychology, Zukav notes, is "soul knowledge," but psychology as an area of learning came to mean the science of the personality. If the world is truly going to evolve, it needs to be built around greater awareness of the soul, as opposed to the personality.

One of the aims of *The Seat of the Soul* is to redefine power so that we do not automatically give greater value to a person who commands external power compared to a person who does not. The person with authentic power is simply one who has achieved an alignment of their soul and their personality—the power of one. We chase fame, money, and position because we feel a lack of power inside, but without soul knowledge real power will always elude us.

To many people, the book will seem full of New Age ideas, none of which can be substantiated. Yet this is precisely Zukav's point: if we live our life solely as a five-sensory being, only accepting the truth of what we can see, hear, taste, smell, or touch, we shut ourselves off to any other type of truth.

Although its style is often ponderous and not always clear (you will have to read many sentences and paragraphs twice), *The Seat of the Soul* was ahead of its time, and is one of those rare books that may just change how you look at life, the universe, and everything.

Gary Zukav

Author of The Dancing Wu Li Masters, *a seminal book that looked at the links between quantum physics and the spiritual, Zukav has been a pioneer of alternative spirituality in the United States. He has a degree from Harvard University and lives in Northern California.*

Zukav's other books include Soul Stories, The Heart of the Soul, *and* The Mind of the Soul.

50 More Spiritual Classics

1 **Adomnan of Iona** *Life of St Columba* **(7th century)**
Celebrated biography with descriptions of early monastic life on the Scottish island of Iona.

2 **St. Anselm** *Proslogion* **(1077)**
Medieval philosopher's famous presentation of arguments to prove the existence of God.

3 **Ibn El-Arabi** *Bezels of Wisdom* **(12th century)**
Known as Sheikh Akbar (the "Greatest Master") in the Islamic world and "Doctor Maximus" in the West, El-Arabi remains one of the great mystical philosophers. Written late in his life, this book reveals divine truths through the lives of the prophets.

4 **Edwin Arnold** *The Light of Asia* **(1879)**
An Englishman's poetic masterpiece on the life of Buddha.

5 **Farid Ud-Din Attar** *The Conference of the Birds* **(12th century)**
A Sufi master's beautiful allegorical poem based around a bird that can lead others to salvation.

6 **Mary Baker Eddy** *Science and Health with Key to the Scriptures* **(1875)**
A landmark work on healing from the founder of the Christian Science Church.

7 **Benedict of Nursia** *Rule of St Benedict* **(515)**
With this book Benedict formalized the daily life of monks, including spiritual exercises and physical work, creating the template for western monastic life for centuries to come.

8 **Helena Petrova Blavatsky** *Isis Unveiled* **(1877)**
Huge work of esoteric wisdom by the Russian-born founder of the Theosophical Society.

9 **Jakob Boehme** *Aurora* **(1612)**
German mystic's influential meditations on the nature of humans and God.

10 **Dietrich Bonhoeffer** *Letters and Papers from Prison* **(1953)**
Covering the German pastor's arrest by the Gestapo in 1943 to his execution in 1945. Here he first raised his idea of "religionless Christianity."

11 Paul Brunton *In Search of Secret India* (1935)
Fascinating account of Indian travels by the English traveler and spiritual teacher, including his meeting with Ramana Maharishi at Arunachala.

12 **Martin Buber** *I and Thou* (1923)
Highly influential work of theology that inspires a new level of communication with God and other people.

13 **John Bunyan** *Grace Abounding* (1666)
Classic account of personal spiritual experience by the author of *The Pilgrim's Progress*.

14 *The Cloud of Unknowing* (14th century)
A foundational work of Christian contemplative prayer and achieving unity with the divine. The medieval author is still unknown.

15 **Lama Surya Das** *Awakening the Buddha Within* (1997)
A perfect introduction to Tibetan Buddhism by an American who spent years as a monk. Enlightenment for the real world.

16 **John Donne** *Devotions upon Emergent Occasions* (1624)
Devotional work by the English metaphysical poet written in the midst of illness and following the deaths of close family.

17 **Meister Eckhart** *Selected Writings* (13th-14th centuries)
The mystical pantheistic writings of this German Dominican priest were too expansive for the Church of his time, but are loved by modern readers.

18 **T. S. Eliot** *The Four Quartets* (1944)
Four poems that reveal the depth of Eliot's spiritual understanding. He considered this his masterpiece.

19 **Ralph Waldo Emerson** *Spiritual Laws* (1841)
An essay from the great Transcendentalist on being in tune with the forces that move the universe.

20 **Richard Foster** *Celebration of Discipline* (1978)
A modern Christian classic that rediscovers the power of spiritual disciplines, e.g. fasting, prayer, solitude, worship.

21 **Graham Greene** *The Power and the Glory* (1940)
A "whiskey priest" is on the run from a Mexican state that has outlawed religion. One of the great spiritual novels of the twentieth century.

22 **Mahendranath Gupta** *Gospel of Sri Ramakrishna* (1942)
A 1,000-page record of conversations with the great sage, considered by Indians to be a continuation of the line of Krishna and Buddha.

23 **Michael Harner** *The Way of the Shaman* (1980)
The book that created a wave of new interest in shamanistic religion, with the author both an anthropologist and a practicing shaman himself.

24 Hildegard of Bingen *Scivias* (1151)
The first work of German Benedictine nun, composer, poet, artist, naturalist, preacher and mystic visionary, who in a male-dominated age advised kings and influenced popes.

25 Ernest Holmes *Science of Mind* (1938)
A "science" of spirituality discussed in terms of mental and spiritual laws.

26 John of the Cross *Dark Night of the Soul* (16th century)
Famous work charting the loss of spiritual connection, by a Spanish Catholic mystic and friend of Teresa of Avila.

27 Julian of Norwich *Showings* (14th century)
An English anchoress's beautiful expression of divine communion, also known as "Revelations of Divine Love."

28 Thomas à Kempis *The Imitation of Christ* (15th century)
Much-loved Christian devotional work by a German cleric.

29 Jack Kerouac *The Dharma Bums* (1958)
Result of the beat writer's exploration into Zen Buddhism, published a year after *On the Road*.

30 Gopi Krishna *Kundalini: The Evolutionary Energy in Man* (1970)
Fascinating account of a householder's experience of the awakening of the "serpent power," or *kundalini* energy, and its effects on his life.

31 Ramana Maharishi *The Spiritual Teachings of Ramana Maharishi* (various dates, 20th century)
This famed South Indian holy man (d. 1950) emphasized self-knowledge as the means to enlightenment.

32 Abraham Maslow *Religions, Values and Peak Experiences* (1964)
A great psychologist's insightful foray into spiritual experience, in the tradition of William James.

33 Thomas Merton *The Seven Storey Mountain* (1946)
Bestselling autobiography of Merton's transformation from American campus intellectual to Trappist monk, with a growing interest in eastern spirituality.

34 P. D. Ouspensky *In Search of the Miraculous* (1950)
Russian mathematician's popularization of the thinking of G. I. Gurdjieff.

35 *Pirkei Avot* ("Ethics of the Fathers")
Ancient Jewish wisdom and sayings included as a part of the Mishnah, or body of oral law.

36 Plotinus *Enneads* (3rd century)
One of the great minds of the classical era, Plotinus combined Platonic ideas with the primeval notion of the oneness of the universe. Appreciated by early Christians and Renaissance thinkers.

37 Paul Reps and Nyogen Senzaki *Zen Flesh, Zen Bones* (1957)
The spirit of Zen in a small book, including stories, *koans*, pictures; influential in the 1960s and still treasured.

38 Sogyal Rinpoche *The Tibetan Book of Living and Dying* (1992)
Elaboration on the original *Tibetan Book of the Dead* that provides an inspiringly positive understanding of death.

39 Jalaludin Rumi *Mathnavi* ("Couplets of Inner Meaning") (13th century)
A Persian poet's masterpiece; literature designed for spiritual awakening.

40 Anne-Marie Schimmel *Mystical Dimensions of Islam* (1975)
Schimmel, who died in 2003 aged 80, devoted her life to furthering understanding of Islam; this book confirmed her as an authority on Islamic mysticism and poetry.

41 Gershom Scholem *Major Trends in Jewish Mysticism* (1941)
The first real scholarly study of Kabbalah from an academic perspective, which sparked the revival of public interest in the field.

42 Rudolf Steiner *How to Know Higher Worlds* (1904–05)
A handbook for the spiritual journey by the Austrian philosopher and founder of anthroposophy, or the science of the spirit.

43 Rabindranath Tagore *Gitanjali* (1913)
Beautiful spiritual verse by a Nobel prize-winning Bengali mystic and polymath.

44 Pierre Teilhard de Chardin *The Phenomenon of Man* (1955)
French Jesuit and paleontologist's sweeping view of the spiritual evolution of humankind. See *50 Self-Help Classics*.

45 St Therese of Lisieux *The Story of a Soul* (1898)
Popular self-told account of a French saint's life with its theme of simple trust in God.

46 Paul Tillich *The Courage to Be* (1952)
Landmark philosophical work dealing with existential questions of finding meaning in modern life. Tillich was a German-born theologian who emigrated to the US after opposing the Nazis.

47 J. R. R. Tolkien *The Lord of the Rings* (1954–55)
Good and evil do battle in Tolkien's alternative universe.

48 Evelyn Underhill *Mysticism* (1911)
Classic study of the subject by an English poet and mystic.

49 Alan Watts *The Wisdom of Insecurity* (1951)
How to live with full acceptance of the absence of security in life, from a western master of eastern religion.

50 *The Way of a Pilgrim* (19th century)
Classic of Russian spirituality that follows the path of a pilgrim who has lost his family and learns the art of constant prayer.

This is only a sprinkling of further classics. As with the main list, another 50 or 100 worthy titles could have been included.

For a selection of more contemporary spiritual classics, see *50 Self-Help Classics*.

Chronological list of titles

St. Augustine *Confessions* (400)
Epictetus *Enchiridion* (1st century)
Chuang Tzu *The Book of Chuang Tzu* (4th century)
Ghazzali *The Alchemy of Happiness* (1097)
Margery Kempe *The Book of Margery Kempe* (1436)
Teresa of Avila *Interior Castle* (1570)
Emanuel Swedenborg *Heaven and Hell* (1758)
Richard Maurice Bucke *Cosmic Consciousness* (1901)
William James *The Varieties of Religious Experience* (1902)
G. K. Chesterton *St Francis of Assisi* (1922)
Hermann Hesse *Siddartha* (1922)
Kahlil Gibran *The Prophet* (1923)
Mohandas Gandhi *An Autobiography: The Story of My Experiments with Truth* (1927)
Black Elk *Black Elk Speaks* (1932)
C. S. Lewis *The Screwtape Letters* (1942)
W. Somerset Maugham *The Razor's Edge* (1944)
Paramahansa Yogananda *Autobiography of a Yogi* (1946)
Abraham Joshua Heschel *The Sabbath: Its Meaning for Modern Man* (1951)
Muhammad Asad *The Road to Mecca* (1954)
Aldous Huxley *The Doors of Perception* (1954)
Carl Gustav Jung *Memories, Dreams, Reflections* (1955)
G. I. Gurdjieff *Meetings with Remarkable Men* (1960)
Dag Hammarskjöld *Markings* (1963)
J. Krishnamurti *Think on These Things* (1964)
Malcolm X *The Autobiography of Malcolm X* (1964)
Idries Shah *The Way of the Sufi* (1968)
Richard Bach *Jonathan Livingston Seagull* (1970)
Shunryu Suzuki *Zen Mind, Beginner's Mind: Informal Talks on Zen Meditation and Practice* (1970)
Ram Dass *Be Here Now* (1971)
Carlos Castaneda *Journey to Ixtlan* (1972)
Chögyam Trungpa *Cutting through Spiritual Materialism* (1973)

Robert M. Pirsig *Zen and the Art of Motorcycle Maintenance* (1974)
Thich Nhat Hanh *The Miracle of Mindfulness: An Introduction to the Practice of Meditation* (1975)
Fritjof Capra *The Tao of Physics: An Exploration of the Parallels between Modern Physics and Eastern Mysticism* (1976)
Helen Schucman & William Thetford *A Course in Miracles* (1976)
Starhawk *The Spiral Dance: A Rebirth of the Ancient Religion of the Great Goddess* (1979)
Simone Weil *Waiting for God* (1979)
Dan Millman *The Way of the Peaceful Warrior: A Book that Changes Lives* (1989)
Gary Zukav *The Seat of the Soul: An Inspiring Vision of Humanity's Spiritual Destiny* (1990)
Daniel C. Matt *The Essential Kabbalah: The Heart of Jewish Mysticism* (1994)
Michael Newton *Journey of Souls: Case Studies of Life between Lives* (1994)
James Redfield *The Celestine Prophecy: An Adventure* (1994)
Mother Teresa *A Simple Path* (1994)
Miguel Ruiz *The Four Agreements: A Practical Guide to Personal Freedom* (1997)
John O'Donohue *Anam Cara: Spiritual Wisdom from the Celtic World* (1998)
Eckhart Tolle *The Power of Now: A Guide to Spiritual Enlightenment* (1998)
Neale Donald Walsch *Conversations with God: An Uncommon Dialogue* (1998)
Ken Wilber *A Theory of Everything: An Integral Vision for Business, Politics, Science and Spirituality* (2000)
Pema Chödrön *The Places That Scare You: A Guide to Fearlessness in Difficult Times* (2001)
Rick Warren *The Purpose-Driven Life* (2002)

Credits

The dates given here are the date of publication of these editions. Original publication dates are stated in each of the 50 commentaries.

Asad, M. (1954) *The Road to Mecca*, New York: Simon & Schuster.
The Confessions of Saint Augustine (1983) trans. E. M. Blaiklock, London: Hodder & Stoughton.
Bach, R. (1973) *Jonathan Livingston Seagull*, London: Pan Books.
Black Elk, N. and Neihardt, J. G. (2000) *Black Elk Speaks*, Lincoln: University of Nebraska Press.
Bucke, R. M. (1991) *Cosmic Consciousness*, London: Arkana.
Capra, F. (1989) *The Tao of Physics: An Exploration of the Parallels between Modern Physics and Eastern Mysticism*, London: Flamingo
Castaneda, C. (1972) *Journey to Ixtlan*, London: Bodley Head.
Chesterton, G. K. (2001) *St Francis of Assisi*, Thirsk: House of Stratus.
Chödrön, P. (2003) *The Places that Scare You: A Guide to Fearlessness in Difficult Times*, London: Element.
The Book of Chuang Tzu (1996) trans Martin Palmer with Elizabeth Breuilly, Chang Wai Ming, & Jay Ramsay, London: Penguin.
Cleary, T. (1992) *The Essential Tao: An Initiation in the Heart of Taoism through the Authentic Tao Te Ching and the Inner Teachings of Chuang-Tzu*, New Jersey: Castle Books.
Dass, R. (1978) *Be Here Now*, Albuquerque: Hanuman Foundation.
Epictetus (1909) *A Selection from the Discourses of Epictetus with The Encheiridion*, trans. George Long, Project Gutenberg, www.gutenberg.org.
Gandhi, M. (1957) *An Autobiography: The Story of My Experiments with Truth*, Beacon Press.
Muhammad Al-Ghazzali (1909) *The Alchemy of Happiness*, trans. Claud Field, London: J. Murray; also at www.sacred-texts.com.
Gibran, K. (1970) *The Prophet*, London: Heinemann.
Gurdjieff, G. I. (1978) *Meetings with Remarkable Men*, London: Picador.
Hammarskjöld, D. (1964) *Markings*, trans. W. H. Auden & L. Sjoberg, London: Faber and Faber.
Heschel, A. J. (1975) *The Sabbath: Its Meaning for Modern Man*, New York: Farrar, Straus and Giroux.
Hesse, H. (2000) *Siddhartha*, Boston: Shambhala Classics.
Huxley, A. (1994) *The Doors of Perception*, London: Flamingo.
James, W. (undated) *The Varieties of Religious Experience*, New York: Dolphin Doubleday.

Jung, C. G. (1978) *Memories, Dreams, Reflections*, Glasgow: William Collins.
The Book of Margery Kempe (1936) trans. W. Butler-Bowdon, London:
  Jonathan Cape.
Krishnamurti, J. (1970) *Think on These Things*, New York: Harper & Row.
Lewis, C. S. (2001) *The Screwtape Letters*, London: HarperCollins.
Malcolm X (2001) *The Autobiography of Malcolm X*, London: Penguin Classics.
Matt, D. C. (1994) *The Essential Kabbalah: The Heart of Jewish Mysticism*,
  New York: HarperCollins.
Maugham, W. S. (2000) *The Razor's Edge*, London: Vintage.
Millman, D. (2000) *Way of the Peaceful Warrior: A Book that Changes Lives*,
  Tiburon: H. J. Kramer.
Newton, M. (2002) *Journey of Souls: Case Studies of Life Between Lives*, St.
  Paul: Llewellyn Publications.
Nhat Hanh, T. (1987) *The Miracle of Mindfulness: An Introduction to the
  Practice of Meditation*, trans. Mobi Ho, Boston: Beacon Press.
O'Donohue, J. (1998) *Anam Cara: Spiritual Wisdom from the Celtic World*,
  London: Bantam.
Pirsig, R. M. (1999) *Zen and the Art of Motorcycle Maintenance*, London: Vintage.
Redfield, J. (1993) *The Celestine Prophecy: An Adventure*, New York: Bantam.
Ruiz, M. (1997) *The Four Agreements: A Practical Guide to Personal
  Freedom*, San Rafael, CA: Amber-Allen Publishing.
Schucman, H. & Thetford, W. (1996) *A Course in Miracles*, New York: Viking.
Shah, I. (1990) *The Way of the Sufi*, London: Penguin.
Starhawk (1999) *The Spiral Dance: A Rebirth of the Ancient Religion of the
  Great Goddess*, New York: HarperCollins.
Suzuki, S. (2003) *Zen Mind, Beginner's Mind: Informal Talks on Zen Medita-
  tion and Practice*, New York: Weatherhill, Inc.
Swedenborg, E. (1976) *Heaven and Hell*, trans. George F. Dole, New York:
  Swedenborg Foundation.
Teresa of Avila (1989) *Interior Castle*, New York: Doubleday.
Mother Teresa (1995) *A Simple Path*, comp. Lucinda Vardey, London: Rider.
Tolle, E. (2001) *The Power of Now: A Guide to Spiritual Enlightenment*,
  Sydney: Hodder.
Trungpa, C. (1987) *Cutting through Spiritual Materialism*, Boston: Shambhala
  Dragon Editions.
Walsch, N. D. (1997) *Conversations with God: An Uncommon Dialogue*,
  London: Hodder & Stoughton.
Warren, R. (2002) *The Purpose-Driven Life,* Grand Rapids: Zondervan.
Weil, S. (2001) *Waiting for God*, New York: HarperCollins.
Wilber, K. A. (2001) A *Theory of Everything: An Integral Vision for Business,
  Politics, Science and Spirituality*, Dublin: Gateway.
Yogananda, P. (2001) *Autobiography of a Yogi*, Los Angeles: Self-Realization
  Fellowship.
Zukav, G. (1991) *The Seat of the Soul: An Inspiring Vision of Humanity's
  Spiritual Destiny*, London: Rider Books.

Acknowledgments

I am very grateful to the following people:

Tamara Butler-Bowdon, my wife: for reading through the book and providing valuable feedback as it came into being.

Andrew Arsenian, Marion Butler-Bowdon, Chris Holland, Deborah Logan and Noah & Beatrice Lucas: for helping to shape particular commentaries through their knowledge or providing crucial books.

At Nicholas Brealey Publishing: Nick Brealey for supporting the concept of the book within the *50 Classics* series; Sally Lansdell for editing and layout; Victoria Bullock for publicity and promotion in the UK; Trish O'Hare, Chuck Dresner, and Erika Heilman in the US office for suggestions on the classics list; and Carmen Mitchell for North American publicity and promotion.

Also to Frances Derricourt at Allen & Unwin for publicity in Australia and New Zealand.

And to anyone who has written to me after reading the first two books – thanks for taking the time, I appreciate every thought and comment.